On Christian Mysticism

On Christian Mysticism

A Conservative Evangelical Perspective

Bruce Norman MacPherson

On Christian Mysticism: A Conservative Evangelical Perspective

Published by Bruce N. MacPherson, Carol Stream, IL 60188.

All URLs verified as of March 15, 2017.

ISBN-13: 978-1544123646
ISBN-10: 1544123647

Contents

Section 2 Biblical Spirituality

Introduction

Juicy wild strawberries stared at me just beyond reach, on the other side of a tall chain-link schoolyard fence. Classes were over for the day. This second grader just couldn't resist and began climbing. With one arm over the fence, my little feet slipped and I fell. In those days, the top wires were not twisted back down as they are today. One of those barbs deeply pierced the bicep of my right arm. My older brother heard my screams, pushed me up and off, and put pressure on that bleeding arm until we got home a few blocks away, and to expert adult help. No doctor ever looked at it, so I lived with a large scar for many years. But that didn't keep me from trying that stunt again, in another town, another school, catching just my hand that time.

Who can say they never foolishly went a wrong way, and of course for all the right reasons. The grass, or strawberries, always look best on the other side of the fence. Many of us follow that wrong path again, and again. How often we all need a big brother or another compassionate friend to step alongside, to rescue us, and to help us heal. To head us in the right direction. To do things better.

All of us occasionally need correcting, or help to do things better. We all need warnings. None is immune from error, in doctrine or in practice. We need to hear and to heed warnings such as, "Bridge out ahead!" "Do not take internally." "Stay on the path." "Beware the dog!" We also need help in the area of "spirituality," like Jesus in that famous Sermon on the Mount saying, "Do not judge," but do "watch out for false prophets" (Matthew 7:1, 14).

My intent is to compassionately warn Christians about some serious dangers associated with Christian mysticism, and to give an urgent call to God's people for much needed revival and renewal. As Genesis 4:7 states: "If you do what is right, will you not be accepted? But if you do not do what is right, sin is crouching at your door; it desires to have you, but you must rule over it."

Many Christians are "climbing over the fence" to reach intimacy with God but are in severe danger because they are entering the dark realm of mysticism. It is the wrong path and will not lead to God. It looks enticing, but *stop! Don't go there!* Christian mysticism is a cancer subtly invading Christianity, and it needs to be unmasked.

John Dreher, a priest, tells the story of a distraught mother who asked him for advice. Her ten-year-old daughter had been introduced to contemplative "centering prayer" in her Catholic school's religion class. This technique involves repetition of a Christian word or phrase as a mantra, to get close to God. She began to hear what she thought was Jesus telling her things. Then she started having trouble going to sleep at night, saying she would see scary things when she closed her eyes. She did not want to stay in her room so was allowed to sleep with her sister. She told her mother that it laughed. Her mother said, "Kristy had used the centering prayer on her own at bedtime for some time before this started."

Dreher says such techniques "can bring people in touch with the spiritual realm" which includes evil spirits. He says, "Laughter is very characteristic of evil spirits." He thinks these mystic practices are "part of a conflict of the Kingdom of God and the kingdom of darkness."[1]

Several leading Catholic mystic writers admit Christian mysticism is not found in the Scriptures. Carl McColman, a lay-Cistercian and expert on Christian mysticism, made a significant admission in a recent book. He said Christian mysticism is "the cross-fertilization between Christianity and mysticism . . . something entirely new. . . . Christian mysticism is not the same thing as basic Christianity."[2]

This book is a call to a return to that basic Christianity! To *Christian Formation* that is truly rooted in the Bible.

Christian mysticism seeks communion with God in the "alpha" state of consciousness. This is only induced by saying a word over and over again, to clear your head of all thoughts.

Now, how did I get involved with such a topic? Soon after relocating to the United States in 2003 after 34 years as a missionary in northwest Argentina, I began learning about the mystic path of "silence and solitude" which Christian mystics claim is the *only way* to finding your true self and entering into deep union with God. I bought and read more than forty-five books about this topic and have now spent more than ten years researching Christian mysticism. My desire is for

---

[1] www.catholiceducation.org/en/religion-and-philosophy/apologetics/the-danger-of-centering-prayer.html (Dreher has left Catholicism and is now Episcopalian, but this article still appears on several Catholic websites).

[2] Carl McColman, *The Big Book of Christian Meditation: The Essential Guide to Contemplative Spirituality* (Newburyport, MA: Hampton Roads Publishing, 2010), 20. McColman learned contemplation at the Shalem Institute for Spiritual Formation. His book comes highly recommended by Richard Rohr, Phyllis Tickle, Brian McLaren, Cynthia Bourgeault, and others.

Christians to really know God, and to reach spiritual intimacy with God. My concern is that the enemy is sneaking into our churches and we are unaware. I saw the effects of mysticism during my first years of ministry among the Mormons in Utah, and then among the Guaraní people group in Argentina. I see myself as a watchman in a guard tower: I have some perspective on this topic, and I feel the urgency to spread a warning.

My wife, Nancy, and I graduated from Wheaton College, Illinois, in 1961. I then earned a master's degree in missions from Denver Seminary. While pastoring a church in Utah after seminary, I learned that Mormonism was founded upon the occult and witchcraft, with rites lifted from Freemasonry. Founder Joseph Smith had involvement also with Jewish mysticism's Kabbalah.

After Utah, we moved to Argentina, where we helped develop church leaders. Some of these people belonged to the Guaraní tribal people not far removed from the jungle. Their "old ways" included *curanderos* and *brujos*, the traditional healers and witch doctors. Once they became Christians, their spiritual antennas went up, and they were quick to see through religious fakes who got people to be "slain in the spirit." One church leader said his grandmother used to do that before she knew Christ.

Later, as director of spiritual formation in the national church's resident seminary, I coordinated a mentoring program for the resident students, guiding them and their church mentors in having a genuine walk with the Lord. In Argentina, we constantly observed Spiritism in varied forms, sometimes attempting to invade the true church, through syncretistic Catholicism, the adoration of Mother Earth (*Pachamama*), *Difunta Correa* shrines along the highways, and many other cultic influences. Those who came to know Christ from those roots were quick to recognize the world of evil spirits when introduced to any form of Christian mysticism.

We eventually relocated to the United States in 2003 and continued in Christian ministry. A friend of mine introduced me to terms such as *contemplative spirituality*, *Christian formation*, *centering prayer*, and *Christian mysticism*. He urged me to read and help him evaluate some books by Christian mystics including Richard Foster, Thomas Merton, Henri Nouwen, and Bruce Demarest. I read about the threefold mystic path which Christian mystics claim is the only way to find your "true self" and enter into deep union with God. These "Christian contemplatives," as some call themselves, claim to have found the essential ingredient for knowing God personally that is lacking in traditional, historic Christianity that is so heavy on Bible study, apologetics, preaching, and teaching. I soon learned this increasingly popular movement has its roots in the "Desert Fathers" of the third and fourth centuries, mainly based in Syria and Egypt. They in turn were highly influenced by Neoplatonism and Greek mystery religions.

I came to wonder about Catholic and Quaker mystics being so critical and disparaging of traditional practices including corporate worship, apologetics, and sincere Bible study. Many of them express the feelings found on the jacket of Ruth Haley Barton's book *Invitation to Solitude and Silence*, which says, "Much of our faith is about words—preaching, teaching, talking with others. *Yet all of these words are not enough to take us into the real presence of God where we can hear his voice*" (emphasis mine). Why then does the Bible tell us to preach and teach? I began to sense something wrong. You mean I am not in God's presence as a Christ-follower when I am praying or praising God? Not even when I am praying through a passage of Scripture and talking with God about it? I also learned that Ruth Haley Barton studied at the Shalem Institute for Spiritual Formation, begun by Tilden Edwards. He calls his institute, "The Western Bridge to Far Eastern Spirituality."

I began asking God for wisdom and discernment. A former pastor of mine says he now prays to God through Mary and the "saints." Is Christ no longer our only mediator? Where is such a practice found in Scripture? Where are the evangelical theologians and apologists when we need them? What are they saying now? At first I could hardly find any Christian leaders or theologians who were evaluating this incoming tide of historic Christian mysticism that is so quickly becoming the latest fad among evangelicals. I also pray much for divine protection from Satan and his forces. He knows his days are numbered and hates to be exposed.

I sometimes feel like Daniel who prayed, "My lord, what will the outcome of all this be?" (Daniel 12:8). Then I recall God telling him, "Those who are wise will shine like the brightness of the heavens, and those who lead many to righteousness, like the stars for ever and ever" (12:3). Our former mission director, Warren Webster, once told us: "National church leaders want missionaries who are experts—experts in knowing God and in helping others to know God. This kind of missionary is never told to go home, and is always needed."

Red flags were now appearing. I began to see that contemplative silence and solitude really means silencing one's mind via a mantra-like use of a word or phrase from the Bible. Christian mystics follow traditional mystic as well as New Age techniques to empty their minds, to move beyond thinking and feeling. They do so by finding a word or phrase to repeat hundreds of times, like an Eastern religious "mantra." This mind-emptying is often with the expressed goal of centering themselves, looking *inward,* at their souls, at their true selves, which they believe is a spark of God within every person. I learned that Tony Campolo repeats the name Jesus for upwards to half an hour each morning to enter a "thin place" and meet with God in the silence, and that he thinks Christian mysticism is a means for bringing about world unity and peace.

Many of these Christian mystics are also followers of Swiss psychiatrist Carl Jung (quoted by Foster and many others). Jung saw our souls as the "divine child." Jung was also obsessed with the occult and eroticism. He studied Hinduism and the pagan cult of Mithras and concluded that their idea of self-deification could repair the damage done by Christianity. Jung even favored producing a master race, using people of Aryan heritage. Jung's stated aim was to change or eliminate Christianity, which he viewed as a myth. I am surprised that many evangelicals are so captivated by Jung. Do we really know what we are getting into?

Every Christian contemplative promoting the mystic path adores and quotes Teresa of Ávila, from Spain. She was a part of the counter-reformation and hated Protestants, saying they were damning themselves by rejecting the Mass and papal authority. Even Richard Foster found her difficult to understand. She thought she was demonized and used holy water to ward off the spirits. Mysterious noises would come from her throat and at times she would thrash about uncontrollably. She claimed to have seen many demons and was seen levitating during Mass.

An increasing number of Christian mystics seek the union of all religions, with contemplative practices being the common ground for such ecumenical union. Almost none of the mystics have any place for a new birth or conversion experience, and many hold to universal salvation, which eliminates any need for evangelism or missions. Many mystic writers see no difference in essence between humans and God.

Mystic Catholic priest Henri Nouwen said everyone has eternal life and is a child of God. Many of them deny the biblical doctrine of the substitutionary atonement of Christ.[3] So did Meister Eckhart, German Catholic theologian who greatly influenced many mystics and philosophers over the centuries, including Carl Jung, Thomas Merton, and Quaker founder George Fox. Richard Foster and other contemplative authors today favorably quote Eckhart without any disclaimers.

Many mystics hold to pluralism, the idea that all religions lead to heaven, that people can find God regardless of their religion. They treat all mystics as brothers whether they are Catholic, Islamic Sufi, Buddhist, Hindu, or any other religion.

Red flags continued to appear, now joined by some warning bells. What seemed so right at first became increasingly frightening. Some websites are now appearing that warn against the heresy and dangers of contemplative spirituality—also called centering prayer, Christian mysticism, and spiritual formation.

If you are at all familiar with or involved in contemplative spirituality, I would sincerely like to know what has led you to your present thinking and if this is truly helping you to have spiritual victory and power and to become more like Jesus Christ. What do I need to know to understand your position better? What elements of traditional Christian mysticism do you reject? And, what are the "old teachings" of Christianity that need replacing? What biblical doctrine and practice is for all people at all times?

The last thing I wish to do is discourage anyone who is earnestly seeking a closer walk with the Lord and longing for true revival and renewal.

I can understand the appeal of Christian mysticism. Parts of it have helped me, too. Some reoccurring themes found in contemplative spirituality resonate with me as being both biblically based and too often overlooked by contemporary evangelicalism. These include simplicity and frugality, unpretentiousness, noteworthy by an absence of hunger for luxury and the latest fads. Other good themes include

---

[3] On pages 58–59 of Brennan Manning's book *Above All* (Brentwood, TN: Integrity Publishers, 2003), he wrote, "The god whose moods alternate between graciousness and fierce anger . . . the god who exacts the last drop of blood from his Son so that his just anger, evoked by sin, may be appeased, is not the God revealed by and in Jesus Christ. And if he is not the God of Jesus, he does not exist." This is quoted with slight modifications from William Shannon's book *Silence on Fire* (New York: Crossroad Publishing, 1991), 109–10.

making time daily for prayer and Bible meditation, good stewardship of the earth's resources, not announcing our good deeds, quieting our minds, and seeking more solitude to unwind so we can concentrate on God and his Word.

In many other ways, Christian mysticism is a significant and growing challenge to biblical Christianity. The main purpose of this book is to expose those dangers.

This book is divided into two parts, the two approaches to walking with God: the mystical path and the biblical path. The first part is about Christian mysticism. I begin with definitions and a glossary of terms; then a description of Christian mysticism's unifying beliefs, countered with my evaluation of each belief, based on biblical Christianity. Then I talk about the historical roots of Christian mysticism, its main attraction, and list some warnings from other sources.

The second section is a description of biblical Christianity. Researching the writings of Christian mystics has driven me to seek the "real thing": a closer and more intimate and cognitive communion with God, living in constant awareness of his presence. I've become aware of the need to avoid intentionally shutting down all thought processes in order to enter the mystic altered state of consciousness. How can I maintain a love relationship with the Creator of our universe? How can I seek intimacy with God? How do I let the word of Christ dwell in me richly while I worship him with "psalms, hymns and spiritual songs"? (Colossians 3:16) How do I avoid the dead orthodoxy and hypocrisy of just going through religious motions? These are the questions that drive the second part of this book, which begins with biblical sanctification, or biblical path for holiness and increased intimacy with God. It is a list that I have been working on for many years, of how to live the Christian life. Then I treat right motives for loving, obeying, and serving God; and then core values and attitudes essential for growth and service. In the Appendices, I talk about following Jesus' example, I pose some questions for reflection, and I have a list of Christian mystic leaders.

Learning about Christian mysticism's historical roots, along with its basic tenets, drives me back to the basics, which begin with the need for genuine conversion in response to the gospel.

This study has motivated me to practice greater humility, honesty, careful biblical hermeneutics, and more Bible reading with both head and heart. It has helped me with being content, being thankful, living a life of constant worship and constant repentance and faith, and showing a greater social concern for all people I meet. I'm constrained to do everything "in Jesus' name" (as representing him) and am increasingly urged on to worldwide evangelism coupled with personal holiness, integrity, and true love for all people.[4]

There are two approaches to seeking intimacy with God, the mystical way and the biblical way. It is my desire to help the church to be aware of the lure of mysticism and to avoid its dangers.

Let's join King David in saying, "My soul thirsts for God, for the living God. When can I go and meet with God?" (Psalm 42) How can we know God intimately and live in his presence? Enoch and Noah "walked with God." So can we!

---

[4] About evangelism: I greatly appreciate Jonathan Dodson's approach. On his blog he discusses his recent book, *Unbelievable Gospel* (Grand Rapids: Zondervan, 2014). He says, "I consider five types of unbelievable evangelism that lead many to avoid sharing their faith, i.e., evangelism that is preachy, impersonal, intolerant, know-it-all, and shallow." Then on the positive side he says, "We must understand how the gospel is worth believing for those around us. Taking up five major gospel metaphors—justification, union with Christ, redemption, adoption, and new creation—I try to show how these different gospel images or doctrines can be applied to different people in different circumstances . . . Like good counselors, we must listen to others well in order to know how to effectively communicate the unsearchable riches of Christ in a way that makes sense to them."

Section 1
Christian Mysticism

Chapter 1:
What Is Christian Mysticism?

There are two basic and distinct approaches to knowing and walking with God: the traditional Christian *mystic* spirituality and the historic Christian *nonmystic* spirituality. For a start, we need to define the term "mysticism" before we look at "Christian mysticism."

Mysticism in General

Mysticism has various meanings. It can be anything nebulous, miraculous, or supernatural. In Catholicism, mysticism can include the doctrine of transubstantiation, where the bread and the cup of the Eucharist are thought to be transformed mystically into the actual body and blood of Christ. Mysticism can also refer to a religious rite, a religious experience, any personal communion with God or divinity, or a search for hidden or allegorical meanings of Scripture like the Desert Father Origen practiced. Mysticism may be found in practices like blessing water to make it holy, or practicing certain rites to keep out of purgatory, or to help someone else out of purgatory, or to save one's soul.

In shamanism, a person accesses the spirit world by a religious ritual that ushers them into an altered state of consciousness. This almost always involves the use of a sacred word, or mantra. Sometimes drugs are used to enter such a trance. All major religions exhibit some form of mysticism that involves religious ecstasies. This includes Islamic Sufism, Jewish Kabbala, Zen Buddhism, Hinduism, Taoism, and New Age practices. See the Wikipedia entry on "mysticism" for a helpful overview.

This is how Professor Doug Groothuis of Denver Seminary defines general mysticism: "The direct experience of the ultimate sacred reality (however understood)."

I am indebted to Groothuis for the following list of four basic types of mysticism. Most Christian mystics figure in the second and fourth categories. Additional comments on each category are my own.[5]

---

[5] www.theconstructivecurmudgeon.blogspot.com/2010/11/outline-for-upcoming-lecture-at-cherry.html

1. Nature: A feeling of oneness with nature, like Wordsworth, with no Creator/creature distinction.
2. Monistic or nondual: The idea that humans are of the same basic *essence* as God. This is found in Advaita Vedanta Hinduism and in Zen Buddhism, and in some Christian mysticism.
3. No-self: A pantheistic belief, without a personal God; a state of negations. This is the idea of being blown out or extinguished, and includes the idea that living beings have no soul.
4. Dualistic theistic: Belief in a distinction between the self (our *soul*) and the divine. The identity of the person will never dissolve. Dualism affirms the radical transcendence of God.

From the second category, monistic or nondualistic Christian mystics include Meister Eckhart, John of the Cross, Julian of Norwich, Thomas Merton, Matthew Fox, Madame Guyon, Henry Suso, and many more.

A few Christian mystics might fit the third category, nirvana mysticism, including the founder of the Catholic *Quietists,* Miguel de Molinos.[6] The idea is that each person will be eventually negated, or annihilated. In the fourth category, *dualistic* theistic Christian mystics follow essentially the same "mystic path," going from a cognitive to a noncognitive, alpha state of consciousness by repeating a word or phrase. They also lean heavily upon the teachings of the monistic and nondual Christian mystics. They are attracted especially to the writings of all varieties of Christian mystics including Eastern Orthodox, Roman Catholic, even those steeped in the occult. They love the literary works of many who deny essentials of Christianity. Examples of such essentials are justification by faith alone and the substitutionary death of Christ. Some Christian mystics, like Richard Foster, enjoy studying

---

[6] In the 1600s Catholic Spanish mystic Miguel de Molinos, founder of Quietism, refers to Christian mysticism's ultimate goal: "By doing nothing the soul annihilates itself and returns to its beginning and to its origin, which is the essence of God, in which it remains transformed and divinized, and God then remains in himself, because then the two things are no more united, but are one alone, and in this manner God lives and reigns in us, and the soul annihilates itself in operative being." The following link leads to a significant article from the *Catholic Encyclopedia* about Quietism: www.newadvent.org/cathen/12608c.htm This article was written by Pascal P. Parente in 1944.

non-Christian mystics of varied religious traditions, for example Lao-Tse of China and Zarathustra of Persia. He values them as people who can "guide us in the spiritual walk."[7]

The New Testament word *mystery* (*mysterion* in Greek) was used in the pagan mystery religions in reference to exclusive, secret knowledge known only to a few. The *NIV Study Bible* note on Colossians 1:26-27 says, "Paul changes that meaning radically by always combining it with words such as 'disclosed' (here), 'made known' (Ephesians 1:9), 'make plain' (3:9) and 'revelation' (Romans 16:25). The Christian mystery . . . is a revelation of divine truths—once hidden but now openly proclaimed."

Christian Mysticism

Christian mysticism may be defined as follows: the search for a personal, unmediated, and direct experience with God that bypasses the mind; an extrasensory and intimate contact with God where a person hears God's voice and receives divine guidance.

Christian mysticism involves seeking and feeling the divine that dwells within all humans, "that of God in everyone," as Richard Foster and other Quakers term it. The portal for entering God's presence is always the repetition of a sacred word or phrase, a mantra-like practice. A person enters "the silence" of God's presence only by disengaging the mind and all senses, thus entering into an altered state of consciousness. This state is sometimes called *alpha*.

Since Christian mystics believe God dwells within *all* people, then all are spiritual children of God, "the beloved" as well-loved mystic Henri Nouwen terms it. Since the time of Desert Father Origen, many Christian mystics have rejected the idea of an eternal hell. Instead, they believe in universal salvation—that all people will eventually end up in heaven. For most Christian mystics, all roads lead to salvation and to heaven, whether or not one knows about Jesus.

Christian mystics are critical and skeptical of historic biblical Christianity. They look askance at traditional "church" so heavy on worship, Bible study, prayer, apologetics, and doctrinal statements. Christian mystics seek an intimate relationship with God, knowing him

---

[7] Richard J. Foster, *Celebration of Discipline: The Path to Spiritual Growth* (HarperSanFrancisco, 1988), 72.

instead of merely knowing about him. They assert that such a relationship with God is found only by suspending rational patterns of thought via a deep mystical contemplation, termed the *silence*.

Christian mysticism is also termed *contemplative spirituality*. Catholics sometimes use the term "spiritual theology" when referring to the study of Christian perfection. The terms *spiritual formation*, *Christian formation*, or *centering prayer* are common synonyms of Christian mysticism.

Many Christian mystic writers, including Thomas Merton and Madame Guyon, are nondualistic, or even monistic. That is, they think that humans are of the same basic *essence* as God with no fundamental separation between Absolute Being and one's soul (or "true self").

Christian mysticism is rooted in Eastern Christianity, especially in the ancient beliefs and practices of the Desert Fathers of the third and fourth centuries who were highly influenced by Neoplatonism,[8] Gnosticism, Jewish Kabbalah, and even Eastern religions such as Hinduism and Buddhism. Many Christian mystics believe that such mysticism is the foundation of all religions, should lead to increased interspirituality, a new world order, and the uniting of all religions.

The reader may find it helpful to read or skim several Wikipedia articles on this and related topics. See for example the following articles:

Christian Mysticism[9]
Centering Prayer[10]
Hesychasm[11]

---

[8] www.thefreedictionary.com/Neoplatonism Neoplatonism originated in third century Egypt, as a blending of Greek and Eastern mysticism with Judaic and Christian influences.

[9] en.wikipedia.org/wiki/Christian_mysticism This is a fairly good, relatively brief overview of this whole topic, including its historical development and main proponents.

[10] en.wikipedia.org/wiki/Centering_prayer

[11] en.wikipedia.org/wiki/Hesychasm This is a significant article which gets to the very heart of Christian mysticism's use of a sacred word, tracing this practice to hesychasm in Eastern Orthodoxy and rooted in the practices of the Desert Fathers of the third and fourth centuries.

Christian *Nonmystic* Spirituality, Based upon the Scriptures

Christianity is all about knowing and loving God—the Father, the one and only Son, and the Holy Spirit. It involves both knowing *about* God and enjoying an intimate relationship *with* God. Chapter 7 unpacks this whole process.

It all begins with personal conversion, being justified by faith in Christ's atoning work on the cross. The new birth and its accompanying *eternal life* is a totally free gift to be received by faith alone. The Christian's good works follow initial salvation and are a result of walking with God. This radical change of life is evidence of personal faith and trust in the infinite, transcendent, and immanent God.

This conversion, or new birth experience, is followed by a lifelong path of sanctification.[12] It is a life of cooperation with God, his grace coupled with our trust and obedience. God's direct work in us is truly miraculous and glorious. We become increasingly like Christ as we walk with him via all the means he has ordained. This includes Bible meditation, adoration and worship, and all kinds of prayer. Special, intimate communion with God can be experienced anywhere, at any time, usually with the mind fully engaged. All three persons of the Godhead dwell in all those who have received Jesus Christ as Savior.

The mind should be steadfast and renewed, but not intentionally silenced by means of lengthy repetition of a sacred word or phrase. At conversion, we enter the Kingdom of God. We pass from darkness into light. God calls us to a life of holiness and obedience under the lordship of Christ. Loving God and people constitutes the fulfillment of God's law, of all that God demands of us (Matthew 22:37-40). God's presence in us, along with our daily yielding to him, result in a life of love, joy, peace, patience, kindness, goodness, faithfulness, gentleness and self-control. It is a life centered in Christ and his daily grace, a life filled with praise and worship, being joyful always, praying continually, and thankful in all circumstances.

The following basic biblical values and attitudes are essential for Christian growth and service: humility, honesty and integrity, love, constant repentance, constant faith in the Lord, and obedience. This is

---

[12] This article compares the Catholic and non-Catholic approaches to spiritual theology: www.gotquestions.org/spiritual-theology.html

part of what it looks like when we meet someone who obviously walks with God and is filled with his Spirit. Biblical "spiritual formation," is to become increasingly like Jesus.

Nonmystic Christianity is rooted exclusively in the Scriptures which constitute the only authority for doctrine and practice. Such a walk with God, really knowing him, as taught and practiced in the Scriptures, is God's divine power at work within us. It is "everything we need for life and godliness through our knowledge of him who called us by his own glory and goodness" (2 Peter 1:3).

In essence, Peter is asking, "What more do you want?"

What more could Christian mysticism offer? The feminine side of deity? Joint meditation and worship with gospel-denying Zen Buddhists? Assurance that all will end up in heaven, even the devil and his angels? Levitations, like Teresa of Ávila often experienced? No need for evangelism or missions, as Henri Nouwen finally concluded?

Let's take an in-depth look at Christian mysticism, and then decide if we really want or need it.

Chapter 2:
Glossary of Terms and Recurring Themes

Now that I've defined Christian mysticism, I am listing the most common terms and themes associated with it. This will be helpful before reading the next chapter, where I describe in detail the unifying beliefs of Christian mysticism.

Ancient Wisdom: A semitechnical term used by theosophy and the occult. One dictionary defines it as "Pre-Christian knowledge, philosophy, and beliefs."[13] John Ortberg says of Richard Foster's 1992 edition of Prayer: Finding the Heart's True Home, "This book is a rare gift—informed by ancient wisdom." Some evangelicals consider "ancient wisdom" to be mere accretions to biblical Christianity.

Apophatic (Dark) Way of Silence: Prayer that is beyond words, thoughts, concepts, images, or any senses, in order to enter God's presence (the opposite of "kataphatic," see below). *Silence* for the mystic means absence of all thought. It is silencing of the mind, instead of merely seeking a quiet place for prayer.

Breath Prayer: "A form of contemplative prayer linked to the rhythms of breathing: (1) breathe in, calling on a biblical name or image of God, and (2) breathe out a simple God-given desire."[14] It is also called "prayer of the heart." It is rooted in the contemplative tradition of Eastern Orthodoxy.

Centering Prayer,[15] Centering Down: This involves repetition of a sacred word to be "present to God." It is kataphatic prayer, *with* words. Teresa Tillson of St. Olaf College says, "Centering Prayer prepares us

---

13 www.dictionary.com/browse/ancient-wisdom
14 Adele Ahlberg Calhoun, *Spiritual Disciplines Handbook: Practices That Transform Us*, (Downers Grove, IL: InterVarsity, 2005), 204.
15 See what Thomas Keating says about centering prayer: gravitycenter.com/practice/centering-prayer/
See also: en.wikipedia.org/wiki/centering_prayer

to receive the gift of God's presence."[16] It prepares us for contemplative prayer. Henri Nouwen said, "The quiet repetition of a single word can help us to descend with the mind into the heart."[17] Adele Calhoun says centering prayer is "taming scattered thoughts by attending to Christ through the use of a prayer word."[18] On a Catholic website Jacqueline Galloway discusses mysticism, saying we come to know God by entering "the superconscious state." This is done "by using a repetitive word . . . something to bring us into the presence of God."[19] Matt Slick, former New Ager, describes centering prayer as similar to what he practiced before his conversion to Christ.[20] A Catholic website says centering prayer "is neither Christian nor prayer."[21]

Christ Consciousness: This is definitely not awareness of Jesus Christ! A term used in pseudo spirituality meaning a state of awareness by means of contemplation, where you realize you are divine, a Christ, and living in enlightenment. Mystic "Christ consciousness" is non-Christian spirituality.[22]

The Cloud of Unknowing: A fourteenth century anonymous English mystical text built upon the mystical tradition of Pseudo–Dionysius the Areopagite. This book describes how a person arrives at an encounter with a "nothing and a nowhere" as we encounter the mysterious and unfathomable being of God himself.

Contemplation, Contemplative Prayer: Apophatic, wordless prayer, when at last we slip into "the silence" of God's presence, or "divine

---

[16] www.stolaf.edu/people/huff/classes/religion/Essay.html
[17] Henri Nouwen, *The Way of the Heart: Desert Spirituality and Contemporary Ministry*, (NY: Ballantine Books, 1981), 64–5.
[18] Adele Ahlberg Calhoun, *Spiritual Disciplines Handbook*, 207.
[19] www.ecatholic2000.com/pray/prayer2.shtml
[20] carm.org/centering-prayer
[21] www.catholicculture.org/culture/library/view.cfm?recnum=7091
   See also: acatholiclife.blogspot.com/2007/05/errors-of-centering-prayer.html
[22] See this website, *Center for Christ Consciousness*: www.ctrforchristcon.org/the-stillness.html This article about *stillness,* as well as the whole website, is frighteningly similar to Christian mysticism's techniques and aims, while openly being "a blend of the Eastern and Western approaches to spirituality." Such a blend is what also characterizes "Christian" mystics like M. Scott Peck, Thomas Merton, Thomas Keating, and Tilden Edwards.

union" which is the last stage of the mystic path and the goal of all Christian mysticism. It is sometimes called "prayer of the heart." See this well-researched article from Christian Research Network about Christian mystic contemplation.[23]

Daily Office, Divine Office, Canonical Hours: Fixed times of prayer during the day. This may vary a lot between denominations.

***Dark Night of the Soul*:** A book by Catholic mystic John of the Cross (1542–1591). British mystic Evelyn Underhill understood this concept as a state of confusion, sensing God's absence or withdrawal before arriving at the final step in the mystic path. Some refer to this as a spiritual desert, absence of light and hope, a time of depression, discouragement, even doubt, spiritual burnout, feeling far from God. Mother Teresa of India admitted she lived in such a state most of her life.

Daily Prayers, Daily Exam: Jesuits instituted this as a verbal prayer at noon and late evening, talking with God about the events of the day.

Divine Union, Transforming Union: The last, wordless stage of the mystic path, where one finally enters "the silence" of intimate communion with God.

Enneagram: An attempt to map one's unconscious and subconscious motivations, so as to find your true self and wellness. An Enneagram is defined as "a geometric figure that delineates the nine basic personality types of human nature and their complex interrelationships." See more at the link below.[24]

False Self: It is a mask we put on, which we all develop in order to cope with the emotional trauma of early childhood; a sort of pathological dependence on what people think of us. Keating says, "In Baptism, the false self is ritually put to death. . . . "[25] Definitions of

---

[23] christianresearchnetwork.org/topic/contemplative-prayer/#identifier_2_42750
[24] www.enneagraminstitute.com
[25] Thomas Keating, *Open Mind, Open Heart: The Contemplative Dimension of the Gospel* (New York: Continuum, 1992), 128.

"false self" vary among Christian mystics. Adele Calhoun in *Spiritual Disciplines Handbook* defines this as "an identity rooted in secondary things like accomplishments, productivity, people pleasing, fame for success."

Holy, or Sacred Rhythms: Setting aside regular times for praying or for practicing spiritual disciplines, for worship and getting closer to God, for spiritual transformation, for serving others and showing mercy, and for the rhythms of the liturgical church calendar.

Interspirituality: A term coined in 1999 by Wayne Teasdale in his book *The Mystic Heart*. He says it involves "identifying and embracing the mystical core or common ground of the world's religions."[26] Interspirituality also involves topics such as global governance and world structures, along with distilling wisdom from all religions. Catholic mystic Father Thomas Keating of the Centering Prayer Movement is closely associated with Interspirituality. So is mystic author Adrian B. Smith. Some have described divinity as one underground river which we access from different wells or traditions, thus making all religions the same at their mystic core. Apparently Pope Francis is also into interspirituality, according to an article titled "New Age Leader Deepak Chopra Asks: 'Will Pope Francis Become a Holy Man for the World?'"[27] He also seems to be involved in historic contemplation, even naming Thomas Merton as one of the four most meaningful people.[28]

Kataphatic (Light) Way:[29] Prayer with words and thoughts (the opposite of apophatic, see above).

---

[26] quotationstreasury.wordpress.com/tag/definition-interspirituality/
[27] www.lighthousetrailsresearch.com/blog/?p=19044
[28] www.lighthousetrailsresearch.com/blog/?p=18379
[29] This article by Frederick G. McLeod explains the difference between "apophatic" and "kataphatic": opcentral.org/resources/2015/01/13/frederick-g-mcleod-apophatic-or-kataphatic-prayer/
See more at: www.ignatianspirituality.com/2026/kataphatic-or-apophatic-prayer#sthash.FktmpMAG.dpuf This last article helps us to better understand St. Ignatius, founder of the Jesuits, and their expression of mysticism.

Kundalini: Yoga and Hindu concept of energy coiled up like a snake and centered at the base of the spine waiting to be awakened by intense meditation and breath control. It can give a feeling of an electric current running along the spine and can be very dangerous with many physical symptoms characteristic of demon possession.[30] It is thought that seven chakras, or energy centers, open up during kundalini practice. Theosophy has promoted this practice, as well as psychologist Carl Jung and some Christian mystics including Thomas Keating.

Labyrinth Prayer: It takes you inward as you slowly walk in concentric paths, to bring your whole self into harmony with God.[31]

***Lectio Divina*:** Divine reading; sacred reading of Scripture that involves reading a text then letting a word or phrase speak to you as a sacred word to repeat, as a mantra, to usher you into wordless contemplation.

Mystical Theology/Spiritual Theology: The Catholic Encyclopedia article about contemplation defines mystical theology as "the science that studies mystical states."[32] This includes especially the mystic path, which comprises the preparatory dispositions and disciplines that trigger the final ecstatic state of union with God.

Metaphysical: That which is beyond the material realm, or is supernatural or immaterial (*meta* is Greek for "beyond").

"Palms Up, Palms Down": What some mystics like to do during centering prayer and may indicate "in with the good, and out with the bad."

Sacred Word: An essential part of "centering prayer" and all mysticism, Christian or otherwise, in which a word or phrase repeated for a period of time serves to free the mind of all thinking and

---

[30] Check out this Catholic website article about Kundalini:
www.churchmilitant.com/news/article/awakening-the-serpent-within
[31] www.lessons4living.com/labyrinth.htm
[32] www.newadvent.org/cathen/04324b.htm

supposedly leads into God's presence. It induces an altered state of consciousness.

Spiritual Director: A mature Christian, sometimes from another faith tradition, who comes alongside you as a mentor or guide. The director gently guides you in your spiritual formation, especially to help you find intimacy with God.

Spiritual Formation, Christian Formation: Spiritual exercises and disciplines including *Lectio Divina* that serve to usher you into God's presence and help you to become more like Christ. Spiritual directors are usually recommended for this process. The Wikipedia article on spiritual formation is somewhat helpful.

Thin Place: Where the boundary is thin between heaven and earth, where God is present in a special way or more easily approachable. It's where time and eternity almost touch.

True self/Christ-self: The image of God in which we are all created, our primal self, our basic core of goodness, our divine center, or "inner light" as Quakers term it. Keating says, "God and our true Self are not separate. Though we are not God, God and our true Self are the same thing."[33] Keating's quote shows his nondualism. Catholic priest Henri Nouwen said, "The God who dwells in our inner sanctuary is the same as the one who dwells in the inner sanctuary of each human being."[34]

Union with God: Ecstasy, the final stage of the mystic path.

Universalism: The idea that all people will eventually be rightly related to God. The Desert Father Origen influenced many people to believe this.

---

[33] Thomas Keating, *Open Mind, Open Heart: The Contemplative Dimension of the Gospel* (New York: Continuum, 1992), 127.

[34] Henry J. M. Nouwen, *Here and Now: Living in the Spirit* (New York: The Crossroad Publishing Company, 1994), 22.

Visualization: Imagining actually seeing Jesus, or gazing at icons and images of saints. It is the belief that sometimes we can create a reality by visualization. At times such images begin to move and talk to us. Ignatius Loyola, founder of the Jesuits, taught people to visualize themselves at events mentioned in the Bible then interact with the characters.[35] Episcopalian mystic Morton Kelsey taught visualization and told people not to be fearful when images begin to move. Catholic writer Randy England warns that "visualization is the attempt to manipulate the physical world or contact the spirit world by use of the imagination. . . . Visualization is the foundation and basis for witchcraft . . . and pagan shamanism."[36]

---

[35] www.ignatianspirituality.com/ignatian-prayer/the-spiritual-exercises/pray-with-your-imagination

[36] Randy England, *The Unicorn in the Sanctuary: The Impact of the New Age Movement on the Catholic Church* (Rockford, IL: Tan Books, 1991).

Chapter 3:
Unifying Beliefs and Practices
of Christian Mysticism

When people learn I am reading about and evaluating Christian mysticism, invariably they ask questions such as, What is it? What are its basic beliefs and practices? What are its roots?

Christian mystics vary widely, from theological liberalism to progressive Protestantism and on to evangelicalism and ultra-conservativism. Their roots are Catholic, Orthodox, Quaker, or Protestant. Those who call themselves evangelical mystics[37] hold to the fundamental doctrines of evangelical Christianity[38] while looking for something more. They read almost all the Christian mystics, then try to hold on to that which is good. Some say, "I eat the fish and spit out the bones." Not everyone who seeks intimacy with God through mystic silence and solitude will affirm all of the following beliefs and practices. Likewise, some noncontemplative followers of Christ, like me, will readily see some points with which they wholly agree. All Christian mystics practice some form of contemplation which

---

[37] See this website for a historical overview of what's termed evangelical mysticism: en.wikademia.org/Evangelical_mysticism Some Christians distinguish between Christian mysticism and evangelical mysticism, as seen in the following article:
en.wikademia.org/Differences_between_Christian_mysticism_and_Evangelical_mysticism Others find it hard to distinguish clearly these two categories since virtually all the evangelicals practicing contemplation also quote extensively from the same traditional mystics, from the Desert Fathers onward. Another link is: wesleygospel.com/2011/03/25/evangelical-mysticism-the-article-that-wikipedia-deleted/

[38] The Evangelical Covenant Church has a helpful list of evangelical emphases: "Evangelicals historically have been characterized by a number of significant emphases: a strong insistence on biblical authority; the absolute necessity of new birth; Christ's mandate to evangelize the world; the continuing need for education and formation in a Christian context; and responsibility for benevolence and the advancement of social justice." The following link unpacks this in detail: www.covchurch.org/resources/wp-content/uploads/sites/2/2015/03/covenant_affirmations_booklet.pdf The first three of these points are denied or greatly distorted by many highly loved and read Christian mystics from the early Church Fathers onward. For another summary of basic evangelical emphases, see: nae.net/statement-of-faith/

historically has involved silencing the mind in order to enter God's presence.[39] The term contemplation was used almost exclusively for this mystic experience until about the fifteenth century. Christian mysticism/contemplation is often associated with the term "spiritual formation." Since 1996 The Association of Theological Schools (ATS) requires its approved institutions to include spiritual formation in their curriculum, although it is not clear what the ATS means by this term.

So, what do *most* of the traditional Christian mystics believe and practice? What is Christian mysticism? What is promoted in virtually all Christian schools under the term spiritual formation?

I have already discussed mysticism in general, and have briefly defined Christian mysticism. I will now attempt to examine Christian mysticism in detail and evaluate each aspect in light of Scripture.

I do not want to harm anyone who is honestly seeking a closer, more intimate walk with God, as we all should be doing. However, some warning is needed, especially when dealing with blatant denial of the most basic biblical teaching and practice.

Direct Experience with God

Christian mysticism involves the search for a personal, unmediated, and direct experience with God that bypasses the mind, an extrasensory and intimate contact with God where a person hears God's voice and receives divine guidance. Christian mystics say it involves both *meditation* and *contemplation*, using these terms somewhat differently than New Age and Eastern religions do.

Meditation in Christian mysticism is cognitive, with the use of words, thoughts, and all our senses. It is pondering the Scriptures and practicing other religious activities that help us know *about* God. Such meditation may even involve thinking about something you have read or experienced. It also involves selecting some word or phrase then repeating it over and over. Christian mystic meditation is *kataphatic* (with words and thoughts), with the intention of preparing us for contemplation which is *apophatic* (without words and thoughts).

---

[39] Former Catholic priest, Richard Bennett, gives us a helpful clarification of what traditional Christian mysticism entails: "Mysticism is an attempt to gain ultimate knowledge of God by a direct experience that bypasses the mind." Read more at: www.christiananswers.net/q-eden/mysticism-bennett.html

Thomas Keating refers to centering prayer as "preparation for contemplative prayer."[40]

Contemplation (contemplative prayer), in contrast, is usually a fleeting, formless prayer without words. It is extrasensory, beyond all thoughts or feelings. This is slipping at last into "the silence" of intimacy with God, where God shows up in a special, mystic way. It is often called "union with God." Others prefer calling it "a loving gaze upon God." Richard Foster calls this "a loving attentiveness to God . . . talk recedes into the background and feeling comes to the foreground."[41] Foster refers to the final stage of contemplation as "spiritual ecstasy." We need to keep in mind that New Age and Eastern Religions use the term meditation differently, to mean the same nonverbal experience that Christian mystics refer to when they talk about contemplation.

Carl McColman discusses normal use of Bible study, worship and prayer, but says, "However . . . as valuable as this knowledge is, be careful not to reduce the Christian mysteries to mere intellectual exploration . . . as joyful as it is to learn *about* God and Christ . . . be careful that these mental gymnastics don't become an obstacle to actually *becoming intimate* with this God you are so busy studying."[42] He says *Lectio Divina*, ending with silent contemplation, "opens you up to allow God to lead you where he chooses," and is "the single most foundational spiritual exercise related to Christian mysticism." He suggests twenty minutes for repeating a sacred word in order to enter into the deep silence of God's presence, an intimacy with God without words and with all senses disengaged. Ruth Haley Barton quotes Thomas Merton as describing this as passing beyond communication

[40] Thomas Keating, *Open Mind, Open Heart: The Contemplative Dimension of the Gospel* (New York: Continuum, 1992), 31. See Teresa Tillson on this: www.stolaf.edu/people/huff/classes/religion/Essay.html

[41] Richard Foster, *Prayer: Finding the Heart's True Home* (HarperSanFrancisco, 1992), 166.

[42] Carl McColman, *The Big Book of Christian Mysticism: The Essential Guide to Contemplative Spirituality* (Newburyport, MA: Hampton Roads Publishing, 2010), 189. On page 219 and following, McColman explains in greater detail how to practice wordless mystic contemplation.

into silent communion.[43] Brennan Manning said, "The first step in faith is to stop thinking about God at the time of prayer."[44]

Christian mystics will ask us how long it's been since we have *sensed* God's presence, while also saying we only meet God with all senses turned off since our minds get in the way of such intimacy.

This ancient mystical practice induces an altered state of consciousness called "the silence," which is a silencing of the mind by entering what is called the alpha state of consciousness. This is the essence of all mysticism, whether New Age, Christian, and otherwise.[45] Contemplation is the final stage of the historic mystic path which we will later describe.

Some leading Christian mystic authors learned and refined this contemplative ability from their close associations with non-Christian Eastern mystics,[46] which mirrors what the ancient Desert Fathers in Egypt also did.

The ancient Christian mystic path involves searching out and discovering those lost secrets of the ancient church, including the Desert Fathers and mystics of the Middle Ages. These secrets include labyrinth prayer, *Lectio Divina*, certain postures and rhythmical breathing, visualization, and virtually always include the repetition of a sacred word or phrase to still the mind and usher us into God's presence. *The Jesus Prayer* is often used, especially by Eastern Orthodoxy where it originated: "Lord Jesus Christ, Son of God, have mercy on me, a sinner."[47]

---

[43] Ruth Haley Barton, *Invitation to Silence and Solitude* (Downers Grove, IL: InterVarsity, 2014), 111.

[44] Brennan Manning, *The Signature of Jesus* (Colorado Springs: Multnomah, 1996), 198.

[45] Laurie Cabot with Tim Cowan, *Power of the Witch* (New York: Delta, 1989), 173, 183. Cabot, a practicing witch for over forty years, says, "The science of Witchcraft is based upon our ability to enter altered states of consciousness we call 'alpha' . . . In alpha the mind opens up to nonordinary forms of communication. . . . It is the heart of Witchcraft."

[46] This includes many of the most famous Christian mystics that all the others freely quote and lean upon, people like Thomas Merton, Henri Nouwen, William Blake, William Menninger, Meister Eckhart, Carl Jung, M. Scott Peck, Thomas Keating, Brennan Manning, and M. Basil Pennington.

[47] According to en.wikipedia.org/wiki/Hesychasm, the goal of the *Hesychast* (mystic) in the repetition of the Jesus Prayer is to arrive at union with God, or ecstasy, and "to acquire, through purification and Grace, the Holy Spirit and salvation."

Biblical Evaluation

Bible-based Christianity includes cognitively knowing about God and truly knowing God in a warm, intimate relationship through faith and trust in Jesus Christ.

The Bible teaches cognitive meditation of Scripture and prayer with words, but insists that a true walk with God involves much more than merely knowing *about* him. I need to keep thinking and remain mentally engaged as I worship, pray, draw near to God, reflect upon all of life, and mull things over. I need to apply God's truth to every area of my life. "Think on these things" (Philippians 4:8). "Let the word of Christ dwell in you richly" (Colossians 3:16). The righteous person of the first psalm delights in God's law and meditates on it at all times. I should not divorce my head from my heart, nor should I meditate on Scripture without also communing with the Author. The Bible *does not* teach the ancient "mystic path" of silencing the mind with constant repetition of a sacred word so as to enter the alpha altered state of consciousness and finally arrive at God's intimate presence. The Bible *does* teach me to love God with all my heart, soul, strength, and mind, and to love my neighbor as myself. A. W. Tozer once said we need to keep close to God, keep close to people, and keep humble. What a good summary of the basics.

Christian mystics/contemplatives rightly seek intimacy with God. They are sick and tired of "talk without the walk"; of the do's and don'ts of "ugly orthodoxy" that is so angry and full of gloom and doom, condemning without caring, with little mercy or love, superficially close to God yet so aloft from people. Like Jonah when he finally arrived at Nineveh. As a result, beautiful heresy becomes increasingly attractive. God-seeking people cringe at all the quarrelling and division over inconsequential ideas—like where the Holy Spirit proceeds from, just the Father or from both the Father and the Son.[48] Or how many "dispensations" there are, if any. Or the meaning of obscure prophetic details.

Church historians tell us early asceticism and monasticism was born out of reaction to the low spiritual state of the Christian church. Perhaps many Christian mystics today are reacting to some church

---

[48] The Eastern church divided from Rome and the Western church over this very question.

21

experiences of dead orthodoxy and hypocrisy, with people just going through the motions without real contact with God.[49] Could this reaction be similar to what Danish Søren Kierkegaard was confronting in cold and formal Lutheranism in the early 1800s? Might these disillusioned Christian mystics need a different kind of church? I fear that in their quest for the real thing, they could easily be recreating just another form of legalism while missing the heart of the biblical gospel. Could they unintentionally be getting themselves involved with some serious heresy, or even the occult, while missing the joy of Spirit-filled living? Where can they today find real New Testament Christianity— intimate contact with God through daily repentance, verbal and cognizant worship, all kinds of sincere prayer, and Scripture meditation? Like what occurred after the Day of Pentecost! Where today should we look to find apostolic doctrine, warm and supportive caring, joyful worship, generosity and true community, continuous evangelism, with everything saturated in prayer? (Acts 2:42-47).

People who are being drawn to contemplative practices sincerely desire to become more like Jesus. They need to experience unconditional acceptance and love from nonmystic Christians who also love Jesus with their whole hearts. They also need to see what God has actually said—God's inspired "ancient wisdom" that trumps all else! For instance, the Bible teaches that "eternal life" is to *know* intimately both the Father and the Son (John 17:3). It involves establishing an initial, personal relationship with him, not merely knowing about him (see 1 John 1:1-4). "Eternal life" is synonymous with "salvation" and with "the Kingdom of God" (See Matthew 19:16-30), which we are to seek first and foremost (Matthew 6:33). This alone is biblical spirituality, united with Christ by repentance and faith alone. But this must be a faith that results in a changed life, as I daily walk with God and enjoy a personal encounter with him. That kind of intimacy with God must translate into loving people and obeying Christ, as James says in his epistle. If I lack either the basics of "the faith" or the fruit of the Spirit, maybe I need to examine myself as Paul warned the Corinthian church: "Examine yourselves to see whether you are in the

---

[49] William Ralph Inge notes that "every historical example of a mystical movement may be expected to exhibit characteristics which are determined by the particular forms of religious deadness in opposition to which it arises." This is from his 1899 lecture, "Christian Mysticism," delivered at Oxford University.

faith: test yourselves" (2 Corinthians 13:5). Paul prays for their perfection in the sense of spiritual maturity (2 Corinthians 13:9, 11). Biblical spirituality begins with conversion/justification, followed by the lifelong process of becoming like Christ and walking with God via all the means he has ordained. Such intimate walking with God is not found exclusively in our "quiet time," as important as that is, but in a life of constant worship, saying "yes" to the Spirit's promptings, talking with God at any moment and about anything, usually with the mind fully engaged. My mind should be steadfast and renewed, but not intentionally silenced by means of lengthy repetition of a sacred word or phrase. Such nonmystic Christian living is rooted exclusively in the Scriptures which constitute my only authority for doctrine and practice.

Every recorded prayer in the Bible is verbal. In 1 Samuel chapter one Anna moves her lips in silent prayer in the tabernacle. Eli mistook this for drunkenness. Anna's silent prayer, *with words*, is recorded in verse 11. Is this real prayer? Of course! In true communion with God? Absolutely! And her prayer for a son was answered as is clear in verse 20: "She named him Samuel, saying, 'Because I asked the Lord for him.'"

Biblical intimacy with God involves both cognitive and noncognitive elements, our minds and our emotions, but never intentionally shutting down our minds or our five senses. Since mysticism's "prayer without words," or "loving attentiveness," is not found in Scripture, we probably should not call it true prayer. If it is not prayer, then what is it? Is such a person smiling at God in companionable silence? Do they have a sense of awe or some other emotion? Could such a person even be receiving a message from God if, as contemplatives claim, it is a state devoid of all thought and sensation? Might such an ecstatic experience involve contact with demonic spirits, as mystic writer Evelyn Underhill warns us about?[50] Teresa of Ávila describes from her own experiences, fully assured she herself was demonized.[51] Foster and Merton openly mention this danger.

---

[50] www.sacred-texts.com/myst/myst/myst19.htm

[51] Frequently Teresa's experiences were frightening. Mysterious noises would come from her throat. People sometimes accused her of being under satanic power. In fact, she herself often feared she was possessed by demons. At least she claimed to have seen many demons. One of these, in her own words, "made me thresh about with my body, head, and arms, and I was powerless to prevent him." *The*

Every time I talk to God, with words and genuine repentance, praise and submission, God hears me and is with me in an elevated degree of intimate communion. This is a direct encounter with the Creator of the universe who has become my Savior and Lord. In so doing I seek God and his glory, not just feelings. Perhaps people around me experience more feelings than I do, as Christ's Spirit produces his love, joy, peace, patience, and so forth in my life.

It is significant that some famous, often quoted Christian mystics like Thomas Merton and Thomas Keating admit that contemplation involving the mystic path of silence is not found in the Bible.[52] We will examine the historic roots of Christian mysticism in the next chapter. Christian mysticism only goes back to the Desert Fathers of the third and fourth centuries after Christ, by Christians who were highly influenced by Greek mysticism and philosophy.

A growing number of evangelical Christian leaders and organizations are awakening to the serious differences between historic Christian mysticism and basic biblical teaching and practices. "Evangelical Resources" is an excellent source of books, articles, and websites dealing with doctrinal deviations of all sorts, including an extremely helpful survey of "mysticism."[53] This link includes both critiques of Christian mysticism and some material about true biblical spirituality. See also the bibliography I have added to this book, along with more links to evaluations of Christian mysticism.

Life of Saint Teresa of Ávila by Herself, trans. J. M. Cohen (London: Penguin Books, 1957), 222. She would use holy water to protect herself from these spirits. She would arrive at a state of ecstasy, a state of complete passiveness where all senses quit, including memory. She described this as sweet, happy pain, alternating between a fearful fiery glow and a spell of strangulation. She was seen levitating during mass.

[52] Keating says, "Jesus did not teach a specific method of meditation or bodily discipline for quieting the imagination, memory, and emotions. . . . The Spirit is above every method or practice." See: Thomas Keating, *Open Mind, Open Heart: The Contemplative Dimension of the Gospel* (New York: Continuum, 1992), 132. Mystic Catholic priest Thomas Merton, quoted by virtually all Christian mystics, recognized that "contemplation" in the historic mystic sense is not mentioned in the New Testament. Thomas Merton, *The Inner Experience: Notes on Contemplation,* (HarperSanFrancisco, 2003), 33. How right he was. Yet he assures us "contemplation is man's highest and most essential spiritual activity."

[53] www.evangelicalresources.org/mysticism.shtml

God is Unknowable

Historic Christian mysticism says God is ultimate reality and ultimate mystery. He is divinity existing in divine darkness. He is totally incomprehensible, "utterly unknowable," and "beyond understanding" by our senses or reason.[54]

Interestingly enough, the influential Catholic mystic Thomas Merton admitted that "in the end the contemplative suffers the anguish of realizing that he no longer knows what God is."[55] Another Catholic mystic writer, Carl McColman, discussing "exploring the unknowable" asks: "How can mysticism be about God when even Christians don't all agree on who or what God is or how knowable he is?"[56]

Many Christian mystics use the term apophatic theology to describe divine darkness, that God is basically inaccessible and unreachable.

Early Desert Fathers, as well as many Christian mystics since then, have agreed with Hinduism in declaring that God is unknown and unknowable.[57] Many Christian mystics think that God is everything (pantheism), or that God is in everything (panentheism). I will explain this some more in the section dealing with union with God, where I treat essential topics like nondualism and monism and the essential nature of all humans.

Early Christian mystics, like the unknown author of *The Book of Privy Counseling,* thought that mindless contemplation leads a person to find out that God is one's being. The companion to this book, *The Cloud of Unknowing,*[58] describes how a person arrives at an encounter with a "nothing and a nowhere" as they encounter the mysterious and

---

[54] Thomas Merton, *The Inner Experience: Notes on Contemplation* (HarperSanFrancisco, 2003), 72, quoting the ancient Christian mystic Pseudo-Dionysius the Areopagite.

[55] www.longpauses.com/new-seeds-of-contemplation/ This book by Merton was reprinted in 2007 with an introduction by Sue Monk Kidd where this quote is found on page 13.

[56] Carl McColman, *The Big Book of Christian Mysticism: The Essential Guide to Contemplative Spirituality* (Newburyport, MA: Hampton Roads Publishing, 2010), 27.

[57] Vergilius Ferm, *Living Schools of Religion,* (Littlefield, Adams & Co., 1958). On page 9, in the chapter on Hinduism, it states: "Hinduism declares that Brahman is unknown and unknowable. . . . Brahman, soul, and universe are one. They are convertible terms. 'I am He.'"

[58] See this short summary of these two books: www.frimmin.com/books/privycounsel.php

unfathomable being of God himself. Most Christian mystics affirm that our "true self" is a bit of divinity residing in everyone, in our divine center which is often termed our "collective soul."[59] Christian mystics who are more conservative hold to a strict dualism: God and people are of two distinct substances, and only true followers of Christ are indwelt by him.[60] At the same time, these conservative Christian mystics lean heavily upon the writings of the nondualistic and monistic Christian mystics including Thomas Merton, Meister Eckhart, Julian of Norwich, John of the Cross, Catherine of Genoa, Matthew Fox, Madame Guyon, Thomas Keating, William Shannon, Jan Ruysbroeck, M. Scott Peck, Richard Rohr, Swiss psychiatrist Carl Jung (not very "Christian" but highly followed by many Christian mystics today), and many more. Dualistic mystic evangelicals freely quote all these authors without qualification or warning.

"Ultimate mystery, ultimate reality" is Thomas Keating's term for "the ground of infinite potentiality and actualization; a term emphasizing the divine transcendence. It is the divine Presence and ground in which our being is rooted."[61]

Biblical Evaluation

In contrast to Christian mysticism's assertion that God is unknowable, the Bible says God is indeed knowable. It also teaches that no humans will ever share God's divine essence.

Some knowledge about God is known from observing nature, although people often distort or suppress such truth (Romans 1:19; Psalm 19:1-6). All people need God's special revelation to avoid

---

[59] Swiss psychiatrist Carl Jung taught we all have a "collective soul" or "true self" and saw this as the "Divine Child" or Christ, and it is connected to all other humans in what he termed a "collective unconscious." See: Richard Noll, *The Jung Cult: Origins of a Charismatic Movement* (Glencoe, IL: Free Press Paperbacks, 1994), 250–54.

[60] We should also note that Christianity denies the eternal existence of good and evil. All matter as well as human souls are totally dependent upon God's creation and sustaining activity. The Bible says only God has immortality (1 Timothy 6:16). Only God is eternally indestructible. Our future "immortality" is imputed by God, not some inherent quality we enjoy. C. S. Lewis argued against any dualism that would equate God with Satan! That they are not opposites. Lewis said, if Satan has an opposite, it might be Michael.

[61] rabbihenochdov.com/pages/snowmass.html (Here's a vivid example of syncretism and ecumenism.)

distorting natural revelation as well as knowing God personally. Dennis Hinks, in his helpful article, "Mankind, the 'Image of God'" says, "We cannot comprehend the *infinite* God, except to the limited extent that he reveals himself in finite creation."[62] Humans share only some of God's attributes. Hinks says, "We acknowledge that humans are only a finite *reflection* of the infinite."

God's attributes that we humans know about yet will never share: God's essential qualities of being all-powerful, glorious, worthy of worship, everywhere present, all-knowing, eternal, immortal, self-sufficient, uncreated, transcendent, creator and sustainer of the universe including all life and matter, unchangeable, and absolutely infinite in all his qualities.

God's attributes that we humans can experience, by God's grace: God is holy and totally separate from sin, just, merciful, loving, gracious, kind, patient, sacrificial, compassionate, trustworthy, never ceasing, and much more.

As we grow and mature in our faith and walk with God, we become increasingly like him in these qualities. We need no hidden, esoteric knowledge from God that is gained in "the silence." Nor will we Christians, or humans in general, ever participate in God's basic *essence*.[63] God originally created humans "in his image." This is what distinguishes humans from the rest of the animals, although the Scriptures never explain what all is included. The Bible does assure Christians that we will be *like Christ* when we see him. We will be holy, will never sin again, will be totally yielded to God and walk in full communion with him for all eternity. As finite creatures we cannot begin to comprehend all God has prepared for us who love him (1 Corinthians 2:9). One thing is for certain: humans will never be

---

[62] www.journal33.org/godworld/html/man-iog.htm Hinks says about the distinction between humans and God: "False religion tends to distort this distinction. It may emphasize only one of these two aspects of God (his transcendence or his immanence). Or it may *lower* God to the level of the creature, or *raise* the creature to the level of God."

[63] On page 95 of his book *Soul Transformation: The Sanctification Experience of the Believer* (Tempe, AZ: Xulon, 2012), Donald Ekstrand discusses "fellowship with God," saying fellowship means being partakers, then quotes 2 Peter 1:4, "partakers of the divine nature." A few sentences later Ekstrand says, "Theologians aren't sure exactly what it means '*to possess the divine essence*'. . . ." replacing the word "nature" with "essence." The fact is, we don't possess God's essence, nor does any English translation use "essence" in 2 Peter 1:4.

objects of worship. But, as Hinks says, "God created humans in such a way, that they are *as much like God as is possible* for a created being . . . in ways that the rest of creation cannot be."

Can humans know God? Of course! The book of Hebrews begins by saying, "In the past, God spoke to our forefathers through the prophets at many times and in various ways, but in these last days he has spoken to us by his Son" (Hebrews 1:1-2). As in marriage, my relationship with God is a covenant, committed to loving God and forsaking all others. In marriage the two partners continue to learn about one another for the rest of their lives together.

When Philip asked our Lord, "Show us the Father," Jesus replied: "Don't you know me, Philip, even after I have been among you such a long time? Anyone who has seen me has seen the Father" (John 14:8-9).

An excellent treatment of the knowability of God says God is knowable, but not exhaustively, and shows how we can know God.[64]

I need to ponder often about all God has revealed, his essential qualities as well as what he has done and will do, and praise him for what he is! Psalm 147:4 says God "determines the number of the stars and calls them each by name." Wow! Then we join the psalmist in the following verse: "Great is our Lord and mighty in power; *his understanding has no limit*" (emphasis added).

Everything God affirms about himself in the Scriptures is true— and is knowable, although "we know in part" (1 Corinthians 13:9). It will take eternity to know God in all his infinite greatness. As a Christ-follower, I also "know" God intimately. This is called "eternal life," knowing the Father and the Son (John 17:3). But like a good marriage, it gets increasingly better as we grow in the grace and knowledge of Jesus Christ (2 Peter 3:18). The apostle Paul kept pressing on, to know Christ more intimately. If Christians needed to repeat a sacred word to accomplish this, Paul surely would have explained to us the mystic path. What could lead a Christian mystic to think God is totally unknowable, unless they reject either the divine inspiration of the Scriptures or the divinity of Jesus Christ, or both? Historic Christian mysticism's distorted concept of the essence of God, and our ability to know anything for certain about him, along with their affirmations

---

[64] www.theopedia.com/knowability-of-god See especially the link at the end, to Wayne Grudem's teaching on this subject.

about all humans, simply shouts "heresy!" Undoubtedly these distorted concepts of divinity and humanity are historic Christian mysticism's greatest deviations. Christian mysticism is an attempt to regain the awe and wonder of intimate communion with God that dead orthodoxy and liberal theology fails to deliver, yet offers a warped and false concept of both God and humans that is more akin to Zen Buddhism and New Age thought and practice—satanic ideas that blur the distinction between Creator and creation.

What we believe about the nature of God is of supreme importance. The biblical "ground of all being" is a personal creator called Jesus Christ who, along with the Father and Holy Spirit, created all matter and sustains it (John 1:3, 10; 1 Corinthians 8:6; Colossians 1:16-17; Hebrews 2:10). Jesus is no mere "Higgs boson" or "god-particle" that scientists are just now discovering. God is indeed ultimate reality, but separate from his creation. Moreover, he is knowable. To us who know him and have received by faith his imputed righteousness, we enjoy eternal life—knowing both the Father and the Son (John 17:3). We will continue to get to know this infinite, loving God for all eternity. Unlike mystic monism and nondualism, biblical Christianity is dualistic. We adore and serve God but will never share in his essential qualities. The Bible repudiates the pantheistic concept of interconnectedness of all reality, that all the universe is one essential reality. This pagan idea is found in Eastern religions, the Neoplatonism that strongly influenced the Christian mystic Desert Fathers, and many nondual Christian mystics since then. The Wikipedia article on nondualism is helpful in understanding this.[65]

As I ponder God's infinite qualities, I respond to him with the words of Mark Altrogge's lovely song, "I Stand in Awe."[66]

---

[65] en.wikipedia.org/wiki/Nondualism#Christianity

[66] Check out this website for the author's account about writing this hymn:
theblazingcenter.com/2015/04/the-story-behind-the-song-i-stand-in-awe.html

The Mystic Path

In Christian mysticism, there are three stages for knowing God intimately: purgation, illumination, and divine union. This is called the mystic path or the mystical way.[67] Maximus the Confessor (580–662) or Dionysius the Areopagite (probably fifth century) first mentioned these stages. The first two are preparatory dispositions that lead to and prepare the way for union.

Purgation is an awareness of sin, purification, cleansing, via various disciplines mainly pertaining to the body including contrition, confession, self-discipline, self-denial, and mortification of appetites. Inge says the early mystics had "an almost morbid desire to suffer." Inge says we must purify ourselves in order to see God. "Purification removes the obstacles to our union with God."[68] In the Christian mystic book *The Cloud of Unknowing*, we are told in Chapter 28 that nobody should practice contemplation "before they have cleansed their consciences of all the particular sinful deeds they have previously committed, according to the accepted requirements of Holy Church."

Illumination is an enlightening of the mind, gaining insights. Inge says "the illuminative life is the concentration of all the faculties, will, intellect, and feeling, upon God." He explains that by now the mystic is learning to perform good works and can now concentrate on his inner life. The *Catholic Encyclopedia* says this stage is: "a constant attention of the mind and of the affections of the heart to thoughts and sentiments which elevate the soul to God."[69]

Mystical or Divine Union is a union of our will, or of our essence, with God. In this altered state of consciousness people often feel a special oneness with all nature, or with all people. Thomas Merton and other Christian mystics have often seen the need for destroying the myth of subject-object duality. Other Christian mystics hold to a strict dualism, insisting that subject and God remain eternally distinct. We will further unpack these different positions under the next topic, about union with God.

---

[67] "Mysticism," *Evangelical Dictionary of Theology* (Grand Rapids: Baker, 1984), 745.

[68] William Ralph Inge, *Christian Mysticism: The Bampton Lectures, 1899: Considered in Eight Lectures Delivered before the University of Oxford* (London: Methuen & Co., 1899), 11.

[69] www.newadvent.org/cathen/14254a.htm

This ultimate stage of Christian experience is induced by a kataphatic preparatory regimen (with the use of words and thoughts) for getting into position for the apophatic (wordless) mystic silence. It is the mystic's exclusive mode for being alone with God and really knowing him intimately. Union is sometimes called contemplation, contemplative prayer, prayer of the heart, prayer of silence, the silence, the stillness, prayer without words, prayer of loving regard, prayer of simplicity, prayer of loving attentiveness,[70]prayer of the heart, prayer of simple gaze, or ecstasy. Divine union sometimes includes visions, revelations, and trances, yet is always ineffable and indescribable, as we learn from the *Stanford Encyclopedia of Philosophy*.[71] Union is the final step or goal of *Lectio Divina*. Bruce Demarest of Denver Seminary calls this final stage "The centerpiece of monastic discipline, which is about listening to God in silence."[72] Sometimes this final step is described as the void, the emptiness, the nothingness, or the absence of thought. Richard Foster calls this the goal of contemplative prayer.[73] He says such union is sometimes experienced as ecstasy, which he says is "contemplative prayer taken to the nth degree."[74] Divine union is accompanied by feelings of love and peace. One writer says, "Unity with God is a gift bestowed only on a small elect."[75]

Adela Ahlberg Calhoun describes this traditional mystic path in her popular book *Spiritual Disciplines Handbook*. To the traditional three stages she adds a beginning stage, awakening, "in which we encounter God and ourselves. This stage can be gradual or radical, a moment of conversion or a long journey to trusting God."[76]

---

[70] "Joyce Huggett," Richard J. Foster and Emilie Griffin, ed., *Spiritual Classics* (New York: HarperOne, 2000), 13.

[71] Pseudo-Dionysius, late fifth or early sixth century AD, asserted all such mystic experience of God is negative. Meister Eckhart and John of the Cross, then later Fr. Thomas Keating insist on the indescribability of God and religion experience. Psychologist William James concurred. A helpful article on mysticism from Stanford University explains this in greater detail, found at: plato.stanford.edu/entries/mysticism/

[72] Bruce Demarest, *Satisfy your Soul: Restoring the Heart of Christian Spirituality* (Colorado Springs: NavPress, 1999), 275.

[73] Richard Foster, *Prayer: Finding the Heart's True Home* (HarperSanFrancisco, 1992), 167.

[74] Ibid., 173.

[75] www.esotericquarterly.com/issues/EQ07/EQ0703/EQ070311-Nash.pdf

[76] Adele Ahlberg Calhoun, *Spiritual Disciplines Handbook: Practices That Transform Us*, (Downers Grove, IL: InterVarsity, 2005), 285. Calhoun's book

The Catholic organization New Advent gives us an in-depth study of this threefold path.[77] Other helpful articles by New Advent include the following topics: contemplation,[78] ecstasy,[79] prayer of quiet,[80] Unitive Way,[81] and mysticism.[82]

Another interesting treatment of the mystic path is a transcript of a video, *Becoming God: The Path of the Christian Mystic - Part I*, by Elizabeth Clare Prophet.[83] She asserts that Christian mystics believe "that all men by nature are like God and that within everyone there is a spark of the divine" and they pursue "direct intercourse with God through contemplation and prayer." Then she describes the traditional "path of ascent to God," that of purgation, illumination, and "union of the soul with her Lord." For her, purgation is "purging of the soul of all that is unlike God" and is "a battle between the false self and the true self . . . The path of purgation is a path of the imitation of Christ." Elizabeth Clare Prophet was definitely not an evangelical, probably more New Age than the Christian mystic she called herself.

The afore mentioned Stanford University's study on mysticism mentions the medieval concept of this final state of union: "Generally, medieval Christian mysticism had at least three stages . . . in the union-consciousness: quiet, essentially a prelude to the union with God, full union, and rapture, the latter involving a feeling of being 'carried away' beyond oneself."[84] This "rapture" stage is probably what Foster describes as "ecstasy." Eastern Orthodoxy refers to this stage as *theosis,* a Greek term meaning deification or divinization. Ancient Celtic religion as well as New Agers, spiritists, and witches sometimes refer

---

leaves out any reference to the biblical gospel, or need for a new birth experience, or anything about the atoning work of Christ.

[77] www.newadvent.org/cathen/14254a.htm

[78] www.newadvent.org/cathen/04324b.htm

[79] www.newadvent.org/cathen/05277a.htm

[80] www.newadvent.org/cathen/12608b.htm

[81] www.newadvent.org/cathen/14254a.htm

[82] www.newadvent.org/cathen/10663b.htm

[83] tsl.org/2011/07/becoming-god-christian-mysticism-youtube-part-4/

[84] plato.stanford.edu/entries/mysticism

to this as the "thin place,"[85] "sacred space," "the silence,"[86] or "alpha state."[87]

If you are up to some thorough investigation into Christian mysticism, and ecstatic trance-like states in general, read the 1911 book, *Mysticism,* by Evelyn Underhill. Her Chapter VIII about ecstasy and rapture is quite revealing about that final step in the mystic path. This chapter is on the Internet.[88] Underhill says that in mystical union a person is deprived of all senses. She distinguishes two kinds of ecstasy:

1) Divine in origin, in which God communicates high things.
   These are healthy ecstasies, resulting in renewed strength.
2) Demonic in origin, morbid ecstasies, psychopathic.

Underhill says levitations sometimes occur. St. Catherine of Siena (1347–1380) says the spirit would raise a body from the earth. Teresa of Ávila also said it can leave considerable mental disorder behind, and that person is unable to function for some time, even for days. One then longs for an eternal union and possession by the "divine bridegroom." Teresa knew this from personal experience. Ignatius of Loyola was also said to have levitated, as have many other Christian mystics.[89]

Tony Campolo describes his practice of entering this state of contemplative union as beginning each day centering down on Jesus: "I say His name over and over again, for as long as fifteen minutes, until I find my soul suspended in what the ancient Celtic Christians called a 'thin place'—a state where the boundary between heaven and earth, divine and human, dissolves."[90] Later on we will consider this process in more detail.

---

[85] www.patheos.com/blogs/markdroberts/series/thin-places/
[86] www.christiananswersforthenewage.org/Articles_BeStillDVD.html
[87] Laurie Cabot with Tim Cowan, *Power of the Witch* (New York: Delta, 1989), 183: "Alpha is the springboard for all psychic and magical workings. It is the heart of witchcraft." Cabot is a Witchcraft high priestess, living in Salem, MA, and has been popularizing witchcraft in the United States for many years. Check out this Christian website about her and witchcraft in general: www.lighthousetrailsresearch.com/alpha.htm
[88] www.sacred-texts.com/myst/myst/myst19.htm
[89] www.tokenrock.com/explain-levitation-64.html
[90] www.azquotes.com/author/2397-Tony_Campolo/tag/heaven

Christian mystics say the ecstatic mystical union with God is always God's initiative beyond our control, an experience that is fleeting, transient, fluctuating, with degrees of intensity. It comes and goes. Merton calls it "infused contemplation" and says: "The deciding factor in contemplation is the free and unpredictable action of God."[91] But, even Merton honestly wonders if such dark experiences are always from God or demonic in origin, since they arc indescribable and uncheckable. Even so, mystic writers cannot keep silent about mysticism!

Biblical Evaluation

If the historic Christian mystic path is the only way to enter God's presence and enjoy intimacy with the Lord, as some people assert, why is the Bible devoid of such teaching? The Bible assures me that from my conversion onward I already have union and intimate communion with God through faith in Jesus Christ. I express this by action, by living in accordance with the Spirit, and by doing what God desires. Therefore, I cry out "Abba, Father." God's Spirit testifies with my spirit (Romans 8:15). This leads to a life of growing communion with God and with all of God's people (1 John 1:1). In place of a complicated, esoteric mystic path for intimacy with God, it's as simple as prayer, prayer that includes pondering the Scriptures and talking with its Author, and doing so with all my senses fully active. Through Jesus' one-for-all sacrifice, my sins have been purged (Hebrews 1:1-3). The outer life of purgation, the inner life of illumination, and the blessed fellowship with God are not meant to be separate steps but a part of my everyday practice. Through continuous repentance, confession to God, coupled with submission and obedience, I maintain full fellowship with God. Daily I turn to God from worthless idols to serve the true and

---

[91] Thomas Merton, *The Inner Experience: Notes on Contemplation* (HarperSanFrancisco, 2003), 73ff. After reading Merton's entire chapter six, "Infused Contemplation," there was no longer any doubt in my mind such union is demonic in origin, as it mentions the anguish, bitterness, even despair one experiences as they "advance quietly into the darkness" that "brings with it a terrible interior revolution. Gone is the sweetness of prayer . . . the interior life is filled with darkness and dryness and pain." On page 76 Merton candidly wonders: "How does one know that he is guided by God and not by the devil? How does one distinguish between grace and illusion?"

living God (1 Thessalonians 1:9). Each day I enjoy the illumination of the Scriptures by God's Spirit.[92]

The Bible says each true Christian is a temple of the Holy Spirit, a temple of God (2 Corinthians 6:16), where the boundary between earth and heaven has dissolved. The veil of the temple has been torn in two by the death of Christ! "Therefore, brothers, since we have confidence to enter the Most Holy Place by the blood of Jesus, by a new and living way opened for us through the curtain, that is, his body, and since we have a great priest over the house of God, let us draw near to God, with a sincere heart, in full assurance of faith" (see whole context of this great text in Hebrews 10:19-22). What other "thin place" do we need? None whatsoever!

For more information about "thin places" see my blog: bruce-shalom.blogspot.com/

Union with God

The Concept of *union with God*, the final stage and goal of Christian mysticism, varies somewhat among the Christian mystics:

Union of Identity

This is monism, or at least nondualism, both of which say all people are essentially divine, having God at their core being or "true self," as clones of God. Union of identity is not the normal view of evangelical Christian mystics, nor of evangelicals in general, yet evangelical mystics rely heavily upon the writings of Christian mystics who hold to the theory of metaphysical monism or nondualism.[93]

---

[92] J. I. Packer gives us this helpful article: www.monergism.com/thethreshold/articles/onsite/packer/Illumination.html
See also this article: www.gotquestions.org/biblical-illumination.html

[93] Later we will thoroughly explain these terms when defining mysticism, but basically monism says there is but a single basic substance or principle as the ground of all reality. Humans are of the same basic essence as God, with no fundamental separation. Nondual means "not two," but neither are they completely one substance. "Same but different" you might say. On page xvi of *The Essential Writings of Christian Mysticism* Bernard McGinn says there are a number of mystics who "claim that God and the soul become identically one, at least on some level . . . who claim to have reached identity with God" yet who

Quakers, including Richard Foster, have said that every human has a spark of the divine within, sometimes called "the inner light." Many Christian mystics go way beyond Foster's concept. Catholic mystic Beatrice Bruteau, founder of The School of Contemplation, was nondualistic and said, "We have realized ourselves as the Self that says only I AM."[94] The idea of deification (divinization or *theosis*) is found in many of the Fathers of the ancient church, especially the Eastern Church. Such ideas reappear often down through history. Thomas Aquinas of the thirteenth century referred to "full participation in divinity which is humankind's true beatitude and the destiny of human life" (*Summa Theologiae e.1.2*).[95] Julian of Norwich (1342–1423), esteemed by modern-day contemplatives, once said, "I saw no difference between God and our Substance: but as it were all God."[96] Meister Eckhart and John of the Cross definitely fit this category (monism/nondualism). John of the Cross wrote, "God dwells and is present substantially in every soul, even in that of the greatest sinner in the world." Meister Eckhart said, "I and God are one."[97]

In this monastic category we could also put Matthew Fox, as well as Catholic Pietist Madame Guyon especially after hearing her say, "So was my soul lost in God, who communicated to it His qualities." Then she spoke of being plunged "wholly into God's own divine essence."[98] Merton was also monistic, calling this our "original nature."[99] He also said the idea of original sin is but a myth. God made all people in his image. People are basically good. In his book *The Inner Experience* Merton says the "Ascension of Christ, the New Adam, completely restored human nature to its spiritual condition and made possible the divinization of every man coming into the world." He says everyone

---

also hold to "some distinction between Creator and creature." This is a good example of nondualism.

[94] cccrmn.org/v2/index.php?option=com_content&view=article&id=344:interview-with-beatrice-bruteau-from-enlightenext&catid=86:articles&Itemid=210

[95] orthodoxwiki.org/Theosis

[96] https://cac.org/julian-of-norwich-part-iii-2015-07-22/

[97] "Meister Eckhart Sermon 52" in *The Essential Writings of Christian Mysticism*, ed. Bernard McGinn (New York: Random House, 2006), 442–43. Eckhart also wrote about himself as a person: "According to my unborn mode I have eternally been, am now, and shall eternally remain. . . . I neither wax nor wane."

[98] logosresourcepages.org/Believers/guyon.htm

[99] apocryphile.org/jrm/articles/merton.html is an insightful article: "False Self and Original Nature: Reflections from Suzuki and Merton."

can become as Christ is, "divinely human, and thus to share His spiritual authority and charismatic power in the world."[100] More recently M. Scott Peck taught that man can become God.[101]

Tony Campolo says in *Partly Right,* "We affirm our divinity by doing what is worthy of gods . . ." He thinks Christ lives in every human being, whether Christian or not. Here is what Campolo said in 1988 at Prestatyn, UK: "One of the most startling discoveries of my life was the realization that the Jesus that I love, the Jesus who died for me on Calvary, that Jesus, is waiting, mystically and wonderfully, in every person I meet. I find Jesus everywhere. The difference between a Christian and non-Christian is not that Jesus is not in the non-Christian—the difference is that the Jesus who is within him is a Jesus to whom he will not surrender his life. You say, 'Are you saying that Jesus is present in everybody?' I am only telling you what it says in John 1:9; 'He is the light that lighteth every man, every woman that cometh into the world.' . . . Erick Fromm, one of the most popular psychoanalysts of our time, recognized the diabolical social consequences that can come about when a person loses sight of his/her own divinity."[102]

Christian mysticism that believes in union of identity no longer has a subject and an object. This nondual and monistic mysticism is not transformational, but makes people extinguishable, like blowing out a candle. An article about mysticism[103] observes that "mystical experiences often, perhaps characteristically, involve what is now called an 'altered state of consciousness'—trances, visions, suppression of cognitive contact with the ordinary world, loss of the usual distinction between subject and object, weakening or loss of the sense of the self." Famous American psychologist and philosopher William James held to nondualism.[104]

---

[100] Thomas Merton, *The Inner Experience: Notes on Contemplation* (HarperSanFrancisco, 2003), 38.

[101] In his book *The Road Less Traveled*, 25th Anniversary edition (NY: Simon & Shuster, 2002), 270, Peck said: "God wants us to become Himself (or Herself or Itself). We are growing toward godhood. God is the goal of evolution. It is God who is the source of the evolutionary force and God who is the destination."

[102] For more of Tony Campolo's heretical ideas, see: battle4truth.wordpress.com/2008/05/05/heretic-quotes-from-tony-campolo/ Campolo practices and promotes Christian mystical centering prayer.

[103] www2.kenyon.edu/Depts/Religion/Fac/Suydam/Reln329/Mysticismdef.html

[104] nonduality.org/2008/06/06/non-duality-of-william-james/

One Christian worker in London, Wes English, says deification is an essential component of Eastern Orthodoxy, saying Timothy Ware's *The Orthodox Church* helps us understand this thinking.[105]

Thomas Merton once said about our divine center: "If only we could see each other that way all the time, there would be no more war, no more hatred, no more cruelty, no more greed. . . . I suppose the big problem would be that we would fall down and worship each other."[106] Interestingly enough, in Hinduism *namaste*, or bowing, means "I bow to the divine in you."[107]

Union of Presence

Other Christian mystics hold to union of presence. This concept of God and humanity is termed Christian dualism that evangelical Christians hold to. There always exists an eternal Creator—creature distinction. This can be termed theistic mysticism. The Christian metaphysic of dualism holds to two realities, but only the God-part is eternal, unlike the Taoist Yin and Yang. Unlike Christian monism and nondualism, Christian dualism affirms the radical transcendence of God. Theologian Millard Erickson says there is "a dualism in which all that is not God has received its existence from him. God preserves in existence the whole creation and is in control of all that happens. . . ."[108]

Union of presence in theistic evangelical Christian mysticism also teaches that Christians seek communion with God and enjoy his presence by arriving at that final stage of the mystic path called "union." Nevertheless, they never expect to become divine. God remains God and people always remain people even when in full communion with God. The identity of the person will never dissolve.

---

[105] Wes English writes: "You do not have to read Eastern Orthodox theology too long before you come across the concept of divinization, deification or *theosis* (all synonyms). Timothy Ware's *The Orthodox Church* provides a very concise understanding of deification: "the final goal at which every Christian must aim: to become god, to attain *theosis*, 'deification' or 'divinization.'" www.theologynetwork.org/christian-beliefs/creation-and-new-creation/getting-stuck-in/deification--the-radical-nature-of-our-relationship-with-god.htm

[106] www.monasteriesoftheheart.org/scriptorium/mertons-revelation

[107] en.wikipedia.org/wiki/Namaste

[108] Millard Erickson, *Christian Theology* (Grand Rapids: Baker, 1994), 54.

Biblical Evaluation

The Bible teaches theistic dualism, and union of presence for all regenerate followers of Christ, whether mystic or not.

In contrast to evangelical mystics seeking union of presence as a final state of the historic mystic path, the Bible says all true followers of Christ, from their conversion onward, can say with Paul, "Christ lives in me" (Galatians 2:20). The Father and the Spirit also indwell me, from conversion onward (John 14:23; Romans 8:9, 11). I am "in Christ Jesus" (Romans 8:1), and seated with Christ in the heavenly realms (Ephesians 2:6). Christian evangelicals, mystic and nonmystic alike, insist they will never share God's unique essence.

The Christian's position from spiritual birth onward is unity of presence, not based upon feelings or degree of sanctification. Yet God calls me to walk with him in intimate communion and to love him with all my heart. This is a *nonmystic* union and communion with Christ. I want to seek his face and bask in his presence. I come before him with singing (Psalm 100) with lots of noise or in quietness. I increasingly see prayer, real prayer, as being the essence of this intimate relation with the Creator and Sustainer of the universe who has become my Savior. God can and should personally guide me, both via his Word and the inward illumination and prodding of his Spirit, all the while avoiding mystic mind-numbing contemplation. The steps of a good person are ordered of the Lord in so many ways, both cognitively and mystically, both consciously and unconsciously. When at last Christ appears, at last I will be perfect, like him (1 John 3:2-3). This blessed assurance drives me to purification, to grow in Christlikeness, for his glory.

People never become God but only become Godlike in character. Ephesians 4:13 talks about our "attaining to the whole measure of the fullness of Christ." Ephesians 4:17ff., especially verse 24, "The new self, created to be like God in true righteousness and holiness." These and other such texts help us understand what Peter means in 2 Peter 1:4, "So that . . . you may participate in the divine nature and escape the corruption in the world caused by evil desires."[109] Hebrews 12:10 reiterates this thought in saying, "So we may share in his holiness."

---

[109] The *NIV Study Bible* note on 2 Peter 1:4 says "*participate in the divine nature* does not indicate that Christians become divine in any sense, but only that we

Mysticism's "forbidden fruit" of becoming divine still looks as appealing today to some people as it did to Adam and Eve (Genesis. 3:5). Satan continues to tempt humans with the very desire he himself had from the time he was banished from heaven.

It's a sad day when people deny the fundamental differences between humans and other animals. It's even more tragic when people deny any fundamental difference between humans and God. Lon Alison recently remarked, "Whenever humans attempt to be God, horrible consequences follow."[110] Instead of humans becoming God, in the incarnation God took on humanity! (See Hebrews 2:14, 17)

The desire and goal of each Christian is expressed by Paul in Philippians 3:10, "I want to know Christ," and knowing God is defined by our Lord as "eternal life" (John 17:3). It is a growing relationship. Someday we'll know God completely, in full spiritual union. Even Buddhists recognize that "union of identity" is the authentic Christian view. One Buddhist website that compares Buddhism with Christianity says, "Man, in the Christian view, can never become God."[111] At least at this one point we can agree with Buddhists. It is unfortunate that many of the Christian mystics never grasp this basic truth.

We imitate God ("Be imitators of God," Ephesians 5:1), walk with him, and begin to reflect his glory and character. 2 Corinthians 3:18 says it well: "Being transformed into his likeness with ever-increasing glory, which comes from the Lord, who is the Spirit." When we finally see the Lord we shall be fully like him in perfect holiness (1 John 3:2-3), but will never share in his infinite, divine essence. Only Jesus is uniquely God's Son. The Greek term for this in John 3:16 and elsewhere is *monogene huion*, or as the NIV translates it, his "one and only Son," meaning one of a kind, sharing the same divine nature as God. This is in contrast to Christ-followers who are God's sons and daughters by adoption, are like God in holiness, will rule with Christ, have a rational mind, and enjoy imputed immortality as something God grants. (1 Timothy 6:16 clearly states that only Christ has immortality,

---

are indwelt by God through his Holy Spirit . . . our humanity and his deity, as well as the human personality and the divine, remain distinct and separate."

[110] Lon Alison, former executive director of the Billy Graham Center at Wheaton College, is on staff at Wheaton Bible Church, West Chicago, IL.

[111] www.bps.lk/olib/wh/wh275-u.html M. O'C. Walshe, "Buddhism and Christianity: A Positive Approach," Vol. XVII, Numbers 239 (Kandy, Sri Lanka: Buddhist Publication Society, 2012), 265–80.

that is, as part of his essence). Christian mystic expert William Ralph Inge says that early Christian mystics, in speaking of human deification, meant people are imperishable, that is, immortal in their essence.[112] The Bible denies this, saying this quality is given followers of Christ, not something innately theirs.

An increasing number of evangelicals are attracted to contemplative spirituality but remain dualistic and hold to the biblical doctrine of union of presence yet strangely enough they love reading the nondual and monistic mystics who hold to the heretical idea of union of identity.

A good summary statement of union with God is found in Wayne Grudem's *Systematic Theology* in which he defines this union as four aspects of the believer's union with Christ: We are in Christ, Christ is in us, we are like Christ, and we are with Christ.[113] He does a masterful job of developing each of these points. He says our fellowship with Christ "can vary in intensity," and this fellowship with both the Father and Son "brings us into fellowship with each other (John 1:3). Another excellent treatment of "union" from an evangelical Christian viewpoint is the article on "Union with Christ" in *Baker's Evangelical Dictionary of Theology.[114]*

Christian mystics often describe their spiritual journey as gradually leaving dualism until they finally wake up to the fact that they are nondual, or even monistic.[115]

All this sounds so much like New Ager Shirley MacLaine who expresses the same ideas in her book *Going Within*. New Age and Eastern religions refer to the true self as your primal self, the god, or

---

[112] William Ralph Inge, *Christian Mysticism: The Bampton Lectures, 1899: Considered in Eight Lectures Delivered before the University of Oxford* (London: Methuen & Co., 1899), 13.

[113] Wayne Grudem, *Systematic Theology* (Downers Grove, IL: InterVarsity, 2000), 840–50. This section is so heartwarming and reads like a good sermon. As in the whole book, this section ends with excellent questions. He gets us to ponder our awareness of Christ in and with us, how we might better imitate him, and what we might do "to increase the intensity of our daily fellowship with Christ."

[114] www.biblestudytools.com/dictionaries/bakers-evangelical-dictionary/union-with-christ.html

[115] William Shannon, expert on Thomas Merton, quoted Merton on dualism/monism as saying: "You have to see your will and God's will dualistically for a long time. *You have to experience duality for a long time until you see it is not there.* In this respect I am a Hindu." *Thomas Merton's Dark Path* (Toronto: Collins Publishers, 1987), 225. (Emphasis mine)

the truth. Plato, like some contemporary Christian mystics, spoke of the human soul as somehow being a part of the universal soul.

Christian mysticism's historic concept of divinity as present in everyone is exactly what New Age, astrology, the occult, and Eastern religions have always taught. New Age advocate and writer, Angelica Danton, says, "To my understanding, the Age of Aquarius is a time of new thoughts and systems of thinking that will ultimately lead to a new wave of consciousness on our planet. Religion as it has been will change, and a different free spirituality will emerge. This new spirituality will truly unite all peoples as they realize that they are all potentially divine beings, and that they are all more alike than they are different from one another."[116]

The Bible teaches that only true followers of Christ are God-indwelt, from their conversion onward (Romans 8:9). Kenneth R. Samples writes an insightful article, "Human Beings: God or Creatures Made in God's Image?" [117] He says, "The Eastern mystical religion of Hinduism makes the amazing claim that the true human self is none other than God himself... the human soul is divine.... Historic Christianity asserts that although God created human beings . . . made in God's expressed image," humans are finite and eternally distinct and separate from God. Like God, humans are moral beings, have a soul, "display knowledge, wisdom, goodness, love, holiness, justice, and truthfulness." Yet "God's divinity makes him differ in *kind* from people . . . self-existence (independence), immortality (eternal existence), immutability (changelessness), infinity (limitlessness), and eternality (timelessness)." Sadly, countless Christian mystics, from the Desert Fathers onward, agree with Hinduism and Buddhism's concept of reality. This huge red flag should leave us stunned and shaking. No quantity of disclaimers can negate the homogeneity of Christian mysticism and Eastern religions in so many aspects.

Christian mysticism's claim, that all people possess a spark of divinity at their core, is termed nondualism or monism. Catholic mystic William Shannon, an expert on Thomas Merton, says "We have to cross the abyss that separates our surface consciousness from the deep and creative realm of the unconscious. Only when we cross over, do we become our true self. At this point, dualistic language simply breaks

---

[116] www.llewellyn.com/journal/article/599
[117] www.reasons.org/articles/human-beings-god-or-creatures-made-in-gods-image

down." He then quotes Merton in saying: "You have to experience duality for a long time until you see it's not there."[118]

Nondualism and Monism

We need to pause here and explain some terms. "Dualism" in metaphysics says there is an eternal distinction between humans and divinity. "Nondualism" (not two) involves a falling away of that distinction between a person and God, short of complete identity. Like a drop of water dropped into wine and taking on the taste of wine. "Monism" (oneness) goes one step further, saying humans, along with all reality, are of the same basic essence as God. Like a drop of water falling into an infinite ocean. It is little wonder that Thomas Merton eventually saw no contradiction between Buddhism and his brand of Catholic mysticism. Merton attempts to justify his monism by saying friendship with God means equality.[119]

True Self and False Self

A mystic website says: "When you awaken to Oneness and personally experience the absolute reality that God is within you as your true Self, you will see through the illusoriness of the sense of separation and discern the error in the belief in two powers. This spiritual awakening to the Truth of Oneness is what mystics refer to as *enlightenment* or *spiritual illumination*."[120]

Heretical monism affirms that all reality is one, that every person in their true self is divine and belongs to the cosmic soul. Hinduism thinks people have a misconception, perceiving themselves as separate from God, thus needing enlightenment.

Christian mysticism, with its heretical nondualism/monism, obviously does not share the Biblical teaching about the nature of either God or humanity. This is an enormous heresy that goes way back, much further than even the Desert Fathers. A biblical rebuttal to this heresy

---

[118] William H. Shannon, *Silence on Fire: Prayer of Awareness* (New York: Crossroad Publishing, 1991), 126–27.

[119] Merton wrote, "Contemplation is that wisdom which makes man the friend of God, a thing which Aristotle thought to be impossible. For how, he said, can a man be God's friend? *Friendship implies equality.* That is precisely the message of the Gospel." Merton, *The New Man*, (Abbey of Gethsemani, 1961), 17.

[120] contemplatingtruth.wordpress.com/2015/05/05/journey_of_awakening/

is found in Jen Wilkin's book *None Like Him: 10 Ways God is Different from Us.*[121]

Marcia Montenegro, converted to Christ out of New Age and astrology, observes that Christian mysticism presents "a gnostic view of knowledge—a secret knowledge obtained only by those able to attain these higher states."[122]

The terms "true self" and "false self" along with the Christian mystic concepts about these do not have any biblical basis. Contrary to what Carl Jung, Quakers, Thomas Merton, and many other mystics think, the heart or soul, that is, our "true self," is *not* divine. The Hebrews of the Old Testament viewed a person as a totality, as one psychophysical organism, with God exerting influence upon people from the outside. The Holy Spirit says through the prophet Jeremiah, "The heart is deceitful above all things and beyond cure" (Jeremiah 17:9). Proverbs 4:23 calls the heart "the wellspring of life." It is the real you. When discussing Ephesians 3:16, Barnes' notes on the Bible refers to "the inner man—in the heart, the mind, the soul." The article on "Heart" in The *New Bible Commentary* (Eerdmans, 1962), tells us this term in the Bible is "used of the center of things . . . the inner man . . . the essence of the whole man, with all his attributes. . . . This means that 'heart' comes the nearest of the New Testament terms to mean 'person.'" This article also stresses the biblical teaching of everyone needing a new heart via repentance and conversion. Only the "pure in heart" (not everyone) will see God.

John Piper says "The human mind, apart from transforming grace (Romans 12:2; Ephesians 4:23), is depraved (1 Timothy 6:5) and debased (Romans 1:28) and hard (2 Corinthians 4:4) and darkened and futile (Ephesians 4:17-18).[123]

---

[121] Jen Wilkin, *None Like Him* (Wheaton, IL, Crossway, 2016). The back cover states, "Our limitations are by design. We were never meant to be God. But at the root of every sin is our rebellious desire to possess attributes that belong to God alone."

[122] www.christiananswersforthenewage.org/Articles_contemplativePrayer1.html (See section on "Beyond self: the false self vs. the true self").

[123] John Piper, *Think: The Life of the Mind and the Love of God* (Wheaton, IL: Crossway, 2010), 100. Mark A. Noll writes the foreword to Piper's book. Noll and Piper have been good friends since they were fellow literature majors at Wheaton College.

An Internet Christian mystic website, *Centers of Light*, proclaims: "As Christian mystics, we find truth in our experiences, not dogma. . . . Come back into union with your divine self."[124]

Should we affirm that all people have a divine self, or higher self as New Agers call it? Or, do we have the courage to trust the Scriptures which affirm that God dwells only in each true follower of Christ? We can choose the mystics' idea or we can trust God's inspired Word. We cannot have both. G. K. Chesterton wrote in *Orthodoxy*, "Of all the conceivable forms of enlightenment the worst is what these people call the Inner Light. Of all horrible religions the most horrible is the worship of the god within."[125]

The presence of God's Spirit in us is *not* synonymous with our "soul" or "spirit," that is, our true self. Sometimes the Bible refers to our true self as our "heart" and sometimes as our "inner man." In a recent *Desiring God* article (1/16/12) John Piper discusses how we should pray for our soul, or heart, or our true self: to be inclined to God and his Word, to have the eyes of our heart opened to understand Scripture, to be wholly united rather than fragmented, and to be satisfied in God's steadfast love. Hebrew and biblical psychology historically treated a person as a whole: body and soul/spirit. Theologian Wayne Grudem refers to Mark 12:30: "You shall love the Lord your God with all your *heart,* and with all your *soul,* and with all your *mind,* and with all your *strength*." About this text Grudem says Jesus is "piling up roughly synonymous terms for emphasis to demonstrate that we must love God with all of our being."[126] Theologian Millard Erickson notes that "Man is to be treated as a unity. . . . The gospel is an appeal to the whole man. . . . God is at work renewing the whole of what we are."[127]

Although we are not divine nor ever will be, we are uniquely created in God's image.[128] We are compelled to reject mysticism's

---

[124] www.centersoflight.org

[125] Randy England, *The Unicorn in the Sanctuary: The Impact of the New Age Movement on the Catholic Church* (Rockford, IL: Tan Books, 1991), 15.

[126] Wayne Grudem, *Systematic Theology* (Downers Grove, IL: InterVarsity, 1994), 479, where he deals with arguments for Trichotomy.

[127] Millard Erickson, *Christian Theology* (Grand Rapids: Baker, 1994), 538–39.

[128] See Douglas Groothuis, *Christian Apologetics* (Downers Grove, IL: InterVarsity, 2011). On page 86 he says: "Humans are not divine—not even when they were in their original and pristine state. With God, they share the

claim that a divine "true self" resides at the core of every human. Genuine followers of Christ have passed from spiritual death to spiritual life and have a redeemed heart via faith in Christ's atoning death for them on the cross. Christ said, "What good will it be for someone to gain the whole world, yet forfeit their soul?" (Matthew 16:26) Our "soul" is us! It needs saving and surely is not divine! The unrepentant soul that sins will experience eternal death. Mysticism's search for our divine true self is neither sane psychology nor biblical Christianity. The New Testament refers to our old and new natures, to the old man and new man, old self and new self (Ephesians 4:22-24; Col. 3:5-10; Rom. 6:6). We are to live in union and communion with Christ, and put to death our former membership in the Old Adam and its inclination to sin. In Ephesians 4 Paul says we are "to put on the new self, created to be like God in true righteousness and holiness" (4:24). Like God, yes, but never divine!

Mystic Darkness

Virtually all Christian contemplative mystics talk about darkness, divine darkness, as we enter God's presence, the darkness of the "cloud of unknowing." They also talk much about the "dark night of the soul" as an essential part of the mystic path. Pseudo-Dionysius the Areopagite, from the fifth or sixth century, greatly influenced mysticism down through the ages. He spoke of mystical contemplation as "the secret silence," arriving at "absolute silence," "divine darkness," arriving finally at the loftiest point a human can attain which he terms the "darkness of unknowing." This person greatly influenced Catholic mysticism for hundreds of years.

Psychologist Carl Jung developed the idea of the "dark side of God," that God also has a dark side since man surely does and man has been created in God's image. One writer says of Jung: "As Carl Jung has pointed out, the orthodox Christian concept of deity in its Trinitarian form does not provide an image of wholeness because it excludes the feminine and the dark side of God."[129]

John of the Cross (1542–1591), famous Spanish priest and mystic involved in the Counter Reformation, wrote about "the dark night of

---

attributes of personality—agency intelligence, creativity, rationality, emotion and relationality—but in form forever finite, limited and contingent."

[129] www.christosophia.org/essaysthegrailofthechristosophia.html

the soul," (in his book by the same title) which, as he says, every believer needs to pass through on the road to illumination and divine union.

Brennan Manning referred to centering prayer as entering into "great darkness." In his book *The Signature of Jesus,* one whole chapter deals with celebrating the darkness.

Jesuit priest and psychotherapist Anthony de Mello refers to centering prayer as "dark contemplation" and going down into "the darkness," into emptiness and nothingness.

Evelyn Underhill also refers to the "dark night of the soul," which she says is a state of confusion, sensing God's absence or withdrawal before that final state of union with God.

It seems significant that many Christian mystics such as Thomas Merton admit that contemplation often leads to dark and foreboding places that are highly dangerous. Merton also says, "Infused contemplation, then, sooner or later brings with it a terrible interior revolution. Gone is the sweetness of prayer. Meditation becomes impossible, even hateful. Liturgical functions seem to be an insupportable burden . . . the will seems unable to love. The interior life is filled with darkness and dryness and pain."[130]

Mother Teresa often mentioned the terrible darkness she continually lived in for as many as fifty years, as if everything was dead.

Episcopal mystic priest Matthew Fox says, "The Black Madonna invites us into the dark . . . into our depths . . . where Divinity lies . . . where the true self lies."[131]

---

[130] Thomas Merton, *The Inner Experience: Notes on Contemplation* (HarperSanFrancisco, 2003), 75.

[131] Matthew Fox says: "The Black Madonna is Dark and calls us to the darkness. . . . Darkness is something we need to get used to again—the 'Enlightenment' has deceived us into being afraid of the dark and distant from it. Light switches are illusory. They feed the notion that we can 'master nature' (Descartes' false promise) and overcome all darkness with a flick of our finger. Meister Eckhart observes that 'the ground of the soul is dark.' Thus to avoid the darkness is to live superficially, cut off from one's ground, one's depth. The Black Madonna invites us into the dark and therefore into our depths. This is what the mystics call the 'inside' of things, the essence of things. This is where Divinity lies. It is where the true self lies." This is found at: rosannj.blogspot.com/2011/03/deep-into-books.html

One Christian mystic writer quotes Isaiah 45:3 in which God says, "I will give you the treasures of darkness."[132] Actually, this probably refers to stolen treasures from vanquished nations that were hidden away, and has no reference whatsoever to the supposed divine darkness that mystics refer to.

Biblical Evaluation

In stark contrast, the Bible teaches that our enemy, not God, is the one who makes us dwell in darkness. In Psalm 143:3 King David says, "The enemy pursues me . . . he makes me dwell in darkness." Then he remembers how wonderful it used to be, meditating on God's works and all God has done. He longs for communion with God: "I spread out my hands to you; my soul thirsts for you like a parched land" (verses 5-6).

Darkness comes in two varieties. One could be termed "common darkness" that God allows in all people, in contrast with lethal, satanic darkness which opposes God and his Kingdom.

Common darkness can include things like hardships, trials of all sorts including persecutions, which Paul describes in detail in 2 Corinthians chapters 4, 6, and 11. Christ predicted the same for his followers (Matthew 10—all of it; John 16:33; Revelation 2:10). In the beatitudes Jesus speaks of our being light as well as being persecuted because of righteousness (Matthew 5). Paul told Timothy what to expect from "evil men and impostors" (2 Timothy 3:10-13). 1 Peter was written in part to prepare God's people for trials of all sorts. Common darkness is all too common. But it is hardly the same as the lethal spiritual kind, the satanic variety, the "dominion of darkness" which is in direct contrast to divine "light"!

As a true follower of Christ, I have been justified by grace and faith alone, have become the light of the world, have peace with God, and have been rescued from the dominion of darkness and placed into the Kingdom of light.

In Scripture "darkness" is a common description of the lethal variety, of rebellion against God. Darkness also describes the eternal state of the lost (Matthew 8:12; 22:13; 25:30). Peter talks about the final destination of false teachers: "Blackest darkness is reserved for them"

---

[132] sigler.org/watson/04_04_come_into_the_darkness.htm

(2 Peter 2:17). Jude says about the angels who fell: "These he has kept in darkness, bound with everlasting chains for judgment on the great Day" (Jude 6). False teachers await that same awful fate (Jude 13).

In his book *Celebration of Discipline*, Richard Foster cites Isaiah 50:10 as saying: "Who among you fears the Lord and obeys the voice of his servant, who walks in darkness and has no light, yet trusts in the name of the Lord and relies upon his God?" (RSV)

Foster goes on to say, "The point of the biblical passage is that it is quite possible to fear, obey, trust, and rely upon the Lord and still 'walk in darkness and have no light.' We are living in obedience but we have entered a dark night of the soul." [133] Foster is quoting from the Revised Standard Version, the only one that gives Isaiah 50:10 this twist. All others say, "let him trust" instead of "yet trusts." Every other translation makes a contrast between those who fear the Lord and those who walk in darkness. For example, the NIV says, "Who among you fears the Lord and obeys the word of his servant? Let him who walks in the dark, who has no light, trust in the name of the Lord and rely on his God."

The next verse continues this contrast, i.e., the difference between those who fear God and those who are involved in wicked practices. The latter "will lie down in torment." Of course, the God-fearers will suffer hardships and trials, but they do not walk in darkness with no light.

Matthew 4:16 quotes Isaiah who describes "people living in darkness" who have now seen a great light. "On those living in the land of the shadow of death a light has dawned." That light is Christ and the true gospel.

The Old Testament saint says: "The Lord is my light and my salvation—whom shall I fear?" (Psalm 27:1). The *NIV Study Bible* on Psalm 27:1 points out that *light* "often symbolizes well-being," as the source of God's salvation and many blessings. Psalm 119:105 says God's Word is a lamp and light to show us the way. God has called true believers "out of darkness into his wonderful light" (1 Peter 2:9). There's no hint in the Bible of universal light in every person, or of universal salvation. Paul told the Colossians that Christ "qualified you to share in the inheritance of the saints *in the kingdom of light*. For he has rescued us from the dominion of darkness and brought us into the

---

[133] Richard J. Foster, *Celebration of Discipline: The Path to Spiritual Growth* (HarperSanFrancisco, 1988), 104.

kingdom of the Son he loves" (Colossians 1:12-13, emphasis added). Note what the *NIV Study Bible* says about this text.[134] Psalm 18:28 says, "My God turns my darkness into light." Psalm 23:4 talks about "the shadow of death," that is, living in mortal danger, but not some dark night of the soul or some such idea. 1 Thessalonians 5:5-6 says, "We do not belong to the night or to the darkness. . . . Let us be alert and self-controlled." (See the whole context of these verses.) 2 Corinthians 6:14-17 asks, "What fellowship can light have with darkness?" then urges believers in Christ to separate ourselves from idolaters. Would not this include Buddhists, Hindus, and Islamic Sufi? Would it include refusing to "dialogue" and learn from, or worship with "Christians" who deny the true gospel of justification by faith alone? Befriend them, yes, and attempt to win them to biblical faith in Christ. These people walk now in darkness and need to see that great light, Christ, that Isaiah prophesied about (Isaiah 9:2). In Paul's conversion testimony (Acts 26:17-18) God tells him, "I am sending you to them to open their eyes and turn them from darkness to light, and from the power of Satan to God."

Jesus says in John 8:12: "I am the light of the world. Whoever follows me will never walk in darkness, but will have the light of life." We need to remember that "God is light; in him there is no darkness at all" (1 John 1:5). This text also says, "If we claim to have fellowship with him (as mystics do) yet walk in the darkness, we lie and do not live by the truth." The IVP New Testament Commentary on John deals well with this text and theme.[135]

Mystic writer Tony Jones aptly describes the final contemplative stage, that "thin space" of mystical union with God, as darkness and spiritual oppression.[136] I never cease to be amazed how Christian mysticism dwells on and even glories in darkness, not unlike an increasing number of contemporary shows and movies such as

---

[134] *The NIV Study Bible* notes: *Light* symbolizes holiness (Mt 5:14; 6:23; Ac 26:18; 1 Jn 1:5, truth (Ps 36:9; 119:105, 130); 2 Co 4:6), love (Jas 1:17; 1 Jn 2:9-10), glory (Isa 60:1-3; 1 Ti 6:16), and life (Jn 1:4). Accordingly, God (1 Jn 1:5), Christ (Jn 8:12) and the Christian (Eph 5:8) are characterized by light. The "kingdom of light" is the opposite of the "dominion of darkness" (v. 13).

[135] www.biblegateway.com/resources/commentaries/intervarsity press-nt/1John/Character-God

[136] In his book *The Sacred Way,* Tony Jones says "It seems one cannot pursue true silence without rather quickly coming to a place of deep, dark doubt." (Grand Rapids: Zondervan, 2005), 41.

"August: Osage Country." Only Satan himself invites us into the dark. In doing so, he shows us his true color! Christian mystics' emphasis upon darkness should be a red flag for us.

A. W. Tozer sometimes refers to "the dark night of the soul" but did not understand this in the mystic sense of emptiness and nothingness, but to the common darkness of times of testing allowed by God, like persecution, pain and confusion, as if God has left us. Job is a classic example of this. Tozer gleaned some things from the mystics but was not a mystic in the traditional sense of shutting down your mind to enter God's dark presence, nor did he practice *Lectio Divina*.[137] A. W. Tozer is one of my favorite authors. It's true he often quoted from many historic Christian mystics. Yet I cannot find him practicing any kind of mind-emptying contemplation, nor did he fall into any of the heresies of the early Desert Fathers. Tozer knew how to walk with God and keep his eyes on Jesus. And so can you and I, my fellow pilgrim.

We should also note that in the Old Testament darkness sometimes refers to the mystery of God's ways, hidden from our understanding, and especially from unbelievers. For the believer, we can say with Psalm 18:28, "You, O Lord, keep my lamp burning; my God turns my darkness into light." In Psalm 97:11 the psalmist says, "Light is shed upon the righteous." I especially like this text in Proverbs 4:18-19: "The path of the righteous is like the first gleam of dawn, shining ever brighter till the full light of day. But the way of the wicked is like deep darkness; they do not know what makes them stumble."

We can say that a biblical "mystery" is something we now understand that was formerly hidden or not yet revealed. Is the gospel still totally hidden? Is God absolutely unknowable? Let Paul answer this for us: "And even if our gospel, is veiled, it is veiled to those who are perishing. The god of this age has blinded the minds of unbelievers, so that they cannot see the light of the gospel of the glory of Christ. . . . For God, who said, 'Let light shine out of darkness,' made his light shine in our hearts to give us the light of the knowledge of the glory of God in the face of Christ" (2 Corinthians 4:3-7).

We should also note that not all the early Church Fathers spoke of darkness as normal and good for us. A sermon included in *The*

---

[137] This website discusses Tozer and his relationship with mysticism, including his references to the dark night of the soul:
www.sermonindex.net/modules/newbb/viewtopic.php?topic_id=3000&forum=35&9

Teaching of the Twelve Apostles talks about having been saved and given light; that *before salvation* we had been wrapped in darkness and mist.[138] (Emphasis added).

On her program *Revive Our Hearts*, Nancy Leigh de Moss with her usual biblical accuracy once said, "Throughout the Scripture darkness is used as metaphor for that which is anti-God. The wicked are called darkness. . . . Now, metaphorically in the Scripture, light is used for God, for life, for salvation. God's Word is said to be light. His presence is associated with light. Truth, goodness, holiness, purity, godliness, these are all concepts in Scripture that are associated with light."[139]

So, come out of the darkness of mysticism and step into the light, the Scriptural spiritual life, the "light of life" (Psalm 49:19; 56:13; 53:11). This image of light that Al Moller says is central to Christianity.[140] Such walking in the light is intimacy with God, is real union and communion with him for us who have turned to God from idols in repentance and faith alone in Jesus. Blameless children of God shine like stars in the universe (Philippians 2:15). We shine because Jesus first shined on us and controls our innermost being. Thus we, too, become the light of the world (Matthew 5:14-16) and help push back the darkness. As children of light we must "have nothing to do with the fruitless deeds of darkness, but rather expose them. For it is shameful even to mention what the disobedient do in secret" (Ephesians 5:8, 11-12). We walk in the light of God's presence, holiness, guidance, truth, grace, and much more. The song "Shine, Jesus, Shine," by Graham Kendrick sums it up well. This song describes truly biblical "spiritual formation"! So does the hymn, "I Want to Walk as a Child of the Light," composed in 1970 by Kathleen Thomerson.

---

[138] "For he has given us light; as a Father he has called us sons; he has rescued us when we were perishing. How, then, shall we praise him, or how repay him for what we have received? Our minds were impaired; we worshiped stone and wood and gold and silver and brass, the works of men; and our whole life was nothing else but death. So when we were wrapped in darkness and our eyes were full of such mist, by his will we recovered our sight and put off the cloud which enfolded us." (An anonymous sermon, commonly titled "Clement's Second Letter to the Corinthians"). christianbookshelf.org/richardson/early_christian_fathers/an_anonymous_sermon_commonly_called_2.htm

[139] www.reviveourhearts.com/radio/revive-our-hearts/light-world/ (4/26/2014)

[140] www.religiontoday.com/columnists/al-mohler/walk-in-darkness-seen-great-light-wonder-christmas.html

Knowing God in the Stillness

Christian mystics love quoting Psalm 46:10: "Be still, and know that I am God." They insist it refers to knowing God intimately by shutting down one's thinking processes. Catholic priest, Thomas Keating, refers to "interior silence" as "the quieting of the imagination, feelings, and rational faculties in the process of recollection; the general, loving attentiveness to God in pure faith."[141]

Biblical Evaluation

As I read this verse in its context, it is not telling me to shut down cognition, but just the opposite! Christian mystics willfully miss the whole milieu of God's people shaking in their boots in panic, with their world "in uproar." Governments are falling, not too unlike our world today. God's people are giving way to fear. They are tempted to forget God's sovereignty and his constant presence with them. "Be still" is God saying in essence, "breath through your nose," quit talking, and begin to reflect! God is telling me to stop talking and starting listening to him for a change, and acknowledge that he is God." I should not worry or panic. God will be exalted among the nations. He is still in charge of this old world. He is always with me and wants to be my fortress, my strength. In this short psalm I find that word *Selah*, telling me to pause, weigh what has been said, reflect, meditate, think, ponder, then lift up my heart in trust and worship of almighty God.

Some commentators think verse 10 is directed to the nations instead of God's people. I find that hard to believe, seeing the word "our" and "us" continually used throughout. Whether this text is spoken to "the nations" or not, is not the question. It is a command to think and consider, and not the opposite. For that matter, it could be directed to both God's people and the rest of the world. Honesty with the Scriptures is always the best way to go. Maybe we need a hermeneutical reformation.

"Be still" is like prophet Samuel telling King Saul, "Stop! Let me tell you what the Lord said to me last night" (1 Samuel 15:16). I highly recommend a commentary on Psalm 46:10 written by Sarah Geis and

---

[141] Thomas Keating, *Open Mind, Open Heart: The Contemplative Dimension of the Gospel* (New York: Continuum, 1992), 146.

Douglas Groothuis of Denver Seminary.[142] Silence is a much needed commodity these days. But never silence *from* God's written Word, but just the opposite. Maybe I need to emphasize and trust the Scriptures more, in place of returning constantly to the human "fathers" from the deserts of Syria and Egypt, or the dogma and interpretations of my favorite theological or denominational tradition.

Stillness and solitude surely have their place, as seen in Jesus' own example (Luke 5:16; 6:12). Yet we can experience God's presence, leading, and power in our lives both in silent devotions and in the middle of noise and much activity, and virtually always cognitive, *with words*. See Marcia Montenegro's article on meditation and Psalm 46:10.[143] Admittedly a racing mind is not very conducive to a prolonged time of prayer. God hears us when troubled in mind or at rest. Repeating a word or phrase for twenty minutes as a mantra is neither biblical nor real prayer, and it can lead us where no true believer should be. There is no place in true Christianity for intentionally shutting down our minds. But surely there is a place for quiet before God that we might term "companionable silence," like what often occurs between two good friends.

God told Job: "Listen to this, Job; stop and consider God's wonders" (Job 37:14). Samuel also had to learn to listen, then say like young Samuel, "Speak, Lord, for your servant hears" (1 Samuel 3:9).

A brief reflection on Psalm 23 would be apropos here: As we allow the Lord, the Good Shepherd, to lead us, we are not in want but are contented and spiritually well fed. He leads us to thrive in green pastures, leads us by quiet and restful waters, and restores our soul. He leads us to righteous living "for his name's sake" (i.e., for God's honor and glory). His presence through tough times is palpable and comforting. These hard times result in the psalmist switching from "he" to "you" and a renewed bond of friendship and communion with God (symbolized by the "table" and eating together). We become the honored guest at God's table! What ecstasy! And not a moment of mind-emptying! All this results in God's glory and a glorious assurance of enjoying God's personal presence forever. We remain sheep, but we enjoy the Lord's imputed righteousness as guests in his house.

---

[142] www.equip.org/PDF/JAP363.pdf
[143] christiananswersforthenewage.org/Articles_MeditationPsalm.html

"Be still and know," but not do not "contemplate" in the Christian mystic sense. No. Normally we use the term contemplate as synonymous with deep reflective observation and thought. Historic Christian mysticism's contemplation is just the opposite—quit thinking! Mystic contemplation probably is not even found in the Bible, unless you look at Saul, in 1 Samuel 18. He is far from God and attempting to kill David, yet "prophesying in his house" under the power of an evil spirit allowed by God. The *NIV Study Bible* notes says about prophesying, "The Hebrew for this word is sometimes used to indicate uncontrolled ecstatic behavior." The Apostle John, even when carried off momentarily to heaven, was not experiencing uncontrolled ecstasy but had full control of his thoughts and body. He even had to be reprimanded for bowing before an angelic being in worship (Revelation 22:8-9).

Is God sending us to a silent, vacant garden or meadow in search of mystic feelings or voices? No! He's saying, "Shut up. Stop! Listen to *me* for a change!"

An Intimate Walk with God

Mystics insist that this mystic path, ending in wordless (apophatic) prayer, is the only way to enter God's blessed and transforming presence and sense real communion with him. Mind-emptying solitude and silence is the mystic's exclusive mode for being alone with God and knowing him intimately. "Contemplation" is the semitechnical term for this wordless prayer. Christian mystics affirm this mystic path is something which no amount of verbal (kataphatic) prayer, worship, church attendance, preaching, apologetics, or Bible study will ever accomplish. It is called the highest form of prayer, and is union with God.

Christian mysticism claims to have found in the mystic path the essential ingredient for knowing God personally that they say is lacking in traditional, historic Christianity. [144]

---

[144] On the back cover of Bruce Demarest's book *Satisfy Your Soul* it urges us to discover "the timeless spiritual guidance of the Christian classics *essential to help us develop an authentic relationship with God today.*" (Emphasis mine). If this were so, then nobody before these writers really knew the Lord since biblical Christianity just isn't enough. Most mystics believe you can't really know God intimately apart from silent contemplation and solitude, along with

Brennan Manning once said: "Intimate knowledge of God only comes through centering prayer."[145]

At Wheaton College I once heard Quaker Richard Foster tell the students that silent, nonverbal meditative prayer is what ushers us into God's presence via "mute language," where we learn from God as we open ourselves to his voice. Foster is describing the traditional mystical theory that God cannot really be known via the intellect and with words, but only via shutting down the mind by use of a mantra.

Quaker leader Mary Blackmar once said, "Quakers believe that no firsthand knowledge of God is possible except through that which is experienced, or inwardly revealed to the individual human being through the working of God's quickening spirit."[146]

Carl Jung said the unconscious is "the only accessible source of religious experience." No wonder so many Christian mystics are followers of Jungian psychology which dovetails easily with Quakerism.

The jacket of Ruth Haley Barton's book *Invitation to Solitude and Silence,* clearly reiterates this: "Much of our faith is about words—preaching, teaching, talking with others. Yet all of these words are not enough to take us into the real presence of God where we can hear his voice." William Ralph Inge wrote, "Ecstasy or vision begins when thought ceases. . . ."[147] As Thomas Merton says, such contemplation is "experiential contact with God beyond the senses and in some way even beyond concepts . . . and flashes out in the darkness of *unknowing.*"[148] Such silence is much more than mere absence of speech. It is even more than mere companionable silence between good friends. Pastor Peter Scazzero of Queens, NY, describes how he had recently learned to practice "apophatic prayer."[149] He says it is "prayer that is beyond words, thoughts, and images."

the aid of "spiritual directors" (which Buddhists call "Masters"), use of mantras, and going through various stages of the mystical way (purification, illumination, then finally the mystical union itself).

[145] Brennan Manning, *Gentle Revolutionaries* (Dimension Books, 1976), 104.

[146] christianexplorations.blogspot.com/2004_07_01_archive.html

[147] William Ralph Inge, *Christian Mysticism: The Bampton Lectures, 1899: Considered in Eight Lectures Delivered before the University of Oxford* (London: Methuen & Co., 1899), 13.

[148] Thomas Merton, *The Inner Experience: Notes on Contemplation* (HarperSanFrancisco, 2003), 71.

[149] www.preachitteachit.org/articles/detail/deep-praying-without-words/

Biblical Evaluation

There's nothing in this world as glorious and fulfilling as knowing God intimately. Such a close walk with him is not in any way dependent upon silencing the mind, nor any other discipline. It is a good relationship with God based upon constant repentance and trust in him, along with loving obedience. It is walking on good terms with him. I hear God's voice whenever I read and meditate on his inspired Word. Even apart from that, I also sense God's Spirit leading and directing my thoughts and actions.

Romans chapter 8 mentions how "those who are in Christ Jesus" who "live in accordance with the Spirit" and with their "mind controlled by the Spirit" are "led by the Spirit of God" and are sons of God. This is intimacy with God.

Jim Reapsome once wrote in the *Evangelical Missions Quarterly*, "The Bible is woefully short on methods. Strong on principles? You bet." He says the Bible has "a strong emphasis on intimacy with God. . . . Jesus turned his contemporary culture of spiritual formation upside down when he told the crowds they had to eat his flesh and drink his blood. . . . Jesus drives us to deeper levels of intimacy with God than we have ever tasted. That was his mission."[150]

The Bible teaches that the church, made up of all who belong to Christ by faith, comprise the bride of Christ. When a husband and wife are on good terms with one another, there is a sense of acceptance, love, and respect. There will be times of verbal communication, or just a companionable silence with occasional smiles, laughs, looks of bewilderment or concern, and all sorts of body language. All this and more without seeking some special mystic, altered state of consciousness! The same goes for the relationship between Christ and his bride. No prayer of protection from evil spirits is needed before such a continual practice of the presence of God. Forget historic contemplative spirituality with its roots in Greek philosophy and mysticism.

Knowing God intimately was high priority for King David. He expresses this as dwelling in the house of the Lord and gazing upon his beauty (Psalm 27:4). In Psalm 15:1 he refers to such communion as

---

[150] Jim Reapsome, "Missiology, Meet Jesus," in *Evangelical Missions Quarterly* (Wheaton, Illinois: EMIS, 1996), 6–7.

dwelling in God's sanctuary. In the New Testament Paul says God calls into "fellowship with his Son Jesus Christ" (1 Corinthians 1:9).

Each day I seek a deeper level of such intimacy with God. I say with Paul, "I want to know Christ and the power of his resurrection and the fellowship of sharing in his suffering, becoming like him" (Philippians 3:10). Peter concludes his second epistle by urging us to a life of holiness and growing "in the grace and knowledge of our Lord and Savior Jesus Christ" (3:18). This is *biblical* spiritual formation. It is a practice for all true Christ-followers, no matter how old they are or how long they have known Christ as Savior.

We can know a lot about God by reading the Scriptures. We can only know him intimately when we receive Jesus as our Lord and Savior. At this new birth experience, we begin a life of consciously walking in communion with God. This process of sanctification is clearly pictured for us in 2 Corinthians 3:18, talking about "ever-increasing glory." We who know the Lord begin to reflect his glory in growing degrees as we are gradually transformed into Christ's likeness. (See also John 17:22).

Along with personal intimacy with God we also need to stimulate communal companionship with the Lord. Contemplative spirituality can all too easily degenerate into a narcissistic me-only relationship with God. Note how after the Day of Pentecost (Acts 2:42ff.) the followers of Christ devoted themselves to communal study of apostolic doctrine. They engaged in joyful worship, loving fellowship and caring for each other, along with continuous evangelism. Note too the place of both gathered and individual worship in the life of the early apostolic church.

Hebrews 10:19 describes how a follower of Christ enters "the Most Holy Place by the blood of Jesus." We are simply to "draw near to God with a sincere heart," by faith and trust, with cleansed hearts and freedom from guilt (10:22).

This is what the Bible means by "the gospel." We have entered into a love relationship with the Creator of this universe! All true followers of Christ comprise the "bride of Christ." Many biblical passages teach that he knows us and we know him. In John 10:14 Jesus says, "I am the good shepherd; I know my sheep and my sheep know me.

John's first epistle gives us a series of tests to show if we really *know* God. Here are a few of these:

- "If we claim to have fellowship with him yet walk in the darkness, we lie and do not live by the truth" (1 John 1:6).
- "We know that we have come to know him if we obey his commands" (1 John 2:3).
- "This is how we know we are in him: Whoever claims to live in him must walk as Jesus did" (1 John 2:5-6).

God longs for intimacy with us. Such an intimate and authentic relationship with God should increase during our lifetime. The Apostle Paul's aim was to *know* Jesus better. Jesus said such knowing is "eternal life" (knowing the Father and the Son, as we read in John 17:3). Furthermore, eternal life is synonymous with the "Kingdom of God"—something we should seek as our highest priority (Matthew 6:33). It is the whole concept of rescuing, redeeming, saving, salvaging, restoring, and renewing.[151] In a word, it is redemption, both of repentant individuals and someday the restoration of the whole universe (see Romans 8:18-25).

It might be profitable for each of us, right now, to pause and analyze how and when we enjoy intimacy with God and how we might experience more of his presence and power in our lives. Do we automatically enjoy it all the time? If not, what is absolutely essential for restoring it? What helps us to become more like Jesus? What helps us to "walk in the Spirit," walk with God, be Spirit filled, and love and obey him?

Every time I pray in the biblical way,[152] with concepts, words and thoughts, I experience authentic, close friendship, and union and communion with him. I welcome him anew into every area of my thinking and living. I do not need to sense or feel his presence and guidance, but am assured that all is well with my soul. By faith I walk

---

[151] To further unpack this concept, check out Matthew 19:16-30. The *NIV Study Bible's* footnotes are helpful on this, too, especially on v. 16. See also Colossians 1:12-13. The Kingdom of God is all about Jesus and the salvation he offers us. This is seen in Acts 28:23, 31 where Paul explained about the Kingdom of God *and* taught about the Lord Jesus. Note the typical Hebrew parallelism in these verses!

[152] Biblical prayer by a true follower of Christ includes repentance and confession, worship, petition, thankfulness, yielded to God's will, through Jesus and his atoning work.

with him, come what may. If I am truly walking with God, sometimes it's others who sense God's presence and the fragrance of Christ.[153]

In Revelation 3:20 Jesus lovingly rebukes people in a lukewarm church. In the same way Jesus stands at our heart's door—waiting, knocking, longing for us to open it so he may enter and have real communion with us. Why do we wait? Why hang on to our sin when we can hang on to the sin-bearer? Let's avoid messing around with dark spiritual powers. Forget the Quaker and Roman Catholic mystics and their mute, noncognitive path. Let's flee Zen, Sufism, Hinduism, and all non-Christian paganism as if it were the plague! Let's forget the centuries of nonbiblical syncretistic accretions and return to authentic biblical Christianity.

The Westminster Shorter Catechism says "The chief end of man is to love God and to enjoy him forever." This seems to fit well into knowing God intimately. This kind of worship is generally underrated in our churches today. Does this indicate we are hardly on speaking terms with God, or hardly thinking about him, or just do not know how to revel in his infinite qualities? I fear that all too often true worship is largely missing in many churches' "worship services." We all need that "loving attentiveness" to God. Worship service leaders especially need to be in tune with the Lord so as to lead the rest of us. Some sort of "call to worship" can be helpful, if nothing more than a choice Bible verse or two. We could get more creative and surprise the congregation with a few people singing something short and appropriate from behind the congregation.

Biblical Christianity surely has elements of "mysticism," if you wish to use that term, but unlike traditional mysticism, such intimacy with God is both cognitive and noncognitive, using both our minds and our hearts. True followers of Christ have fellowship with other true believers and with the Father and Son (1 John 1:3). This communion with God should be constant, not just a part of our "quiet time" or some mindless state of contemplation. Brother Lawrence wrote about this in *The Practice of the Presence of God*. Unlike most mystics, he seemed to stress cerebral, cognitive communion with God all day long, while washing pots and pans, and not some fleeting ecstatic experience with all senses silenced. An esoteric, mind-emptying mystical experience is

---

[153] Paul told the Corinthians: "For we are to God the aroma of Christ" (2 Corinthians 2:15).

neither divinely described nor proscribed in order to have real contact with God.

Here's a practical assignment: Examine a few psalms, for instance Psalms 32–37 or most any other of the psalms. Note the author's warm, verbal, and personal relationship with God. We note the author's singing joyfully to God, repenting and confessing sin to God, praising and extolling God, personally seeking the Lord, crying out to Him, walking in the fear of the Lord, being still before the Lord and waiting patiently for him, content with simplicity and with the lack of wealth, and so forth. Both the biblical examples of piety and our own daily experiences should serve to destroy the mistaken notion of the Christian mystics.

We just need basic, biblical Christianity as found in the Scriptures, not a blend of Christianity with ancient Greek philosophy and pagan religion combined with insights and practices of the mystic elements of Hinduism, Buddhism, Islam, Judaism, and gospel-denying influence of Protestant liberalism and traditional Quakerism.

German Lutheran pastor, hymn writer and mystic, Gerhard Tersteegen, born in Moers, Germany in 1697, is referred to as a mystic since he sensed the nearness of God but not quite in the traditional mystic noncognitive manner. He was part of the Protestant Pietistic movement. He was assured that hymn singing could and should be true communion with God.[154]

The hymn, "I Heard the Voice of Jesus Say," by Horatius Bonar of Scotland expresses so well the biblical teaching on this topic. Bonar composed more than 600 hymns, as pastor in the Free Church of Scotland. On the topic of prayer, he says, "A believing man will be a praying man. To say "I believe," and make this supposed faith an

---

[154] He says: "The pious, reverential singing of hymns has something angelic about it and is accompanied by divine blessing. It quiets and subdues the troubled emotions; it drives away cares and anxieties; it strengthens, refreshes and encourages the soul; it draws the mind unconsciously from external things, lifts up the soul to joyful adoration, and thus prepares us to worship in spirit and in truth. We should sing with the spirit of reverence, with sincerity, simplicity and hearty desire. www.ccel.org/ccel/ryden/hymnstory.p2.c19.html

. . . When you sing, O soul, remember that you are as truly communing with the holy and omnipresent God as when you are praying. Consider that you are standing in spirit before the throne of God with countless thousands of angels and spirits of the just and that you are blending your weak praises with the music of heaven." (Emphasis added)

excuse for unprayerfulness is to deny the very end and object for which we believe, viz., *that we may come into the presence of God and have unceasing fellowship with Him.*"[155] (Emphasis mine)

Inducing Mystic Silence

In order to induce mystic silence, that final stage of the mystic path termed union, Christian mystics utilize some basic techniques for arriving at the silence of God's presence. These serve as triggers for shifting one's state of consciousness. This process is sometimes termed centering down, prayer of presence, or recollection.

As already noted, union is induced by a kataphatic preparatory regimen (with the use of words and thoughts) for getting into position for the apophatic (wordless) mystic silence. Although it is entirely up to God when he chooses to show up in a special way, it is essential for people to prepare themselves for this to happen. The following are some of those basic techniques:

- **Repetition of a Christian word or phrase**, as a mantra,[156] which clears the head of all words, thoughts, and feelings and which allegedly leads a person into Jesus' presence. This is what contemplatives call the silence and is what they seek in retreats of "silence and solitude." Christian mystics say this is the centerpiece, the heart of monasticism, to silence the mind and all sensations, where they arrive at alpha. Some Christian mystics assert this is the foundation of all religion, Christian or non-Christian.[157] In

---

[155] www.gracegems.org/Bonar/true_faith.htm

[156] During Christian mystic "centering prayer" Catholic mystic and monk, Brennan Manning, urged people to stop thinking about God and to "enter into the great silence of God . . . [to] choose a single, sacred word . . . repeat the sacred word inwardly, slowly, and often." (*The Signature of Jesus* [Colorado Springs: Multnomah, 1996], 212, 215, and 218). Henri Nouwen said, "The quiet repetition of a single word can help us to descend with the mind into the heart" (*The Way of the Heart* [HarperSanFrancisco, 1981], 62). Adele Calhoun says centering prayer is "taming scattered thoughts by attending to Christ through the use of a prayer word." *Spiritual Disciplines Handbook* (Downers Grove, IL: InterVarsity, 2005), 207. On a Catholic website, Jacqueline Galloway discusses mysticism, saying we come to know God by entering "the superconscious state." This is done "by using a repetitive word . . . something to bring us into the presence of God, such as: Abba Father. . . . This mantra will be the only words used." See: www.ecatholic2000.com/pray/prayer2.shtml

[157] www.inplainsite.org/html/contemplating_the_alternative.html#10Man

Orthodox Christian tradition the Hesychast (mystic) uses the Jesus Prayer as a mantra, in his or her path to union with God (*theosis*), the Holy Spirit, and salvation.[158] The repetition of a sacred word is comparable to turning off our smart phones by pressing the "off" until it completely turns off. Richard Foster says, "Repetition by itself is not wrong.[159] All mysticism, Christian or otherwise, aims at silencing the mind, to what they term "prayer without thoughts or words."[160] The contemplative Network, associated with Trappist monk Thomas Keating, describes their form of contemplative prayer, calling it centering prayer.[161] They say "this method of prayer is a movement beyond conversation with Christ to communion with Him." Bruce Demarest describes how to enter into the contemplative state of communion with the Lord by repetition of a word or phrase for ten or more minutes.[162]

- **Sitting comfortably**, upright and erect in a chair, with eyes closed, and body relaxed.[163]

- **Rhythmic breathing**, perhaps tilting the head back while inhaling and tilting it forward when exhaling, and focusing on your breathing along with saying your sacred word. Some like to hold their palms up when inhaling and hold them down when exhaling,

---

[158] en.wikipedia.org/wiki/Hesychasm

[159] Richard Foster, *Prayer: Finding the Heart's True Home* (HarperSanFrancisco, 1992), 135. He cites the biblical examples of Jesus' parables of importunity and his form of praying in the Garden, of Abraham praying over Sodom, and Paul praying repeatedly for healing. I wonder if there is any comparison between that sort of repeated prayer and Christian mysticism's repeating a holy phrase for upwards to twenty minutes! As some mystics readily admit, the mystic path, with its mantric praying and seeking an alpha state of consciousness, is not found in the Scriptures. Praying three or four times is no comparison with repeating a few words about 400 times for the express purpose of silencing the mind and all bodily senses.

[160] An example of this found in this pseudo-Christian mystic website: mysticalprinciples.wordpress.com/2015/01/11/prayer-without-words-or-thoughts/

[161] www.contemplative.net/

[162] Bruce Demarest, *Satisfy your Soul: Restoring the Heart of Christian Spirituality* (Colorado Springs: NavPress, 1999), 184. For further reading on this topic, Demarest suggests books by Richard Foster, Thomas Merton, and Henri Nouwen.

[163] On page 20 of his book *An Invitation to Centering Prayer* (Liguori, MO: Cistercian Abbey of Spencer, Inc., 2001), Basil Pennington says, "The important thing is that we are relaxed and our back is straight so that the vitalizing energies can flow freely."

while inhaling God's presence and peace and exhaling all anxiety and evil. A rhythm of breathing as a meditative technique began by the thirteenth century. Christian mystics, like non-Christian mystics, are quite aware of their breathing. Note Karis's reaction to someone's blog about breath prayers.[164]

- **Walking the Labyrinth.** They say this takes you inward as you slowly walk in concentric paths, to bring your whole self into harmony with God. "A labyrinth is an ancient symbol that relates to wholeness. It combines the imagery of the circle and the spiral into a meandering but purposeful path. The Labyrinth represents a journey to our own center and back again out into the world. Labyrinths have long been used as meditation and prayer tools."[165]

- **Meditative music.** Richard Foster says worshiping God through music is an entryway to God's presence.[166] Once we arrive there, words and music become unnecessary.

- Sometimes a **geographic "thin place"** is helpful.

- **Visualization.** Some mystics use their imagination, or they look at icons and images of saints, as part of the mystical process leading to a meditative trance that bypasses normal thinking and ushers us into God's presence. Some think it helps them create their own reality, or conjure up things.[167] Ignatius Loyola, founder of the Jesuits, emphasized the importance of this kind of visualization.[168]

- **Spiritual Direction** is virtually essential for spiritual formation. An increasing number of evangelical Christians are using Catholic directors as personal spiritual trainers, sometimes of the opposite gender.

---

[164] lovenotestoyahweh.blogspot.com/2007/11/what-is-breath-prayer.html Read this! (Especially what Karis says in this blog)

[165] www.lessons4living.com/labyrinth.htm

[166] Richard Foster, *Sanctuary of the Soul* (Downers Grove, IL: InterVarsity, 2011), 75.

[167] christiananswersforthenewage.org/Articles_Meditation.html

[168] www.ignatianspirituality.com/ignatian-prayer/the-spiritual-exercises/pray-with-your-imagination
See also this book for biblically balanced treatment of visualization: Gene Edward Veith Jr. and Matthew P. Ristuccia, *Imagination Redeemed* (Wheaton, IL: Crossway, 2015).

Biblical Evaluation

The Bible teaches that as a Christ-follower, I may "approach the throne of grace with confidence" and do so anytime, anywhere, confessing my sins, worshiping and praising our loving triune God, praying all throughout Bible reading, without the need of the above mentioned techniques. This above list, believed to be essential for approaching God, is not found in the Scriptures. I cannot recall any Scripture about keeping a straight back so that "vitalizing energies" might flow freely. Nor the need for keeping one's eyes closed for prayer although generally this is done today. As I draw near to God in the biblical pattern of words and thoughts, I enjoy everything that the most pious and sincere contemplating Christian mystic has ever longed for! Even prominent Christian mystic Thomas Merton admits the historic mystic path of contemplation is not found in the New Testament yet he says "it is man's highest and most essential spiritual activity."[169] Sadly, many contemplatives are unaware that something else, dark and evil, may be lurking there in "the silence" beyond the fully conscious mind. Demon activity is always a possibility in such a state, as contemplative mystic leaders Richard Foster[170] and Thomas Merton[171] have mentioned. Christ-followers who seek intimacy with

---

[169] Thomas Merton, *The Inner Experience: Notes on Contemplation* (HarperSanFrancisco, 2003), 33–34.

[170] In his book *Prayer: Finding the Heart's True Home* (HarperSanFrancisco, 1992), 164–66, Richard Foster gives us a word of "warning and precaution" about contemplative prayer, i.e., prayer without words that leading to spiritual ecstasy. Foster says: "In the silent contemplation of God we are entering deeply into the spiritual realm, and there is such a thing as supernatural guidance that is not divine guidance. . . . There are various orders of spiritual beings, and some of them are definitely not in cooperation with God and his way!" He then offers us a suggested prayer of protection and suggests we pray: "All dark and evil spirits must now leave" when practicing contemplative prayer.

[171] Merton writes: "My brother, perhaps in my solitude I have become as it were an explorer for you, a searcher in realms which you are not able to visit—except perhaps in the company of your psychiatrist. I have been summoned to explore a desert area of a man's heart in which explanations no longer suffice, and in which one learns that only experience counts. An arid, rocky, dark land of the soul, sometimes illuminated by strange fires which men fear and peopled by specters which men studiously avoid except in their nightmares." Cunningham, Lawrence, ed., *Thomas Merton: Spiritual Master, The Essential Writings* (New York: Paulist Press: 1992), 424.

God via Christian mysticism need to hear: "Danger ahead!" Watch out!" "Enter at your own risk!"

I should center on Christ, not on some supposed spark of divinity that mystics affirm is at the center of every human. The mystic path, involving repetitive prayer, or "mantra meditation"[172] as Catholic priest John Main calls it, is said to be foundational for all religions. John Witcombe notes the use of mantras in all contemplative praying.[173] This idea motivates an increasing number of Christian mystics to seek "interspirituality," that of "identifying and embracing the mystical core or common ground of the world's religions"[174] Magic always seeks power and domination by some form of incantation, to create a "spell" or ecstatic state. It uses rituals to force spiritual powers to do one's will, like control of the weather or people, or even to create reality. Biblical Christianity is a worshipful intimacy with God that results in personal holiness and Christlikeness. It is submission to God. It is not dependent upon rituals or all sorts of disciplines, as important as many of them are. Biblical sanctification/spirituality never seeks some distinct state of consciousness or "spell" as required for enjoying an intimate relationship with God.

"Modern mystics use labyrinths to help them achieve a contemplative state. Walking among the turnings, one loses track of direction and of the outside world, and thus the mind quiets.[175] For some, the labyrinth is symbolic of the journey to one's center, or toward enlightenment or salvation. The idea of labyrinths dates from the time of Greek mythology. Bruce Demarest of Denver Seminary says "the theory behind the labyrinth diverges considerably from orthodox Christian belief. . . . Christians who buy into the symbolism and theory of the labyrinth . . . expose themselves to serious error. . . . Faithful

---

[172] www.innerexplorations.com/chmystext/john.htm This link takes us to a discussion by Catholics about Benedictine monk, John Main's "mantra meditation," a slightly modified form of practice he learned from Hindus. Some Catholic theologians wonder if it is the same as centering prayer. They ask, "Is it identical with the teaching of John Cassion, and *The Cloud of Unknowing?*" John Main explains: "For the Swami, the aim of meditation was the coming to awareness of the Spirit of the universe who dwells in our hearts." Main saw the two as seeking the same end.

[173] amazingdiscoveries.org/S-deception_New-Age_meditation_centering

[174] quotationtreasury.wordpress.com/tag/definition-interspirituality/ quoting Brother Wayne in his book *The Mystic Heart.*

[175] en.wikipedia.org/wiki/Labyrinth#Christian_use

Christians must exercise caution when dealing with the Labyrinth Walk."[176] The labyrinth has no biblical basis or prototype. Former New Ager Marcia Montenegro warns Christians to avoid its use.[177]

Lectio Divina is divine reading, a devotional reading of Scripture that involves the four stages of reading a text, meditation, prayer, then mystic's final stage of contemplation. The prayer stage often includes repetition of a word or phrase that speaks to you, used as a mantra to usher you into wordless contemplation.[178] *Lectio Divina* began in Egypt, with third century Desert Father Origen, who thought the Bible contains meanings which are hidden from most people.

I need to be praying before, during, and at the end of Bible meditation, thinking about and talking with the Author, trusting him and his Holy Spirit to illuminate and help me apply his Word to my thinking and every action. God's Word then reveals what is within me (see Hebrews 4:12). It lights my path, convicts me of sin, and guides me in worship and thankfulness, then to relaxing and basking in God's presence. Such divine reading, bathed in prayer, leads me to engage in intercession and supplication, wanting God's Kingdom to come instead of constructing my own.

The final step of the Christian mystic path, the silence, can easily open me to the world of the occult. I have to ask myself: Is there really something lacking in New Testament Christianity, the kind I find in the Bible? What more do I need? Is it essential I enter such a dangerous spirit world to really know God? Even when prominent mystic leaders assure us this path is not mentioned in the Bible?

I do laud Christian mysticism's longing for God, for their strong yearning for sensing God's presence, and for following Jesus' example of seeking out a quiet place to commune with the Father without the normal distractions. Jesus often slipped out while it was still dark to seek such a solitary place (for example, Mark 1:35). If Christ needed such undivided communion with the Father, how much more do I! One church we worked alongside of in Argentina made a trail to the top of a small knoll near their village, a place for prayer and meditation on

---

[176] Bruce Demarest, *Satisfy Your Soul: Restoring the Heart of Christian Spirituality* (Colorado Springs: NavPress, 1999), 178–80.
[177] christiananswersforthenewage.org/Articles_Labyrinth.html
[178] en.wikipedia.org/wiki/Lectio_Divina

God's Word. Some churches and Christian schools where we now live have such a room.

I find that I need to quit talking (Psalm 46:10) and draw near to God, listening to him for a change, with my mind and heart full engaged. "Do not ever separate the head from the heart . . . not even with something as thin as a razor blade," so said Dr. Gordon Lewis to us students at Denver Seminary. Dr. Vernon Grounds would go for long walks each evening near his home to seek solitude. In Argentina I would grab a butterfly net and head for the jungle trails in the middle of the day, to supply the American Museum of Natural History with some new species. Those Andean foothills were ideal for meditation and prayer, among the wild orchids, toucans, occasional monkeys, and miniature deer. I also prayed the pumas, snakes, and some other critters would not find me overly interesting. God gave me some important insights while strolling with net in hand.

Nothing in this world compares with genuine, intimate communion with God. Enoch and Noah walked with God. So did Samuel's mother, Anna, and so many other men and women of faith, like the ones listed in Hebrews 11. I am still finding what really helps me know Christ better and walk with him in love and worship coupled with obedience. God calls me to radical discipleship. "Radical" means getting back to the roots. I do not intend to be rooted in any Desert Fathers or idolize any other Christian whom God is using, but rooted firmly only in Christ himself, my divine Savior, Lord, friend, example, power. What a glorious eternity awaits each of us who knows him personally. What glory it is to walk with God now.

Salvation and the New Birth

The majority of Christian mystics say Christianity is a journey with no precise initiation. Most Christian mystics reject any idea of Christ dying as their substitute, or that justification is by grace alone and received by repentance and faith alone.[179] Some Christian mystics say salvation is enlightenment, a process of becoming discontented with

---

[179] Episcopal contemplative priest Brian C. Taylor ridicules the idea originating in primitive Jewish religion about "the substitutionary theory of the atonement" which he says "has more in common with ancient Aztec and other blood centered religions than its proponents would care to admit." Brian Taylor, *Setting the Gospel Free* (New York: Continuum, 1996), 90.

our false self, and awakening to the presence of God in everything and everybody. Salvation is by knowledge of our inner divinity. We are not saved from hell but from living hellishly. John H. Westerhoff is quoted in *A Spiritual Formation Journal,* "No aspect of thinking on conversion is more foreign to the American evangelical experience than this stress on conversion as a process.... But Christian tradition does not agree.... Conversion is a continuous and lifelong process."[180]

In his book *Life of the Beloved,* Catholic mystic priest Henri Nouwen says all people are God's beloved, chosen, have eternal life, and are children of God. Richard Foster believes that by shedding his blood on the cross "Jesus took into himself all the evil and all the hostility of all the ages and redeemed it. He reconciled us to God, restoring the infinitely valuable personal relationship that had been shattered by sin."[181] Foster says, "The resurrection is God's abrupt absolution!" Hence there's no place for personal conversion or evangelism to begin a life with God, but just a lifetime of daily repentance and what they term spiritual formation including following Jesus' example. Most Christian mystics believe they are saved by God's grace and their good works.[182] They seek to purify themselves by practicing and nurturing virtues like love, self-control, prayer, penance, and seeking to be pure. Flemish Christian mystic John Ruusbroec said, "All good people are united with God by means of the grace of God and their virtuous life."[183]

Desert Father Origen did not teach that Christ died as the sinner's substitute. Christian mystic Maestro Eckhart believed in reincarnation and denied Christ's substitutionary atonement. A Catholic website affirms, "Even though only God's grace enables us to love others, these

---

[180] Jana Rea with Richard J. Foster, *A Spiritual Formation Journal, A Renovaré Resource for Spiritual Renewal* (HarperSanFrancisco, 1996), 53. Note: The term "Christian tradition" in this quotation refers to historic Christian mysticism, instead of historic Christian teaching found in the Scriptures.

[181] Richard Foster, *Prayer: Finding the Heart's True Home* (HarperSanFrancisco, 1992), 42–43.

[182] Many Catholics pray as did Teresa of Ávila: "Look not upon our sins but upon our redemption by Thy Most Sacred Son, upon His merits and upon those of His Glorious Mother and of all the saints and martyrs who have died for Thee." See: www.ecatholic2000.com/stteresa/way9.shtml

[183] "John Ruusbroec: The Little Book of Enlightenment" in *The Essential Writings of Christian Mysticism,* ed. Bernard McGinn (New York: Random House, 2006), 449.

acts of love please him, and he promises to reward them with eternal life (Romans 2:6-7; Galatians 6:6-10). Thus good works are meritorious."[184]

Biblical Evaluation

The Bible teaches that everyone is alienated and separated from God until their personal conversion, when they get onto God's side. A personal relationship with God must have a precise initiation,[185] although the exact moment is known only to God who sees our heart. Heaven rejoices "over one sinner who repents" (Luke 15:7, 10). An old hymn says, "Oh Happy Day . . . when Jesus washed my sins away. He taught me how to watch and pray, and live rejoicing every day. . . ."

Christ told the Jewish religious leader, "You must be born again" (John 3:7)—not born of water again, but of the Spirit. This results in spiritual, everlasting life, entering God's Kingdom, and becoming a spiritual child of God (John 1:12). Conversion involves adoption into God's family, the "body of Christ." It means passing from spiritual death to spiritual life, from darkness into God's marvelous light, from the mire into the choir, from despair to assurance, "hope so" to "know so," and from being "sinners" to being "saints" who enjoy God's imputed righteousness. At conversion we were branded with the Holy Spirit, that invisible seal, the very presence of God's Spirit! We are now under new ownership. So we sing: "Amazing grace, how sweet the sound, that saved a wretch like me. I once was lost but now am found, was blind but now I see." Believer's baptism then lets the world know we belong to Christ (see Acts 10:44-48).

---

[184] www.catholic.com/documents/pillar-of-fire-pillar-of-truth A very interesting website, *Catholic Answers: To Explain and Defend the Faith*. If you wonder what Catholicism still teaches, check this out.

[185] Timothy Phillips and Donald Bloesch discuss counterfeit spirituality in chapter five of *The Christian Educator's handbook of Spiritual Formation*. I find this a much needed corrective today, especially their emphasis of a spirituality based upon justification and a new birth experience. On page 64 they note, "The perennial spiritual counterfeit called pelagianism dismisses the need for God's regenerative work." Dallas Seminary professor, Robert Lightner, in Chapter three of the same book also discusses the need for initial salvation, since "all humankind is spiritually lost and therefore needs to be found or saved." Biblical spiritual formation begins at that point. Kenneth O. Gangle, and James C. Wilhoit, ed. (Grand Rapids: Baker Books, 1994).

The term *salvation*, as used in the Scriptures, has three aspects or stages. The person who repents and trusts in God has been saved from the penalty of sin, is now being saved from the power of sin, and one day in glory they will be saved from the presence of sin. These stages are justification, sanctification, and glorification. That last stage is salvation from the coming wrath. Note: *wrath* is the opposite of salvation, and refers to final judgment and eternal separation from God (see 1 Thessalonians 5:9; John 3:36; Revelation 19:15; Romans 1:18; 5:9).

This spiritual birth is by grace and by faith alone in Jesus Christ, my sin-bearer. It is a free gift, but results in a life of good works (see Ephesians 2:8-10; Titus 3:5, 8). Paul wrote, "This righteousness from God comes through faith in Jesus Christ to all who believe" (Romans 3:22).

Spiritual birth is essential for growth in Christlikeness, a process that is impossible if we are climbing a legalistic ladder in order to merit union with God. Apart from salvation by faith alone a person gropes along seeking merit, seeking how to appease God by their good deeds and religious rites. They attempt to purify themselves by means of spiritual disciplines in order to know God. As mystic expert William Ralph Inge wrote, "Purification removes the obstacles to our union with God."[186] Until people trust wholly in God's mercy through Christ's death for them on the cross, they merely have a hope-so religion instead of a know-so assurance. Trying to imitate Christ without initial conversion is like taking a filthy shirt, starching and ironing it, then putting it on. First I need to get on God's side. I need washing! Christ said, "Whoever hears my word and believes him who sent me has eternal life and will not be condemned; he has crossed over from death to life" (John 5:24). Growth in holiness, i.e. spiritual formation and becoming like Jesus, flows from this new birth. We must never confuse initial justification with the lifelong process of sanctification. In John chapter 13 Jesus explained to Peter he had been washed, i.e., spiritually bathed, but just needed his feet washed, which symbolizes daily cleansing as part of biblical spiritual formation.

---

[186] William Ralph Inge, *Christian Mysticism: The Bampton Lectures, 1899: Considered in Eight Lectures Delivered before the University of Oxford* (London: Methuen & Co., 1899), 11.

Sad to say, most Christian mystics reject God's diagnosis of the human predicament of total depravity so they miss God's gracious solution via repentance and faith. Too many "theologians" today are confused about the biblical term *gospel*.[187] Professor Michael Horton rightly asks: "Are we working *toward* our justification or *from* it?"[188]

Theologian Millard Erickson helps us define the term "gospel" in *Christian Theology*, included in his chapter on "The Role of the Church."[189] He says, "Without doubt . . . the gospel lies at the root of all that the church does." The gospel is good news! We are no longer without hope and without God. That old hymn puts it well: "My hope is built on nothing less, than Jesus' blood and righteousness . . . On Christ the solid Rock I stand . . . all other ground is sinking sand." This is worth preaching and proclaiming! If we get this wrong, we get everything wrong. Michael Horton notes we are not only to believe the gospel but called to obey it. 2 Thessalonians 1:8 says Christ will someday "punish those who do not know God and do not obey the gospel of our Lord Jesus." Such disobedience refers to their rejection of the gospel, and likewise obedience means acceptance of the good news. The gospel surely must lead to a changed life, one of walking with God in holiness. Horton says, "But obedience must not be confused with the gospel."[190] In Philippians 1:27 Paul says, "Conduct yourselves in a manner worthy of the gospel of Christ." In other words, a life that validates our profession of faith. Be a credit to God! The gospel must lead to a changed life, avoiding "faith without works" that the Bible disparages. We live for him who died for us and was raised again, constantly amazed at his love and grace. This is what drives true holiness and the mission Christ gave the church. It is all rooted in the

---

[187] Reformed theologian Michael Horton says an increasing number of evangelicals are denying belief in the substitutionary atonement of Christ for personal conversion. Some even say you can eventually get to heaven without knowing anything about Jesus. He sees this as the greatest theological challenge facing Christian leaders today. See this article about Horton versus Foster about contemplative spirituality: puritanreformed.blogspot.com/2009/10/michael-horton-versus-richard-foster-on.html

[188] Michael Horton, The Gospel-Driven Life (Grand Rapids: Baker Books, 2009), 149.

[189] Millard J. Erickson, *Christian Theology* (Grand Rapids: Baker, 1994), 1059–67.

[190] www.patheos.com/blogs/euangelion/2014/05/what-does-it-mean-to-obey-the-gospel/

good news promised in Genesis and fulfilled on Calvary. Christ's love compels us! (2 Corinthians 5:14ff.).

Good News—we no longer struggle and agonize over what we need to do to earn God's approval and presence. The gospel is Jesus! It comes from him and is him! All about him! It is news of victory! Full pardon and sonship is provided by God himself on the cross, to all who believe and receive it. Union—yes, united with Christ, from the moment we repent and turn to Christ and turn from our former gods. No ancient, mindless mystic path needed! Just the biblical gospel. The cross, the empty tomb, and a loving God awaiting our trust, our obedience, and a daily walk with him. Now that's really good news!

That same divine power and grace that initially saved me is readily available to me each day! That's very good news. It is God still at work in me in so many ways, "to will and to act according to his good purpose" (Philippians 2:12-13). Jerry Bridges of The Navigators called this a "gospel-driven sanctification." He stressed, "It is the gospel believed every day that is the only enduring motivation to pursue progressive sanctification. . . ."[191]

The gospel (good news) is all about Calvary, Jesus Christ becoming our sin-bearer through his death, burial, and resurrection. Jesus came from heaven "to give his life as a ransom for many" (Mark 10:45). Initial conversion/justification/regeneration is getting on God's side. It involves God's grace and my faith, as I receive what God provided for all who repent and get on his side. Progressive sanctification then kicks in for the whole race, and involves God's grace, my faith, *and my obedience*. Sanctification is not working *for* our justification but *from* it. This is truly good news. If we get this wrong, we get everything wrong.

Helen Roseveare, British medical doctor in the Congo, explained the gospel by saying the "Entrance [fee] to the Kingdom of God is nothing; but the annual subscription is all that you are and have." She left her Anglo-Catholic background at Cambridge and became an evangelical, serving as a doctor in Congo. The Bible teaches salvation by grace alone and by faith alone, but salvation is *unto* good works, which Roseveare terms the *annual subscription*.

---

[191] Quoted from Jerry Bridges's article, "The Gospel-Driven Sanctification." See: www.pcabakersfield.com/articles/gospel-driven_sanctification.pdf

Ed Hayes of Denver Seminary wrote a short article, "Who is Jesus?" He refers to the book *The Imitation of Christ*, written in the thirteenth century by Thomas a Kempis. Hayes encourages us to meditate on the life of Jesus Christ and follow his example. He says, "This means to live as he lived, to think as he thought and to conform ourselves to His image." But, he adds a much needed corrective in saying, "Single-hearted focus reaps great reward, but it does not guarantee our salvation. We do not become saints by imitation, but by transformation. Martin Luther, who was profoundly influenced by Thomas a Kempis, gave a gentle warning, "it is not imitation that makes sons, but sonship makes imitators." Luther "discovered" that hidden gem of truth while reading Romans in the original Greek, "For in the gospel a righteousness from God is revealed, a righteousness that is by faith from first to last, just as it is written: 'The righteous will live by faith'" (Romans 1:17).

Many mystics decry the "judgmentalism" of classifying people as Christians or non-Christians, in effect denying our Lord's teaching about the sheep and the goats, the broad and narrow road, the saved and the lost and the need for a new birth experience, i.e., a spiritual bath (see Jesus' word to Peter about this, found in John 13). Today's Rob Bell along with mystics like Henri Nouwen simply reiterate the satanic lie of universal salvation that Desert Father Origen of Alexandria, Egypt, taught back in the third century. I cannot imagine any doctrine that is more "core" and basic to biblical Christian faith as personal conversion via repentance and faith in Christ's atoning work for us on the cross. Therefore, we heartily sing "Rescue the perishing; care for the dying . . . tell them of Jesus the mighty to save." Everyone needs to fall in love with God in a decisive way—via repentance and faith, and become part of the bride of Christ! Religious leader Nicodemus needed a "new birth." Baptism then follows, to let the world know we are on God's side (Acts 10:44-48). Christian growth in grace (i.e. "spiritual formation") then follows that spiritual birth, as seen in Ephesians 2:10 and Titus 3:8.

Syncretism, Pluralism, and Ecumenism

Many Christian mystics practice religious syncretism, can find God regardless of their religion, and believe in broad ecumenism. Such mystics say all people who practice contemplative spirituality are our brothers, whether they are Catholic, Protestant, Jewish Kabbalah, Islamic Sufi, Buddhist, Hindu, or whatever. They assert we should learn from all religious traditions and even worship together. Religious syncretism is a blending, amalgam, a fusing of elements borrowed from various religions. Christian mysticism/centering prayer has its roots in this sort of blending and interspirituality. One Christian mystic website says, "We can learn a lot from our spiritual brothers and sisters in the East. . . . Respected Christian leaders . . . have seen the benefit in becoming acquainted with Eastern philosophies. Such voices include Morton Kelsey, Henri Nouwen, Father Thomas Keating, Thomas Merton . . . and so many more."[192]

A Buddhist website publishes an article by Episcopal priest Tilden Edwards, founder of Shalem Institute for Spiritual Formation. Edwards says, "Many members of Roman Catholic religious orders have taken the lead in recent decades in 'passing over' to Buddhist practices and standpoints and returning with a fresh perspective on Christian faith and practice."[193] Buddhist practices have taught him to be much more inclusive, to learn from one another's religious tradition.

In the 1970s Trappist Abbot Thomas Keating ministered at St. Joseph's monastery in Spencer, Massachusetts. He, along with William Menninger and M. Basil Pennington, invited Buddhist and Hindu monks to their monastery for dialogue and joint retreats. Much like Catholic mystic priest Thomas Merton, they too found much commonality with Eastern mysticism, especially in the mystic practices. They called this form of contemplation "centering prayer," which is basically the same as historic Christian mysticism or Christian contemplation as practiced since its inception in the third and fourth centuries among the Desert Fathers. It is now being promoted and practiced by many evangelical Christians including most Christian organizations and denominations as well as Bible Schools and Seminaries.

M. Basil Pennington made this amazing and stunning admission: "It is my sense, from having meditated with persons from many different traditions (including Eastern religions), that in the silence we

---

[192] ascendingthehills.blogspot.com/2011/11/use-of-mantras-for-christian.html
[193] www.upanishad.org/dialogue/jesus_buddha.htm (A truly significant, revealing article!)

experience a deep unity. When we go beyond the portals of the rational mind into the experience, there is only one God to be experienced."[194]

Christian mysticism advocate Carl McColman notes, "Throughout the history of Christianity, Christian mystics have displayed an unusual openness to the wisdom of non-Christian philosophy and religion. . . . Mysticism is a form of unity that transcends religious difference." He illustrates this by mentioning a long line of ecumenicity including Greek philosophy's influence on the Desert Fathers Origen and Clement of Alexandria, the Druid influence on Irish and Scottish Christian spirituality, Spanish mystics being influenced by the Jewish Kabbalah, and the interreligious spirituality today in mystics like Thomas Merton, Cynthia Bourgeault, and many others who are influenced by Sufism, Vedanta, or Zen. McColman thinks "no absolutely clear distinction can be drawn between Christian and non-Christian mysticism." [195]

The back cover of Robert Webber's book *Common Roots*, says Webber "challenges contemporary evangelical beliefs and practices that are out of harmony with historic Christianity." This sounds good until we realize he compares contemporary beliefs and practices with those of historic Christianity of AD 100–500 instead of truly historic Christianity found in the inspired Scriptures. He urges us back to the ancient patterns he thinks we need to recover, including the areas of "worship, theology, mission, and spirituality."

A website *Empty Bel* lists many Internet articles about early Buddhist-Christian links.[196] Such links are today on the increase.

The website *Christian Healing Arts* is a clear example of syncretistic interspirituality, accepting all types of religious spirituality as we see on their home page and list of articles. The article on "Christian Meditation" quotes the Bible and likes Christian mystics like John Cassian and Meister Eckhart along with the book *The Cloud of Unknowing*."[197]

---

[194] M. Basil Pennington, *Centered Living: The Way of Centering Prayer* (Liguori, MO: Liguori/Triumph, 1999), 192.

[195] Carl McColman, *The Big Book of Christian Mysticism: The Essential Guide to Contemplative Spirituality* (Newburyport, MA: Hampton Roads Publishing, 2010), 63–64.

[196] www.emptybell.org/articles/links.html

[197] easternhealingarts.com/Articles/ChristianMeditation.html

One example of Catholic ecumenism is found in the "Monastic Interreligious Dialogue."[198] We can also get a feel for this in an article by Beatrice Bruteau.[199] Bruteau was a pioneer in interspirituality, as a Catholic mystic and expert in Hindu Vedanta.[200]

Meister Eckhart said: "Theologians may quarrel, but the mystics of the world speak the same language." Thomas Merton said monks of all religions are "brothers." Many Christian mystics long for a new kind of deep ecumenism, not union of doctrine but built upon what we all have in common while traveling the historic mystic path. Christian mystics easily move into interspirituality. Much-quoted Catholic mystic Thomas Merton once said: "I intend to become as good a Buddhist as I can." Just before his death he told John Moffitt: "Zen and Christianity are the same."[201] Mother Teresa said, "I love all religions." She just wanted to bring her patients closer to the "god" in whom they already believed.

Tony Campolo questions that Christ is the only way to God. In a TV interview with Charlie Rose in 1997 Campolo said: "I am not convinced that Jesus only lives in Christians."[202] In 2005 the head of the Franciscan order told Tony Campolo of a worldwide meeting of Franciscan leaders in Thailand which included some meetings with Buddhist theologians and mystics. The Catholic and Buddhist theologians could find no common ground. But Catholic and Buddhist monks prayed together and came back hugging each other. Campolo says: "In a mystical relationship with God, there is a coming together of people *where theology is left behind* and in this spirituality they found a commonality."[203] (Emphasis mine) Campolo also writes, "A

---

[198] www.dimmid.org/

[199] www.crosscurrents.org/eucharist.htm She quotes Raimundo Panikkar as saying in *The Silence of God*, "No culture, and no religion, can solve the human problem all by itself. . . . Hence the need for a mutual fertilization of human traditions." This mutual fertilization he now sees as including not only the various religions and spiritualties, but also the relationship between humanity as religious (whether theistic or nontheistic) and humanity as secular. So even our ecumenism is expanding and evolving. We are shifting and adjusting, mutating and suffering extinctions; the human *ecology* is in motion, groping for adaptation.

[200] ncronline.org/news/people/interspiritual-pioneer-beatrice-bruteau-loomed-large-contemplative-universe

[201] www.thomasmertonsociety.org/altany2.htm

[202] www.bigchurch.me/blog/8492/post_89526.html

[203] www.crosscurrents.org/CompoloSpring2005.htm

theology of mysticism provides some hope for common ground between Christianity and Islam. Both religions have within their histories examples of ecstatic union with God. . . . I do not know what to make of the Muslim mystics, especially those who have come to be known as the Sufis. What do they experience in their mystical experiences? Could they have encountered the same God we do in our Christian mysticism?"[204]

Christian mystics are generally less negative or critical, and more loving and affirmative of all people, irrespective of their doctrine or practices.

As professor at Denver Seminary, contemplative spirituality expert Bruce Demarest used to take students to a Catholic Abbey for joint study and worship including the Eucharist, "soaking in spiritual traditions, views, practices, and insights as ancient and true as the church." [205]

In his book *Celebration of Discipline,* Foster encourages us to read ancient Chinese mysticism of Lao-tzu as well as Zarathustra of ancient Persia (Iran) who founded the Zoroastrian religion. Such reading serves to "guide us in the spiritual walk." Foster is promoting a vision of an all-inclusive community he thinks God is forming today, via the common ground of contemplative spirituality (Christian mysticism). A friend of mine who has read most of Foster's books says Foster has cozied up too closely to Hindu philosophy in an attempt to make the spiritual disciplines "work."

Note this article from a Catholic website (see footnote), written by Fr. John D. Dreher, comparing Christian spirituality with Eastern spirituality.[206] This is a *must read.* Regarding the topic of New Age, Dreher writes, "The similarities between centering prayer and Transcendental Meditation are striking. 'As an ex-TM mediator,' says Fr. Finbarr Flanagan, O.F.M., 'I find it hard to see any differences between centering prayer and Transcendental Meditation.' Frs. Keating, Menninger, and Pennington authored *Centering Prayer* at a

---

[204] christianapologeticsalliance.com/2013/11/17/mysticism-tony-campolo-and-the-hope-of-world-unity/

[205] Bruce Demarest, *Satisfy your Soul: Restoring the Heart of Christian Spirituality* (Colorado Springs: NavPress, 1999), 26ff. See also Chapter nine, "Wisdom of the Spiritual Classics."

[206] www.catholiceducation.org/en/religion-and-philosophy/apologetics/the-danger-of-centering-prayer.html

time when St. Joseph Abbey had received several retreats involving Eastern religions, including Transcendental Meditation."

Catholic mystic Carl McColman promotes ecumenical unity and practices syncretism. He says, "Those who drink deeply from the wells of Christian contemplation tend, like mystics from all paths, to be far more interested in what unites people of different traditions, rather than what separates us."[207] Philip Yancey was quoted in *Christianity Today* (Nov. 2004) as saying: "Perhaps our day calls for a new kind of ecumenical movement: not of doctrine, nor even of religious unity, but one that builds on what Jews, Christians, and Muslims hold in common. . . . Indeed, Jews, Christians, and Muslims have much in common."

Biblical Evaluation

The Bible says: "Do not learn the ways of the nations" (Jeremiah 10:2), including their religious rites.[208] We should avoid cultic Christianity as well, i.e. any religious expression that teaches another gospel, which means anyone who teaches justification before God by means of rites or human merit. Paul asks the Corinthians: "What fellowship can light have with darkness?" (2 Corinthians 6:14 and context). Are there any spiritual lessons to be learned from the heretical cults and non-Christian religions? Note this warning found in 1 Corinthians 10:20-21: "The sacrifices of pagans are offered to demons, not to God, and I do not want you to be participants with demons. You cannot drink the cup of the Lord and the cup of demons too; you cannot have a part in both the Lord's table and the table of demons." Demons are not divine, yet seek our worship.

In Psalm 16:4 (NLT), David says, "Those who chase after other gods will be filled with sorrow. I will not take part in their sacrifices or

---

[207] www.carlmccolman.net/2014/07/30/the-hidden-tradition-of-christian-mysticism/

[208] Deuteronomy 7:6 says: "For you are a people holy to the Lord your God. The Lord your God has chosen you out of all the peoples on the face of the earth to be his people, his treasured possession." In the context God is telling them to drive out the idolatrous pagans. "Do not intermarry with them . . . for they will turn your sons away from following me to serve other gods" (7:3-4). Isaiah 2:6 says, "You have abandoned your people, the house of Jacob. They are full of superstitions from the East; they practice divination like the Philistines, and clasp hands with pagans."

even speak the names of their gods." King David knew what it was to walk with God in precious intimacy, as expressed in this psalm. He was not about to dialogue with followers of Molech or learn from Canaanite religions! Contrast David's joy and assurance with the scary experience mystic Thomas Merton writes about, the fear and darkness associated with the contemplative mystic path.[209]

I need to follow our Lord and the apostles' example of loving people while warning them about heresy. See Matthew 7:17-23; Matthew 23; Romans 16:17-18; Titus 3:9-11; 1 Timothy 1:19-20 (Hymenaeus and Alexander); 2 Timothy 2:17-18, 4:14 ("Alexander the metalworker . . . strongly opposed our message"); 2 Peter 2; Titus 1:10-16; and the whole book of Jude. Jesus was always a friend of sinners without participating in their sin. He came to seek and to save the lost. He ate with them and joined them in their family events. I must avoid the "ways" of the pagans while seeking their friendship and total well-being. When I live like this, I become a follower of him who is "the way, the truth, and the life."

God calls us to doctrinal and moral purity. He also demands social justice and true concern and love for all people. All the Old Testament prophets decried unjust weights, or making people work without paying them at the end of the day. God calls us to care especially for the widows and fatherless, even the immigrants, the disadvantaged, and all the poor and needy. When we do what is right and just, God says, "Is that not what it means to know me?" (Jeremiah 22:16). God says

---

[209] Merton writes about "The experience of contemplative prayer" saying, "There is . . . a special anguish in the acute sense of one's own helplessness and dereliction, when one is powerless to do anything for himself. When our faculties can no longer serve us in their ordinary way, we are bound to pass through periods of strange incapacity, bitterness, and even apparent despair. . . . Infused contemplation, then, sooner or later brings with it a terrible interior revolution. Gone is the sweetness of prayer. Meditation becomes impossible, even hateful. . . . The mind cannot think. The will seems unable to love. The interior life is filled with darkness and dryness and pain." (Quoted from Thomas Merton, *The Inner Experience: Notes on Contemplation* (HarperSanFrancisco, 2003), 74–75). On page 76 Merton says such experiences are "fraught with great risk. *How does one know that he is guided by God and not by the devil?*" (emphasis added) If you could have given Merton a biblical answer to this, what might it have been? Even Merton and Foster warn about entering into such a mind-emptying state. Why do people seek such a paranormal state? If it is for us, why doesn't God's Word clearly instruct us about seeking and entering such subjective "silence"?

we get to *know* him as we work alongside of him in caring for others and seeking their well-being. Jesus went about doing good . . . and so will I if living in communion with him and empowered by his Spirit.

Some people with open minds dislike any words of correction or warning, even when done biblically with love and humility. They say, "Don't be negative." If we follow their advice we'd never have the Old Testament prophetic writings like what we just read. Nor would we have our Lord's letters to the seven churches of Asia Minor (Revelation 2 and 3), where he first mentions what they are doing well then admonishes them about false teachers and syncretistic practices. Galatians 6:1 tells us to restore someone gently, and the last verses of James urge us to bring someone back who wanders from the truth. Isaiah 30:10 describes the Israelites wandering from the Lord: "They say to the seers, 'See no more visions!' and to the prophets, 'Give us no more visions of what is right! Tell us pleasant things.'" They were learning the ways of the nations.

The Shalem Institute for Spiritual Formation, founded by Tilden Edwards (where Ruth Haley Barton studied) is what Whit Edwards calls, "The Western bridge to Far Eastern spirituality." In their intent to produce a kind of hybrid religion, many Christian mystics like Tilden Edwards are learning from Buddhists, Muslim Sufi, Hindus, and other non-Christian religions. Nouwen, for instance, says he learned some meditation techniques from the Hindu writer Eknath Easwaran.

So, why do we think we need to hang out with, or hang on to every word of mystics who deny basic biblical doctrine? I never cease to be amazed at how soon we, like the Galatians, can become bewitched (see Galatians 3:1). Psalm 1 mentions the happy and blessed condition of the person "who does not walk in the counsel of the wicked or stand in the way of sinners" (i.e., hang out with them) "or sit in the seat of mockers" (i.e., join in and be a part of them). In contrast, "his delight is in the law of the Lord, and on his law he meditates day and night," and he ends up quite fruitful!

I think Richard Lovelace gives us shaky advice when he writes, "We need to listen carefully to other kinds of Christians. Mainline Protestants, Roman Catholics, and Orthodox believers have preserved biblical values that we lack. . . . We need to listen to . . . the body of tradition that has nourished other movements. The early fathers, the medieval mystics . . . Counter-Reformation . . . prophets of liberal social reform. . . ."[210] Then Demarest adds, "As we read the spiritual classics with open minds and hearts, we learn to appreciate the unity of *God's believing people* through the centuries." Wow. I do not think so! Some of those ancient mystics may have really known Christ and the true gospel, but surely not all of them. Read them if you must, but use much biblical discernment! Not everyone who prays to God, or says "Lord, Lord," or who practices contemplation in mindless silence and solitude, has truly entered the Kingdom of God. The Lord knows those who are his, but we sometimes have serious reasons to doubt they belong to the Lord, especially when they decry the substitutionary atonement and deny salvation by faith alone, or are messed up with the occult and Eastern religions. We may even find some inherent truth in what they write and may wish to quote them, like Paul who quoted Job's "friend" Eliphaz (1 Corinthians 3:19). But this does not mean we buy in to everything they express.

Canadian pastor Jim Challies says, "As I survey the contemporary church, one of my gravest concerns is the power and prevalence of mysticism. It appears in pulpits, books, and conversation. . . . It fills the pages of so many books on spiritual disciplines or spiritual formation. . . . Mysticism has wormed its way inside evangelicalism so that the two have become integrated and almost inseparable. In an age of syncretism, we fail to spot the contradiction and opposition.[211]

Cross-fertilization of ideas and practices with paganism can be dangerous to one's spiritual health and is definitely prohibited in Scripture. What fellowship can light have with darkness? All people need the Lord: his Word, his salvation, constant trust in him, his leading and power. A growing number of Christians are wondering if nonbiblical mystic ecumenism and syncretism may be preparing our world for "Babylon," that supreme, ultimate rebellion and opposition to God's Kingdom that includes an enforced one-world religion.

Former Catholic T. A. Mahon says, "Apostasy is growing rapidly, the religion of the Antichrist is taking shape, and mysticism, whether it's the Catholic variety, the Sufism of Islam, Yoga and the gurus of

---

[210] Quoted by Bruce Demarest, *Satisfy your Soul: Restoring the Heart of Christian Spirituality* (Colorado Springs: NavPress, 1999), 279.

[211] www.challies.com/articles/the-boundaries-of-evangelicalism

Eastern mysticism, the Shamanism of native religions, or otherwise, is a common yet powerful magnet that draws all religions together."[212]

Universal Salvation

Universal salvation (i.e., universalism) is a corollary of the above point, the idea that all people will eventually make it to heaven. Hell, if it exists, will someday be emptied. Many Christian mystics say we have no right to be exclusive, that personally knowing Jesus is not the only way to heaven and to God. Desert Father Origen thought maybe even the devil and demons will someday repent and be saved. Like Origen, most Christian mystics think all people will eventually be saved, in the next life if not this one. Julian of Norwich (1342–1423) thought God was all love, that there is no wrath in him.

The idea of universal salvation and no eternal hell then eliminates the essential need for evangelism and missions. During the last year of his life, Henri Nouwen said, "[I used to believe] that there is no salvation outside the Catholic Church and that it was my task to bring all 'nonbelievers' into the one true church. . . . Today I personally believe that while Jesus came to open the door to God's house, all human beings can walk through that door, whether they know about Jesus or not. Today I see it as my call to help every person claim his or her own way to God."[213] Nouwen had once expressed that all people are already God's chosen, are God's beloved, and on the way to heaven.[214]

In his book *Further Along the Road Less Traveled*, M. Scott Peck said, "Christianity's greatest sin is to think that other religions are not saved." Tony Campolo questions that Christ is the only way to God, and believes that Christ is in every human whether Christian or not.[215] He thinks people can experience Jesus without even being aware of it,

---

[212] www.thebereancall.org/content/evangelical-mysticism
[213] Henri Nouwen, *Sabbatical Journey* (New York: The Crossroad Publishing Company, 1998), 51. Nouwen died in 1996, soon after writing this journal.
[214] Henri J. M. Nouwen, *Life of the Beloved* (The Crossroad Publishing Company, 1992). This book, written to a secular Jewish friend, assures him and all humans that we are God's beloved children, have eternal life, and are chosen ones. Our task is to assure everyone of their chosenness, then to get in touch with that chosenness.
[215] Tony Campolo, *A Reasonable Faith* (Nashville: Nelson, 1983), 192.

under a different god's name. He says, "I've got to believe that Jesus is the only Savior but being a Christian is not the only way to be saved."[216]

Much quoted Catholic mystic Thomas Merton thought the monks of all religions share the same light as he did. Foster cites Merton favorably and says Merton "has perhaps done more than any other twentieth-century figure to make the life of prayer widely known and understood."[217] In another book, Foster says, "I am constantly pleased at how applicable Merton's writings are to the nonmonastic world in which most of us live."[218]

Biblical Evaluation

The Bible teaches: In Christ's death, provision is made for the salvation of all who by repentance and faith receive God's offer of sonship and eternal life with him.

Belief in universal salvation eliminates the judgmentalism of classifying people as Christians or non-Christians, or speaking of the broad and narrow road, or the saved and the lost. I'd rather be judgmental on this point and agree with God! Some evangelical Christian mystics would disagree at this vital point yet they still love reading all the mystics who do make this terribly mistaken assertion. And refuse to warn people who are headed for an eternal separation from God.

Do all people on our globe have eternal life and an eternal destiny with God? Is there but one road, instead of two? (See Matthew 7:13-14). Was Jesus mistaken in saying he is "the way, the truth, and the life"? John writes, "He who has the Son has life; he who does not have the Son of God does not have life" (1 John 5:12). Is this clear enough? Apparently there are people who do not have the Son. Or how about John 3:16, 18, and 36 and many similar texts? Jesus said, "If you hold to my teaching, you are really my disciples. . . . If you were Abraham's children . . . then you would do the things Abraham did. . . . If God were your Father, you would love me. . . . He who belongs to God hears what God says" (John 8:31, 39, 42, 47). Obviously Jesus did not think those religious leaders belonged to God! In fact, he boldly told them,

---

[216] www.crosscurrents.org/CompoloSpring2005.htm
[217] Richard Foster, *Spiritual Classics* (New York: HarperOne, 2000), 17.
[218] Richard Foster, *Devotional Classics* (HarperSanFrancisco, 1993), 66.

"You belong to your father, the devil." Wow. No wonder they wanted to kill him. Jesus gives us the parable of the four kinds of soil to show that not all people will respond to the gospel.

Some would argue for universal salvation quoting Paul who wrote, "For as in Adam all die, so in Christ *all* will be made alive" (1 Corinthians 15:22). But don't stop there. The very next verse says, "But each in his own turn: Christ the firstfruits; then, when he comes, *those who belong to him.*" In Romans 5:17 Paul does something similar in stressing *"Those who receive* God's abundant provision of grace and of the gift of righteousness reign in life through the one man, Jesus Christ." Provision is made for all; justification is applied to all who receive that gift. (emphasis added in verses above)

Paul tells Timothy that the living God "is the Savior of all men, and *especially of those who believe.*" That last emphasized phrase qualifies the first part that, if alone, would promote universalism.[219]

The book *Operation World*, a definitive guide for praying for God's work in each country of the world, mentions some global trends including "growing religious pluralism and post-modernity. Even among Christians, a creeping universalism can be observed as gaining ground."[220] In 1993, former executive director of WorldVenture, Hans Finzel, speaking at the National Association of Evangelicals (NAE) national convention, said that universalism is one of the top theological problems facing us in missions, calling it "a rampant disease," being the idea that "God is so loving that there is no way He would truly banish people to an eternal hell. I believe that he will."[221] More than two decades later this is an even more pervasive heresy.

Some Bible expositors, including Dallas Willard, pointed to Acts 10:34-35 as eliminating the need for knowing about Christ.[222] Acts 10:35 says "God does not show favoritism but accepts men from every

---

[219] The *NIV Study Bible* note on this verse, 1 Timothy 4:10, says: "Obviously this does not mean that God saves every person from eternal punishment, for such universalism would contradict the clear testimony of Scripture. God is, however, the Savior of all in that he offers salvation to all and saves all who come to him."

[220] *Operation World*, 7th Edition, (Downers Grove, IL: InterVarsity, 2010), 16.

[221] *Covenanter Witness*, May 1993, 5.

[222] www.christianitytoday.com/ct/2009/june/18.55.html?start=1 is a review of Willard's book *More Than Deep Feelings,* by W. Jay Wood of Wheaton College. On the final page Wood discusses Willard's defense of Christian pluralism.

nation who fear him and do what is right." Such expositors fail to realize Cornelius was already "devout and God-fearing" (v. 2), already worshiping the one and true God, as seen in this context. Furthermore, he needed to believe in Christ (v. 43). The rest of the New Testament clearly teaches the need to believe and receive Christ and his offer of salvation, which is why Christ sends his disciples to preach the gospel to all people.

Jesus is still the only way, the truth, and the life. Faith still comes only through hearing, and hearing by the word of God (Romans 10). Christianity is exclusive. To think otherwise is to call God a liar, is to invalidate worldwide evangelism and missions, and allow people to stay on that broad road that leads to eternal separation from God. Degrees of reward await each true follower of Jesus. Likewise, degrees of punishment await others, eternally separated from God. Our Righteous Judge knows what to do with each person. I'm glad this is God's task and not my problem. Maybe I should trust him, and keep on obeying the "Great Commission" of Matthew 28:18-20.

Contemplative mysticism is the common ground for global religious ecumenism, not only among factions of Islam but among all religions. What do all religions have in common? For one, it is a hatred of biblical faith in God through trust only in Jesus Christ as Savior and Lord. Satan hates God and the true gospel, but religion is just fine with him. Note how Paul in Romans 10:1-3 refers to the zealous Jewish leaders who attempted to establish their own righteousness. Paul prays for their *salvation* instead of trying to learn from them.

John Piper, speaking at the 2010 Third Lausanne Congress on World Evangelization, asserted at a plenary session that Christians need to "care about all suffering, especially eternal suffering." Apparently not all attendees agreed with this statement! But I do. So do the Scriptures! How a just and loving God will work out the details is not our concern. Ours is the privilege of being on his side, by God's grace and through faith. Ours is the God-given task of being "light" and "salt" among people who need the Lord and need to hear the good news, the gospel (See Romans 10:9ff.). Paul has but disparaging words for the Jews who "keep us from speaking to the Gentiles so that they may be saved" (1 Thessalonians 2:16).

The kind of unity Jesus prayed about in John 17 is not for all religions but for the segment of human population who enjoys "eternal life," and knows the Father and the Son (2-3). He prays for our protection (11) and to be guarded from the evil one (15). Christ prays for our sanctification *by God's truth* (17), not by mindless contemplation. Our spiritual unity on earth should be a powerful testimony to an unbelieving world (20-23) so that they, too, might believe. Jesus reveals the Father to us each of us who loves God (26). What basic, glorious theology is found in Christ's intercessory prayer for us. This is the only ecumenicity that glorifies God. So let's express *that* unity in order that the world might believe.

Simplicity

Many Christian mystics believe in practicing good stewardship of earth's resources, including a simple lifestyle. A few practice a vow of poverty.[223] Richard Foster has included a whole chapter on "Simplicity" in his book *Celebration of Discipline*.

Biblical Evaluation

The Bible teaches that I need to be content with what I have (Philippians 4:10-13) and avoid the idols of my culture of greed, avarice, covetousness, and self-indulgence that daily assault me. Jesus says I should not worry as do the pagans (Matthew 6:25-34). At the same time the Scriptures teach me that work is a virtue. I haven't yet found any biblical basis for not working if I'm still able to do so, while I avoid becoming a workaholic.

Jesus created all matter and life and still sustains it (John 1:3; Colossians 1:16-17), and while on earth he worked as a carpenter. After healing a man born blind, Jesus said, "As long as it is day, we must do the work of him who sent me. Night is coming, when no one can work" (John 9:4).

Paul made tents, and said, "We were not idle when we were among you," and gave them this rule: "If a man will not work, he shall not eat." We remember how God placed Adam and Eve in a garden to care for it, along with subduing and caring for the world (Genesis 2:15; 1:28).

Even caring for a flower or vegetable garden is work, but what pleasure and beauty it brings. The story is told of a lady who turned a

---

[223] www.christianperfection.info/tta63.php

weed-infested vacant lot into a flower garden. One day a passing minister saw her in the middle of it and said, "It's amazing what you and the Lord have done here." And she replied, "Thank you, Pastor, but you should have seen it when the Lord had it all to himself!"

An excellent article by Donald S. Whitney stresses the purpose of a simplified lifestyle, removing hindrances to knowing Christ better and obeying him.[224] See also Jim Challies's article, *The Heart of Frugality*, about learning to live with less while not becoming obsessed and enslaved to saving money.[225]

God calls me to faithful stewardship and maintenance of my possessions, and avoiding wastefulness. Proverbs condemns laziness. I should even store up like the ants, preparing for the future and not wasting, yet not hoarding unnecessarily. I should work so as to help those who are truly in need (Ephesians 4:28). The Apostle Paul said that too many people "live as enemies of the cross of Christ. . . . Their mind is on earthly things" (Philippians 3:18-19). God condemns gluttony, but has given us all things to enjoy—for the glory of God (1 Corinthians 10:31). He also puts no premium on intentional poverty, but calls me to help the poor, a hard thing to do if I virtually have nothing to contribute to the crying needs in my world.

Gene Edward Veith said the following in his article, "The Protestant Work Ethic": "Medieval Catholicism taught that spiritual perfection is to be found in celibacy, poverty, and the monastic withdrawal from the world, where higher spiritual life is found. . . . The pioneering sociologist Max Weber was the first to draw attention to the Protestant work ethic. In his book *The Protestant Ethic and the Spirit of Capitalism*, published in 1904, Weber studied the phenomenal economic growth, social mobility, and cultural change that accompanied the Reformation."[226]

As in all of life, God calls us to be balanced and sensible. Carol Reid, responding to an article about living with less, says: "I enjoy hospitality and pampering and making my guests feel special. Bottom

---

[224] bso.larryandpriscilla.com/wp-content/uploads/2011/01/Know-Why-You-Simplify.pdf

[225] www.challies.com/christian-living/the-heart-of-frugality Check out other helpful articles from this author!

[226] www.ligonier.org/learn/articles/protestant-work-ethic/

line: Joy is in Jesus and not things. Materialism and minimalism can both become idols."[227]

Sacred Rhythms

These are set hours for devotional activities, and are sometimes called Liturgy of the Hours, or Divine Office. In the Catholic Church this refers to daily prayers prescribed by the Church for use at set hours. Some other churches also use this pattern. Perhaps from the examples found in the Bible (see Acts 3:1) where God followers prayed at about 9 a.m., 3 p.m., and at sunset. Associated with this are what some people term the *sacred rhythms* where we schedule essential disciplines like Scripture meditation, prayer, worship, rest, ministry, and service. Daily Office, Divine Office, and Canonical Hours are fixed times of prayer during the day and may vary a lot between denominations.

Biblical Evaluation

The Bible does give us examples of this type of set hours for prayer although it was never commanded by God. Daniel prayed three times a day. Acts 3:1 mentions going to the temple "at the time of prayer—at three in the afternoon." At that time in history it was customary for Jews to pray at 9 a.m., 3 p.m., and at sunset. Set hours for prayer and devotion can be of great help in praying more, and more consistently and specifically, not only with a list of petitions but also a brief worship and Scriptural meditation guide.

View of Scripture

"The ultimate authority of my life is not the Bible. My ultimate authority is the divine voice in my own soul. Period." This quote by Christian mystic Sue Monk Kidd, in her book *The Dance of the Dissident Daughter* (p. 76), represents the view of many Christian mystics regarding Scripture.

Years ago Philip Yancey wrote in *Moody Monthly* magazine, "The Psalms primarily communicate not concepts, but the record of how a relationship is maintained."[228]

---

[227] *Christianity Today*, September 2015, 10.
[228] Philip Yancey, "Guidance," *Moody Monthly*, November 1984, 22–23.

Catholic mystic Brennan Manning wrote, "I am deeply distressed by what I only can call in our Christian culture the idolatry of the Scriptures. . . . I develop a nasty rash around people who speak as if mere scrutiny of its pages will reveal precisely how God thinks and precisely what God wants."[229] Modern-day Quakers say, "Like our predecessors, we point to the living Spirit among us as the final source of all authority."[230] One Quaker writer says, "To the Quakers, the Bible is *a* word of God, but not *the* Word of God."[231]

Elsa McInnes describes many people's journeys into contemplative spirituality as involving "stripping and reassembling core beliefs" and "looking for God beyond their church and the Bible." She follows Egypt's Christian mystic Origen in seeking the spiritual teaching of Scripture that goes beyond what is written, and listening "for the living word whether from the Bible or beyond its sacred pages."[232] Like Foster, she sees the need to introduce "evangelicals to other church traditions, to church history and a range of classics of Christian spirituality." In this way they "felt they had been given the missing pieces of a jigsaw puzzle." She notes how Foster's book *Streams of Living Water* is helpful in this regard.

Gerald McDermott wrote in *Christianity Today*, "We need the help of the creeds, councils, and the theologians to interpret [the Bible] properly," calling this the "Great Tradition." He includes people like John of the Cross, Teresa of Ávila, and Mother Teresa, along with heavyweights like Jonathan Edwards and Bonhoeffer.[233] Bruce Demarest of Denver Seminary would have us learn from Catholic, Quaker, and Eastern Orthodox mystics in a search for "authentic Christian insights and practices from the older tradition. . . . "[234] Demarest thinks we need to soak in "spiritual traditions, views, practices, and insights as ancient and true as the church" and absorb the Christian spirituality through spiritual masters of history. His favorites

---

[229] Brennan Manning, *The Signature of Jesus* (Colorado Springs: Multnomah, 1996), 188–89.

[230] 21stcenturyquaker.com/wp-content/uploads/2013/01/Modern-mystics-Section-1.pdf

[231] Vergilius Ferm, *Living Schools of Religion* (Littlefield, Adams & Co., 1958), 230.

[232] studylib.net/doc/7629339/bridges-for-evangelicals---spiritual-growth-ministries

[233] *Christianity Today,* November 2014, 54–57

[234] Bruce Demarest, *Satisfy your Soul: Restoring the Heart of Christian Spirituality* (Colorado Springs: NavPress, 1999).

include Thomas Merton, Teresa of Ávila, Henri Nouwen, Catherine of Siena, Brennan Manning, Basil Pennington, heretic Meister Eckhart, Morton Kelsey, Mother Teresa, and the list goes on.

Christian mysticism has deep roots in Eastern Orthodoxy and the Desert Fathers. Vergilus Ferm, in his textbook *Living Schools of Religion* says of Orthodoxy, "The Holy scripture is not considered a sufficient rule of faith. The Holy tradition, on the other hand, assumes a greater importance than in the Roman Church.... Tradition is considered by enlightened theologians as *living,* that is, ever moving and enriching itself in the collective experience of the Church ... the veneration of the Holy Virgin and the Saints, the doctrine and practice of Sacraments and 'Sacramentalia' and so on."[235]

Biblical Evaluation

The Bible is God's inspired Word, our ultimate authority for doctrine and practice. Our attitude toward the Judeo-Christian Scriptures is so pivotal and basic. Adam and Eve rejected God's authority and momentarily lost their friendship with God and their lovely garden paradise. Their first son totally rejected God's personal warning: "sin is crouching at your door; it desires to have you, but you must master it" (Genesis 4:7).

We often hear that saying, "Preach the gospel at all times, and if necessary use words." Lon Alison of Wheaton Bible Church did a nice spin-off on this by saying, "Feed the poor, and if you must, give food." Of course words are necessary! Christ commands us to go and preach the gospel, backed up of course with compassion and integrity, just as he did.

Misuse and rejection of God's Word lands us on a slippery slope, away from God's grace and from all that God desires for us. According to the first psalm, how do we receive God's blessings and become fruitful? By avoiding the counsel of the wicked and by delighting in and meditating on God's law, the Scriptures. The personal relationship with God—called faith, trust, belief—is based squarely upon what God has said, verbal *concepts* which we call "doctrine." Saving faith still comes by hearing, and hearing by the Word of God (Romans 10:17).

---

[235] Vergilius Ferm, *Living Schools of Religion* (Littlefield, Adams & Co., 1958), 181ff.

Martyn Lloyd-Jones of London rejected the mystic way, expressing his feeling in this significant quote: "How do I know it is God who is speaking to me? . . . How do I know I am not perhaps being deluded by Satan? . . ." Then he asks: "What is the evangelical way in order that I may come to this knowledge and fellowship with God?" His answer is, we should not look into ourselves but into the Word of God.[236] I well remember a church divided over its pastor. One lady stood up and said, "God told me the pastor needs to leave our church." Then another lady jumped up saying, "God told me the pastor should stay." At least one of these Christians was confused about God's message.

Some say that when God speaks to us in the mystic silence we can distinguish truth from error. Foster says, "Satan pushes and condemns, God draws and encourages. You can tell the difference."[237] Dallas Willard admitted that in the mystic silence we hear both God's voice and the voice of our adversary, Satan. Willard said we need to learn to recognize the quality of God's voice and that other voice.

Every Christian contemplative should wonder, as did Thomas Merton, "How does one know that he is guided by God and not by the devil?"[238] "Who am I really in contact with, there in the dark? Who am I loving and listening to? There is no real "checkability."

The Protestant Reformers got it right about what they termed *sola scriptura*—that the sixty-six books of the Bible are the only inspired Scriptures and the only basis both for what we should believe and what we should do. Jews today turn to the *halakhah*. In biblical times the rabbinic literature, including the Talmud, Mishnah, and Gemara ("the tradition of the elders," Matthew 15:1), trumped the Scriptures. For us the Bible must remain our default position—we constantly return to God's inspired Word, not to any fourth century Desert Fathers or any other writer or theological system. We have in Christ an excellent example of this in Matthew 19:5 where Jesus quotes Genesis 2:24 about God's original plan for marriage. We also recall how he resisted Satan with Scripture. He ended the Sermon on the Mount urging us to be as a wise person who builds upon a rock instead of sand, hearing and

---

[236] Martin Lloyd-Jones, *Fellowship with God* (Wheaton, IL: Crossway Books, 1993), 95.

[237] Richard Foster, *Sanctuary of the Soul, Journey into Meditative Prayer* (Downers Grove, IL: InterVarsity, 2011), 128.

[238] Thomas Merton, *The Inner Experience: Notes on Contemplation* (HarperSanFrancisco, 2003), 76.

obeying Christ's Word. The Scriptures are still "God-breathed and . . . useful for teaching, rebuking, correcting and training in righteousness" so that we may be "thoroughly equipped for every good work" (2 Timothy 3:16-17). From the beginning Satan has tried to get humans to ignore, doubt, misuse, distort, or openly deny God's Word. He's still up to his old tricks.

Only through the Scriptures can we know how to enter into a personal relationship with Christ via repentance and faith. In John 20:31 we read, "But these are written that you may believe that Jesus is the Christ, the Son of God, and that by believing you may have life in his name." Subjective feelings can be fickle and untrustworthy. So can human traditions, as Paul told the Colossians (Colossians 2:8). Psalm 119 exalts the place of God's Word which gives us more insight than all our teachers when we meditate all day long on God's law *and keep* his precepts (verses 97-104). This long psalm is really a prayer—intimate fellowship with God! It begins in verse 2 with seeking *God* with all our heart, not merely his Word. But surely not apart from his Word either! We enjoy and worship God with our brains engaged and love him with our whole being, heart, soul, strength and mind. We take God at his word, and take it literally when God isn't speaking symbolically. Genesis chapters 1–11 is real history, just like Christ and the biblical writers understood it. The Desert Fathers twisted Scripture with allegorical interpretations so as to find the supposed deep spiritual meaning. If Satan can't get us to quit reading and believing the Scriptures, he will get us to take it lightly or twist its clear meaning. In contrast to the false teachers bothering the Corinthian Christians Paul says, "We have renounced secret and shameful ways; we do not use deception, nor do we distort the word of God" (2 Corinthians 4:2).

I need the courage to take God at his word, to saturate myself with it, memorize key verses, mull it over, and to put it into practice. I need to both talk *about* God and talk *with* God. I need to see what God has said and discuss it with him. Have you ever noticed how often a biblical psalm switches quickly from theology to addressing God in prayer? Then back again. Psalm 23 is a good example of this, even making the switch within one verse. A call to God's people quickly turns into actual worship of God. Or an admonition or correction ends up as a chat with God about it. Expressing fear and doubt is often followed by trustful prayer.

Real prayer does not go inward to a supposed spark of divinity within us as Christian mysticism purports. Biblical prayer does not usher me to the alpha state of consciousness "beyond the realm of words and ideas" as Thomas Merton termed it. God's Word is a lamp to my feet and a light to my path, as the ultimate GPS. Its headlights, taillights, and horn for warning, keeps us from getting lost, even tells us when to stop and turn around. A sure sign of spiritual maturity is loving God and being attentive to all he has said. God has spoken and did not stutter. What he has said about human rebellion and redemption through repentance and faith is so very true. Such faith still comes by hearing the Word of God.

Now, having said all this about the importance of the Bible as our ultimate authority, I do not disparage broad reading, but urge discernment and caution, like the Bereans of old. Ask God for discernment. Go ahead and listen to what the best minds of the ages have said, but hold on to that which agrees with what God has said through those forty people he inspired. Then have the courage to take him at his word! Enjoy a good sermon or other good Christian literature, but do your own thinking! Enjoy the fish, but don't swallow the bones!

I still urge caution, however. I wonder why we need to immerse ourselves in heresy to look for a tidbit of truth. Why remove the lid of that smelly garbage can and stick my head inside in search for something edible? I might be able to do so, but my "weaker brother" might not yet have the needed discernment, or know where that author is coming from. Jesus warns us: "If anyone causes one of these little ones who believe in me to sin, it would be better for him to have a large millstone hung around his neck and to be drowned in the depths of the sea" (Matthew 18:6; see also Mark 9:42 and Luke 17:2). Wow. Pretty serious stuff.

I must let Christ be my true Teacher, my only authority in all matters of faith and practice (Matthew 23:8-10). Nobody should take my word for it! I am just another fellow pilgrim, with much yet to learn.

Talking about God is essential and God-commanded. But there's nothing quite like really talking *with* God. These two activities are intertwined in the Psalms and all throughout Scripture. I need to walk openly with him through all my mood swings, both in the storms and afterward, on the raging sea and in the quiet harbor. I also need to become more expert at helping others to know and love our Lord.

As a Christ-follower, I always have Jesus' Spirit in me. This is called a permanent *anointing,* an *unction* as we see in 1 John 2:20, 27 and 2 Corinthians 1:21. I do not need more of God's Spirit, or a new *unction.* God's Spirit wants more of me! With Bible in hand, I need to test all prophecies and test the spirits (1 Thessalonians 5:19-22; 1 John 4:1). I should never quench or grieve the Spirit. The same Holy Spirit who inspired the Scriptures indwells me. He illuminates the Bible and gives me power to obey it. To God be all the glory.

Summary

It is so easy to be mistaken and miss some of the most obvious biblical truths, even while our goals and intentions are good. Apollos is a good example, as is the Samaritan woman at the well to whom Jesus said, "You Samaritans worship what you do not know" (John 4:10, 21ff.). Sometimes we "do not know the Scriptures or the power of God" (Mark 12:24). Or, we do know the Scriptures but we don't know and love the Lord who inspired them. Or, we may be filled with disparaging comments about serious Bible study, as if such activity and real contact with God are somehow mutually exclusive.

Sooner or later Christian mysticism ends up distorting virtually every area of Christian teaching—every major doctrine found in the Scriptures.

In the earnest search for intimacy and union with God, and becoming like Jesus, some essential doctrinal topics and God-instituted practices are often left untouched or denied outright. These include the following: basic eschatology, human depravity, substitutionary atonement of Christ, the need for personal conversion, sin as personal rebellion against God, doctrine of the church, the need for evangelism and missions, systematic or biblical theology, hermeneutics, inerrancy of the Scriptures, the essential nature of God including both his immanence and transcendence, Satan and evil spirits, angels, work of the Holy Spirit, the Lord's Supper, baptism, *and much more.* Christian mystics seek God, but in all the wrong places and in the wrong ways. Theirs is an ancient path for sure, but lacking any biblical precedent.

Dr. Earl F. Palmer warns us all about nonbiblical meditation. In his message on Philippians 4, Dr. Palmer notes how the peace of God will guard both our hearts and our minds in Christ Jesus. God wants to work with our *minds* as well as with our hearts. He then notes how Paul, in verse 8, "invites them to meditate." He goes on to explain:

> You know the Judeo-Christian tradition has meditation tradition. Some people aren't aware of that. Meditation is *not* the empty garden type of meditation like you see in many religious movements, with an empty garden or the empty field . . . where you say a word over and over again, to clear your head of any thoughts. . . . Our Lord warned against that. He said, don't empty a house of all spirits because if you empty it the evil spirits will come in the side doors. Rather, fill the house with something you care about. So that's the meditation tradition that's the Judeo-Christian meditation tradition you see in the Psalms. Our tradition is to focus your mind on things that are true in the face of things that are stressful, and that's what he does now. 'Finally, brothers, whatever is true, whatever is noble, whatever is right, whatever is pure, whatever is lovely, whatever is admirable—if anything is excellent or praiseworthy—think about such things' (v. 8). He uses a very strong word for *think* now. It's the Greek word *logizeste*. We get the English word *logical* from that. In other words, compute those things, press the 'save' button on those for sure . . . and keep on doing those things."[239]

It is so easy to miss the obvious! Sherlock Holmes and Dr. Watson decide to go camping. After dinner and some wine, they go off to sleep. A few hours later Holmes wakes up and nudges his good friend.

"Watson, wake up. Look at that sky! What do you make of it?"

Watson gazes a few moments then replies, "I see thousands of stars. And, Saturn is in Leo. It's about 3 a.m. Looks like we'll have good weather in the—"

"Watson, you idiot!" says Holmes, "Someone has stolen our tent!"

Christian mysticism has "stolen the tent!" Stolen the heart out of the biblical good news, the gospel. No longer are all people lost sinners

---

[239] January 3, 2016, at University Presbyterian Church, Chapel Hill, Seattle, WA. His sermon is entitled "The Words of St. Paul for Such a Windy Place."

but children of God and indwelt by a spark of divinity. We only lack eye-opening illumination, suspension of our minds, and contemplative ecstasy to enter God's presence and become just like him. Or worse, even *above* God, as Christian mystic Meister Eckhart once preached.[240] It is Genesis chapter 3 all over again.

Christian mysticism/contemplation is a cancer that is seriously weakening the Church via the mystic path to intimacy with God that bypasses the mind via a sacred word, and leads to a dangerous spirit world. When we listen to the serpent's lies and eat of the forbidden tree, we begin to distort, even deny God's revealed truth. Non-Christian religions like Islamic Sufi, Zen Buddhism, and Hinduism no longer look so bad. We start to agree with a Vatican Council II statement: "The Catholic Church rejects nothing of what is true and holy in these religions."

At first it all sounds so good and right, like wanting intimacy with God and sensing his presence through silence and solitude, fasting, palms up and palms down as we concentrate on our breathing, enjoy walking and meditating a labyrinth, true and false self, the daily office, centering, *Lectio Divina,* visualization that creates reality, apophatic and kataphatic, ancient wisdom, enneagrams, chakras, kundalini, thin places, repetition of a sacred word till one enters an ecstatic state and hears God's voice. It is so nice to think that everyone will eventually make it to heaven and that hell will be finally emptied, as many of the early Church Fathers believed.

In a book review found in *Christianity Today*, Christopher Benson refers to "the contemporary regimen for getting closer to God" that is becoming so burdensome, then recommends the timely message from Phillip Cary's book *Good News for Anxious Christians.*[241] This book emphasizes that "Servants of Christ grow through repetition of the gospel (which turns the heart outward), not through experimentation with techniques (which turns the heart inward)." This review says,

---

[240] "Meister Eckhart Sermon 52" in *The Essential Writings of Christian Mysticism,* ed. Bernard McGinn (New York: Random House, 2006), 438–43.

[241] Christopher Benson, "Christ is Enough", *Christianity Today*, Vol. 54, No. 12, December, 2010, 67. Here is a link to the online article: www.christianitytoday.com/ct/2010/december/30.67.html Someone else's review of this book says, "Cary skillfully unpacks the riches of traditional Christian spirituality, bringing the real good news to Christians of all ages." (Anonymous review on Amazon.com)

"Cary submits that the Lutheran doctrine of *sola fide* (faith alone) offers a powerful corrective to the strangely Catholicized and psychologized evangelicalism that oppresses us." And, I might add, the strangely Quakerized and mysticized evangelicalism!

Chapter 4:
Historical Roots of Christian Mysticism

Importance of History

John Piper says, "The little book of Jude teaches us something about the value of learning history." He notes how Jude warns us of people creeping in unnoticed and perverting the grace of God. They deny "Jesus Christ our only Sovereign and Lord." Piper says, "Jude wants them . . . spotted for who they really are, so that the church is not deceived and ruined by their false teaching and immoral behavior."[242]

Jude proceeds to compare these ungodly people to those from the early Old Testament times, including murderous Cain, the many immoral and idolatrous Hebrews during the Exodus, and Balaam who urged the Midianite women to entice the Hebrew men. The Bible does not whitewash such apostasy. Jude then says we need to "remember what the apostles of our Lord Jesus Christ foretold" about scoffers yet to come, "in the last times," i.e., from apostolic times onward.

Then Jude urges them, and us, to return to the Scriptures, which he calls the "most holy faith." He urges us to "pray in the Holy Spirit," and to remain in God's love. The Bible, prayer, and love. Three huge essentials. Once we do this, we are then able to show God's mercy to people who doubt, and to snatch them from eternal perdition. Return to some Desert Fathers? No. Return to the Scriptures, including the biblical teaching about God, humans, the desperate state of those without faith in Christ, and the need of showing compassion coupled with evangelism.

God often gives us inspired lessons from history. The Bible is full of such lessons and warnings. Now it is time for us to delve briefly into church history, specifically the history of doctrine, the major factors in the development of Christian mysticism, and of Christian spiritual theology. A bit of historical theology.

Eastern style meditation began sneaking into the Christian church around the second century AD, from Clement of Alexandria onward.

---

[242] http://www.desiringgod.org/articles/the-value-of-learning-history

Some contemporary Christian mystics try to find precedence for their contemplative methods in the Bible. If this is so, I have yet to find such roots. Thomas Merton said that contemplation "is not mentioned in the New Testament. . . ."[243] In order to get a handle on Richard Foster, Henri Nouwen, Thomas Merton, and much of what is today termed *Christian formation,* we need to look first at the Desert Fathers who were highly influenced by Greek Neoplatonism. These were Christians of the third and fourth centuries, especially in Egypt, Syria, and Palestine.

Most Christian mystics readily admit to these roots. An article on the Patheos website says, "Christian mysticism can be traced back to the earliest stages of Christianity, including the experiences of many of the early Desert Fathers in the third and fourth centuries."[244]

Many Christians are unaware that these Desert Fathers were also deeply rooted in the Greek mystery religions and philosophy that had been invading Christianity from the time of the apostles. The New Testament church and its apostles had already begun resisting this rising invasion of heresy. The book of Colossians was written in part to combat this false teaching. Then we see Paul warning believers about two false teachers, Hymenaeus and Philetus (2 Timothy 2:17). The *NIV Study Bible* note on 2 Timothy 2:14-18 says they belonged to Gnosticism, which interpreted the Resurrection allegorically instead of literally. Desert Father Origen did the same later, saying Christ arose only spiritually.

Paul warned the Ephesian elders of coming "savage wolves" who would soon come in among them to "distort the truth" (Acts 20:29). So he commits them to God's Word and his grace. Several New Testament books refute early Gnostic inroads. In Revelation 2 and 3 we observe Jesus' concern for seven churches with varying degrees of apostasy in both doctrine and practice. By AD 150 some Christians began baptizing both adults and infants in order to redeem their souls. They thought all people have imputed guilt, as well as a sinful tendency inherited from Adam. Justin Martyr (AD 110–167) said new converts are to pray and fast "for the remission of their sins . . . then they are brought by us to

---

[243] Thomas Merton, *The Inner Experience: Notes on Contemplation* (HarperSanFrancisco, 2003), 32. He says, "The Christian contemplative tradition owes much, however, to classical Greece" and refers to the Desert Fathers of Egypt and the Near East and "the great practitioners of contemplation."

[244] www.patheos.com/Library/Christian-Mysticism.html

where there is water, and are regenerated in the same manner in which we ourselves were regenerated." By AD 202 Irenaeus was teaching that remission of sins actually occurred during the baptismal act. The idea of baptismal regeneration was a very early apostasy from the biblical teaching of justification by faith alone apart from external rites.[245]

Major Factors in the Development of Christian Mysticism

When I am asked to define Christian mysticism, the next question invariably revolves around its source and development. Then people want to know about the major promoters. Church history, along with what's termed "spiritual theology" and "mystical theology," shows how Christian mysticism began and was modified. This section briefly traces this development.

The Desert Fathers and Hellenism

A profound blending of Greek mysticism and Christianity had a deep influence over the life of the Christian church, having begun with Gnosticism in apostolic times then continuing with the monastic Desert Fathers. Christian mysticism/contemplation first appears in the deserts of Palestine and Egypt, with a form of Christianity developed by these Desert Fathers of the third and fourth Centuries after Christ. They were highly educated in Greek philosophy and mysticism. So, let's take a quick look at some of these Greek mystery religions.

William Inge says the Orphic Mysteries (about sixth century BC) had long taught the doctrine of deification, i.e., the acquisition by man of divine attributes. Some tombstones of the mystics would say "Happy and blessed one! Thou shalt be a god instead of a mortal," or something similar. The idea of deification is found in most of the fathers of the ancient church. Inge notes that "this notion grew within the Church as

---

[245] Paul wrote to the Ephesian Christians, "And you also were included in Christ when you heard the word of truth, the gospel of your salvation. Having believed, you were marked in him with a seal, the promised Holy Spirit." (Ephesians 1:13). See also Acts 10:47–48, a clear example of regeneration *prior* to baptism.

chiliastic (ideas of a Millennium) and apocalyptic Christianity faded away."[246]

Some 400 years before Christ's birth, Plato, who held to nondualism, said our minds need to be suspended to arrive at ecstasy. Plato spoke of the human soul as somehow being a part of the universal soul.

At the time of Christ, Philo (20 BC–AD 41), a Jew living in Alexandria, Egypt, taught that an ecstatic state helps absorb us into the divinity, a process called *theosis* and *hesychism*.[247] Later, Christian Eastern Orthodoxy picked up on this. Jeffery Mishlove says, "Philo advocated using forms of asceticism in order to free oneself from the grip of sensory reality and enter into communion with spiritual reality." Mishlove also notes, "The Neoplatonic school, centered in Alexandria, combined mystical elements found in Judaism with Greek philosophy."[248]

Christian Desert Father Clement of Alexandria, Egypt, (who died in AD 215) was steeped in Greek mythology.[249] He held to universal salvation, helped develop the idea of purgatory, and viewed Christians as "true Gnostics." He also introduced mystic "contemplation" to Christian practice, that of repeating a word or phrase from the Bible to attain an ecstatic state. The "Jesus Prayer" probably developed at this time, with its mantra-like repetition as a spiritual discipline to still the mind and enter into union with God.[250]

Origen (AD 185–254), one of Clement's students, held to the preexistence of human souls and universal salvation including the demons and devil. He is well known for spiritualizing and allegorizing Scripture. Origen thought that neither the Genesis account of Creation nor the Resurrection story of Jesus should be taken literally. He never mentions the substitutionary atonement of Christ. There is little room

---

[246] William Ralph Inge, *Christian Mysticism: The Bampton Lectures, 1899: Considered in Eight Lectures Delivered before the University of Oxford* (London: Methuen & Co., 1899).

[247] en.wikipedia.org/wiki/Hesychasm#Hesychastic_practice

[248] Jeffery Mishlove, *The Roots of Consciousness* (New York: Random House, 1975). Online version at: www.williamjames.com/History/GREECE.htm

[249] See Henny Fiska Haag, *Clement of Alexandria and the Beginnings of Christian Apophaticism*, part of the *Oxford Early Christian Studies* (Oxford Press: 2006).

[250] www.orthodoxprayer.org/Jesus%20Prayer.html "The Jesus Prayer," not to be confused with "The Lord's Prayer," was composed a few hundred years after the time of Christ and the apostles, as an aid to help people encounter a personal and direct relationship with God.

in his thinking for sin, divine judgment, or salvation. Origen sometimes used erotic imagery and symbolism when speaking of union with Christ. Many mystics over the ages have followed his example. Professor Bruce B. Janz, University of Central Florida, says of Origin: "He Christianized and theologized Neoplatonism. . . . Origen looks quite Gnostic at times."[251]

Plotinus in Egypt, AD 205–270, although non-Christian, was a major mover in all this, exerting an influence on Jewish, Christian, Islamic, and non-Christian mysticism. He visited Persia (present-day Iran) to study their religious ideas. As Plato, Plotinus held to nondualism, seeing no essential difference between humans and the divine. Plotinus taught that union with divinity can be realized only by arriving at a state of ecstasy where the soul becomes one with God. It is noteworthy that hundreds of years later the Islamic mystic Sufi were also influenced by Neoplatonism.[252]

Eerdmans' Handbook to the History of Christianity says, "Clement and Origen used the concepts of Platonism and Pythagoreanism—and Christian Gnosticism. Origen, and even Tertullian, may at times have been so heavily influenced by them as to cross the narrow frontier that separates orthodoxy from heresy."[253]

Anthony the Great (AD 251–356) said, "He who knows himself, knows God." Although not the actual founder of Christian monasticism, Anthony, a Coptic peasant from central Egypt, gave up all he owned and became a hermit, living in solitude. "He believed himself tormented by demons in every imaginable form. He fasted and practiced the strictest self-denial. He prayed constantly."[254]

---

[251] mysticson.blogspot.com/2013/04/western-mysticism.html To see more of Janz's research, check out pegasus.cc.ucf.edu/~janzb/

[252] persian.packhum.org/persian/main?url=pf%3Ffile%3D02602030%26ct%3D7 Select "Next" at top-left until you come to "INFLUENCE OF NEO-PLATONISM." Or select "Contents" to see many other articles about Sufism. Apparently there existed much cross-pollination, starting with Plotinus of Egypt visiting the Persian court in about the third century AD, more than 300 years before the beginning of Islam. This article says, "Sufism is more indebted to the school of Plotinus than to any other influence." Another question raised by this article is "What elements of their philosophy did the Neoplatonists originally borrow from the East and especially from Persia, which country Plotinus visited expressly to study the system there taught?"

[253] *Eerdmans' Handbook to the History of Christianity* (Grand Rapids: Eerdmans, 1977), 109.

[254] Williston Walker, *A History of the Christian Church* (New York: Scribner, 1918), 125.

John Cassian (360–435), through his writings, was another huge influence on St. Benedict and Loyola. He spent some time in Egypt. He writes about the three-step mystic path, was very hospitable, and stressed perpetual awareness of God. Cassion practiced the mantra-like use of a word or phrase to enter the stillness needed for mystic prayer.[255]

Basing our form of spirituality on the Desert Fathers could be termed spiritual quicksand and should be rejected for the chief cornerstone of the foundation, Jesus Christ. Even Solomon once wrote: "Do not say, 'Why were the old days better than these? For it is not wise to ask such questions'" (Ecclesiastes 7:10). The Guaraní people of Northwest Argentina would tell us of the horrendous "old ways" from which God had delivered them, like living in fear of tribal warfare, fear of evil spirits and witch doctors, fear of starvation, and fear of sickness and dying without hope and without God.

Christian mystics are totally right in asserting their form of contemplation is rooted in the ancient wisdom of the Desert Fathers. Now we see more clearly what influenced those early church leaders, including Greek mysticism influenced by Persian paganism. Could Christian mysticism's reliance upon the Desert Fathers be similar to the rabbinic traditions of Christ's day with the elevation of the Talmud and other traditions and commentaries instead of the inspired writings of Moses? Or is the mystic path more analogous to Eliphaz's hair-raising account found in Job 4:12 and following? We need to go back, much further back even than the Desert Fathers, all the way back to the forty inspired writers of the Bible. To "recall the words spoken in the past by the holy prophets and the command given by our Lord and Savior through your apostles"—Peter's stated goal in writing his two epistles (2 Peter 3:1-2).

The Fathers called contemplative prayer *ruminatio* or rumination. "The Jesus Prayer" originated with them, in Nitria and Scetis of fourth century Egypt. This prayer is: "Lord Jesus Christ have mercy on me." Richard Foster mentions a longer form: "Lord Jesus Christ, Son of God, have mercy on me, a sinner."[256] This prayer is still often repeated for ten or more minutes to enter "the silence" of the spirit world. Orthodox theologian Kallistos Ware says about contemplation: "We use The

[255] wccm.org/content/john-cassian

[256] Richard Foster, *Prayer: Finding the Heart's True Home* (HarperSanFrancisco, 1992), 128.

Jesus Prayer and apophatic practice to move beyond words and images into the fullness of union with God. . . ."[257]

Augustine (AD 354–430) strongly influenced medieval mysticism. He too had been influenced by Plato and Plotinus. Augustine's contemporary, Evagrius Ponticus (AD 346–399), was a prominent Christian mystic writer, influenced by Origen. He greatly influenced John Cassian who in turn took Eastern mysticism to monks of Western Europe.

Much later, after the Desert Fathers, Dionysius the Areopagite, or "Pseudo-Dionysius," most likely sixth century and possibly Syrian, was exceptionally influential. He was an anonymous mystic whose writings influenced Christians for about ten centuries.[258] Gregory the Great (540–604) and the Lateran Council of 649 thought his writings were truly from the first century. John Scotus Eriugena (810–877) translated Pseudo-Dionysius from Greek to Latin. Pseudo-Dionysius taught that there is an inward way to God that is open to all people via personal experience rather than Scripture, an experience of Reality that transcends head knowledge. He spoke of mystical contemplation as "the secret silence," arriving at "absolute silence," "divine darkness," arriving finally at the loftiest point a human can attain which he terms the "Darkness of Unknowing." Dionysius said, "We pray that we may come unto this Darkness which is beyond light."

Pseudo-Dionysius wrote about mystical contemplation: "Leave behind the senses and the operations of the intellect, and all things sensible and intellectual . . . that thou mayest arise by unknowing toward the union, as far as is attainable, with Him who transcends all being and all knowledge. For by the unceasing and absolute renunciation of thyself and of all things thou mayest be borne on high, through pure and entire self-abnegation, into the super essential Radiance of the Divine Darkness." He also taught three stages of spiritual life: purification, illumination, and union. These, he said, are advances in "unknowing." David F. Wright says, "This synthesis of Christian and Neoplatonist concepts enormously influenced Byzantine theologies of mysticism and liturgy. . . . Lorenzo Valla first questioned their authenticity in the fifteenth century."[259] (The Byzantine era lasted approximately from 330 to 1453 AD.)

---

[257] www.clarion-journal.com/files/orthodox-contemplation-2.pdf

[258] www.esotericarchives.com/oracle/dionys1.htm

[259] *Eerdmans' Handbook to the History of Christianity* (Grand Rapids: Eerdmans, 1977), 242.

Mystic expert William Inge says, "No writer had more influence upon the growth of mysticism in the Church than Dionysius the Areopagite, whose main object is to present Christianity in the light of a Platonic mysteriosophy. The same purpose is evident in Clement, and in other Christian Platonists between Clement and Dionysius."[260]

I am now fully convinced that Christian mysticism did not originate with biblical Christianity but arose a few hundred years after the apostles, by the Desert Fathers, highly influenced by Greek mystery religions and Neoplatonism that included seeking an altered state of consciousness. Christianity slowly morphed into a Christian-veneered paganism.

Shall we return to the Desert Fathers and ancient spiritual wisdom? A clue might come from Matthew 5 where we hear Jesus saying six times, "You have heard that it was said . . . but I tell you . . ." He is not referring to the Old Testament Scriptures but the perverted interpretations of those Scriptures, the rabbinic literature, including the Talmud and Midrash. The religious leaders in Jesus' day honored God with their lips but their hearts were far from him. Jesus boldly and openly denounced these "snakes" and "blind guides" (Matthew 23). When questioned about marriage and divorce, Jesus went all the way back to Genesis 1:27 and chided the Pharisees saying, "Haven't you read . . .?" We might be better off following Jesus' example, especially that of going back to the Scriptures as our final authority. Let's quit trusting any "desert fathers and mothers" who, like each of us, are often mistaken. We could start resisting the devil with Scripture, another good example our Lord Jesus left us.

Eastern Religions

Buddhism and Hinduism also influenced the development of Christian mysticism, quite possibly from the early days in Egypt as some scholars are claiming.[261] Some have called the Desert Fathers the first Christian Buddhists.

---

[260] William Ralph Inge, *Christian Mysticism: The Bampton Lectures, 1899: Considered in Eight Lectures Delivered before the University of Oxford* (London: Methuen & Co., 1899).

[261] www.john-uebersax.com/plato/origen1.htm This author says "Origen was an influential Church Father—the most influential, perhaps, up until St. Augustine. He began his career in Alexandria, Egypt which, at the time, was a cosmopolitan melting pot brewing with religious and philosophical ideas—Christian, Greek, Roman, Jewish, Neoplatonist, Egyptian, even Buddhist and Brahmanist."

Mixing Christianity and Far Eastern religions does not end with that era. William Blake, who highly influenced Thomas Merton and Carl Jung, was influenced by Hinduism as well as the Theosophical Society, and was steeped in the occult. Catholic monks Basil Pennington and Thomas Keating, known for promoting mysticism under the term "centering prayer," have incorporated ideas from Eastern religions,[262] often meeting to learn from one another and for joint meditation. Robert A. Jonas, director of a contemplative Christian retreat center near Boston, holds Buddhist-Christian retreats. In 2011, I met a Buddhist who said many Protestants in Elmhurst, Illinois, join with Buddhists to meditate. This Buddhist is well aware of Catholic mystic Thomas Merton who was highly influenced by Buddhism. Near the end of his life Merton was saying he was probably more Buddhist than Christian. He thought the monks of all religions share the same light as he did— and he was probably right. Merton died tragically while visiting Buddhist monks in Thailand. Ruth Haley Barton, once a staff member at Willow Creek Church, later trained at the ecumenical, religiously inclusive Shalem Institute for Spiritual Formation, begun by Tilden Edwards. Edwards calls his institute, "The Western Bridge to Far Eastern Spirituality."

A Canadian teacher of Buddhism notes that "The Desert Fathers . . . practiced a form of prayer which could be described as meditation. In Buddhist terms, this ancient Christian meditation practice included both mantra meditation and nonconceptual meditation. They would take a word, sentence, or phrase from the Bible and repeat it over and over again."[263] Does this sound familiar? Little wonder modern contemplatives are continually returning to the Desert Fathers.

Another article further confirms this connection, noting that Buddhist gravestones in Alexandria indicate that "Buddhists were living in Hellenistic Egypt at the time Christianity began."
en.wikipedia.org/wiki/Buddhist_influences_on_Christianity

[262] Basil Pennington and Thomas Keating, *Finding Grace at the Center* (Petersham, MA: St. Bede's Publications: 1978). All their writings are filled with syncretistic blending of Catholicism and Eastern religious ideas. On page 23 of this book they say, "We should not hesitate to take the fruit of the age old wisdom of the East and capture it for Christ. Indeed, those of us who are in ministry should make the necessary effort to acquaint ourselves with as many of these Eastern techniques as possible."

[263] Brian Ruhe, lives in Vancouver, BC, teaches Buddhism at Douglas College, and his wife is a shaman from Thailand. This quote is found at: desertfathers.blogspot.com/2011/04/teachings–and–practices–of–desert.html and comes from his book *Christian Meditation* (New Delhi, 2003).

Former Jesuit priest Richard Bennett says, "For centuries, the Roman Catholic Church has assimilated to herself the mystery elements of pagan religions. Subjective religious experience, or mysticism, continues to be the meeting point of pagan religions and Catholicism, particularly so since Vatican Council II, when Rome changed her major strategy in an attempt to bring Protestants back under the papal fold."[264] Bennett's articles quotes a Vatican II document talking about Buddhism and Hinduism. That document states, "The Catholic Church rejects nothing of what is true and holy in these religions." This same article by Bennett quotes Catholic monk William Johnson who says about Vatican II, "The Spirit of God is at work in all peoples and in all religions. Since then, most theologians recognize non-Christian religions as 'valid ways.'"

Theologian J. Sidlow Baxter says the biblical teaching of dying to our old nature is not some sort of modified or Christianized Buddhism that says, "Selfhood has to be killed before reality can be attained."[265] Baxter points out that my "self" is my basic *ego*. It is *me*. I will never cease to exist as a person or be absorbed into the Absolute.

Baxter is right about the non-Christian mystic concept that a person's self must disappear or somehow merge with divinity, making this our goal. My research led me to these English articles about Islamic mystic Sufism of Persia, especially one in particular, *The Gospel of Self-loss*.[266] This article says: "Selfhood has to be killed before reality can be attained. The I, the Me and the Mine must be ejected from the centre of one's consciousness. . . . The Western as well as the Eastern mystics call this achievement headlessness, that is, self-negation, total nescience. Thus Jalal-ud-din Rumi sings: In me there is no 'I' and 'we'; I am nought, without head and without feet; I have sacrificed head and soul to gain the Beloved."

The same Persian article quotes other Sufi Masters on the need of self-loss, including, "Self is suppressed by self-annihilation. The nearer nothing, so much more divine."

---

[264] christiananswers.net/q-eden/mysticism-bennett.html#ref2 This is an excellent, brief overview of Christian mysticism.

[265] J. Sidlow Baxter, *Our Higher Calling* (Grand Rapids: Zondervan, 1967), 182–83. Note: Another book by this same author, *His Deeper Work in Us* (1967), shows from Scripture that the follower of Christ has but one basic nature. I well remember as a child his staying in our home on several occasions when he would visit our church for special meetings. He impressed me as being friendly, kind, godly, and interesting to listen to.

[266] persian.packhum.org/persian/main?url=pf%3Ffile%3D02602030%26ct%3D7

Then to my surprise, J. Sidlow Baxter cites some historic Catholic mystics who share this same heretical error, citing such well-known and quoted people like Meister Eckhart and Madame Guyon.

The Catholic website, *New Advent*, confirms Baxter's assertions and defines Catholic Quietism: "Quietism (Latin *quies, quietus*, passivity) in the *broadest sense* is the doctrine which declares that man's highest perfection consists in a sort of psychical self-annihilation and a consequent absorption of the soul into the Divine Essence even during the present life. . . . In its essential features Quietism is a characteristic of the religions of India."[267] Some of the main Quietist leaders were Molinos, Fénelon, and Madame Guyon.

Another Catholic website, CatholicCulture.org, discusses the Quietist heresy taught by Miguel de Molinos. The 1687 Apostolic Constitution of Pope Innocent XI condemned sixty-eight propositions of Molinos. In the fifth one Molinos taught, "By doing nothing the soul annihilates itself and returns to its beginning and to its origin, which is the essence of God, in which it remains transformed and divinized, and God then remains in himself, because then the two things are no more united, but are one alone, and in this manner God lives and reigns in us, and the soul annihilates itself in operative being." This heresy is still common among many Christian mystics. It involves what is termed *monism*, or *nondualism*, and sometimes approximates Theravada Buddhism's mystic idea of being blown out or extinguished.

Mysticism and Buddhism teach self-annihilation, death to one's selfhood, i.e., my essential self, in order to be absorbed into the divine. Christianity teaches daily death to *selfishness* and a godless lifestyle. I die daily to the old deeds of darkness, but not the death of self!

Eastern Orthodoxy

Christian mysticism is deeply rooted in Eastern Orthodoxy. The Desert Fathers lived in what later became part of the Eastern Orthodox church. This church split from the Latin, or Roman church in AD 1054 after many years of bickering over seemingly minor issues. Richard Foster and Gayle Beebe, in their book *Longing for God*, discuss the Eastern Orthodox Church's contribution to mysticism that downplays

---

[267] www.newadvent.org/cathen/12608c.htm This article was written by Pascal P. Parente in 1944.

the place of reasoning.[268] Furthermore, Eastern Orthodoxy apparently has no place for an initial conversion, or "new birth" experience.[269] Eastern Orthodoxy's initial influence still permeates Christian mysticism, including total rejection of the idea of *sola scriptura*. Holy tradition, on the other hand, is much more important.[270] Mystic contemplation is deeply rooted in Eastern Orthodoxy.

Roman Catholic Mysticism

Catholic mystics down through the ages are still a powerful influence upon virtually all Christian mystics today. Hundreds of significant mystics could be mentioned. The Wikipedia article on Christian mysticism lists many such Catholics as well as other mystics.[271] The Early Middle Ages includes mystics such as Gregory the Great and Bede, along with Celtic Christianity. The Late Middle Ages include the Rhineland (German) mystics such as Meister Eckhart, Italian Catherine of Siena, and English mystics such as Richard Rolle, Walter Hilton, and Juliana of Norwich. Influential books include *Theologia Germanica* (late fourteenth century), *The Cloud of Unknowing* (fourteenth century anonymous English mystical text built upon the mystical tradition of Pseudo–Dionysius the Areopagite), and *The Imitation of Christ* by Thomas à Kempis (1380–1471).

The Catholic Counter Reformation began in reaction to the Protestant Reformation. This began with the Council of Trent (1545–1563) which reaffirmed salvation by grace alone but adamantly rejected salvation by faith alone. New religious orders were established along with a renewed interest in mysticism. Among the Spanish were Ignatius Loyola, Teresa of Ávila, Anthony of Jesus, John of the Cross, and Miguel de Molinos. Among the Italians was Lorenzo Scupoli. Among the French were Francis de Sales, Francois Fénelon, Madame Guyon, Brother Lawrence, and Blaise Pascal. Jakob Boehme was a

---

[268] Richard J. Foster and Gayle D. Beebe, *Longing for God* (Downers Grove, IL: InterVarsity, 2009), 315.

[269] Foster and Beebe point out, "The Eastern Church emphasizes a great reverence for mystery coupled with a distrust of reason. . . . The East asserts that theologians first should know God through prayer, contemplation and spiritual disciplines, and then build their theology from intimate communion with him . . . The Orthodox also resonate with the 'spiritual life as a journey.' . . . They view our salvation as a journey of not just being 'saved' but as continually being saved as we move toward the goal of *theosis*, or becoming like Christ."

[270] www.catholicapologetics.info/apologetics/protestantism/sola.htm

[271] en.wikipedia.org/wiki/Christian_mysticism

German mystic of great influence. All these Catholic mystics have been extensively quoted by Renovaré materials and by virtually all modern-day contemplatives like Richard Foster, Dallas Willard, Adele Calhoun, Evelyn Underhill, Sue Monk Kidd, and many evangelical professors of spiritual formation in Bible schools and seminaries all over the world.

The Counter Reformation saw the intensification of the infamous Inquisition that had sprung up in the 1200s. The Spanish Inquisition was particularly severe and involved torture and execution of people who rejected Papal authority and refused to convert to Catholicism, including many Muslims and Jews as well as Protestants. About 300 years prior to the Counter Reformation, the famous Catholic Dominican monk Thomas Aquinas wrote his *Summa Theologica, Volume 3,* in which he taught the persecution and killing of religious dissidents. He said if someone refuses to convert, the church then "delivers him to the secular tribunal to be exterminated thereby from the world by death."[272] Dominicans and Franciscans were the first to serve as inquisitors.

The Protestant Reformation

This reformation did not encourage mysticism. One church historian says of this: "Luther may well have been a mystic in the sense of a believer who rooted his faith in a unique and direct inner encounter with God; but, viewed in the context of the Western mystical tradition, there are reasons for questioning the appellation of Luther as a mystical author. For one thing, Luther never wrote a mystical work in the sense of a commentary or treatise designed to guide the soul through the various practices designed to reach loving union with God."[273] Luther read the traditional mystics along with the Scriptures, taking what he could use and rejecting the rest. McGinn notes that "Luther decisively rejected the mysticism of Dionysius by about 1519." This date is about two years after he posted his famous ninety-five theses on the church door at Wittenberg. McGinn quotes Luther as saying about Dionysius: "But in his *Theology,* which is rightly called *mystical,* of which certain very ignorant theologians make so much, he is downright dangerous,

---

[272] www.ironmaidencommentary.com/?url=album10_xfactor/inquisition&lang=eng&link=albums

[273] www.scielo.org.za/scielo.php?script=sci_arttext&pid=S1015-87582015000400004 This author, Bernard McGinn, is retired from teaching church history at the University of Chicago. He continues to research and write extensively about Christian mysticism.

for he is more of a Platonist than a Christian. So if I had my way, no believing soul would give the least attention to these books." For Luther, union with Christ is expressed in the biblical concept of Ephesians 5:33, a "profound mystery" as this text states, of our being the bride of Christ. Luther notes this relationship begins from the day of our initial justification by faith alone and is the source of our sanctification. John Calvin definitely was not a Christian mystic, but referred to the biblical concept of the believer's union with Christ.

The Quakerism Connection

Quakerism's influence on present-day Christian mysticism is huge, larger than most of us realize. In the 1600s George Fox founded Quakerism in England. Quakers have always taught that each person, Christian or not, has light and God's spirit within them, "that of God in everyone" as they say. John Bunyan warned everyone of Quakers' reliance on their "inner light" instead of the Scriptures. C. K. Chesterton strongly warns us of relying upon any "inner light."[274] Richard Foster is probably the major Quaker factor in the renaissance of Ancient Wisdom of Christian mysticism. Others include John Wimber, Dallas Willard, Peter Wagner, along with Thomas Merton's mother. John Yungblut is another, and points out the affinities between Quakerism and Jungian psychology.[275]

Spiritism and the Occult

These satanic influences are absolutely chilling. Carl Gustav Jung also figures prominently here. This Swiss psychiatrist who dabbled in the occult and eroticism considered himself a spiritist. He said you had to cooperate with the dark side in order to become whole. He studied Hinduism and pagan cults of Mithras and concluded that their ideas of self-deification could repair the damage done by Christianity, which he considered a myth. He also favored producing a master race and was

---

[274] www.catholic.com/blog/todd-aglialoro/me-my-god-and-i In his book *Orthodoxy*, Chesterton says: "Of all conceivable forms of enlightenment the worst is what these people call the Inner Light. Of all horrible religions the most horrible is the worship of the god within. That Jones shall worship the god within him turns out ultimately to mean that Jones shall worship Jones."
[275] www.southerncrossreview.org/19/yungblut.htm

anti-Semitic.[276] Jung's theories continue to exert an enormous influence on psychological, religious, and spiritual thinking today.[277] Jung himself stated his psychology was rooted in ancient Gnosticism. I am astounded so many Christians today are fond of Jung, a man who was bent on destroying Christianity. He is still a huge and growing influence on Christians, especially those with leanings toward Christian mysticism. Jung was especially interested in the mysticism of Ignatius Loyola.

New Age writer Ronald S. Miller says, "Christianity has its own time-honored form of mantra meditation."

New Age university professor Timothy Conway writes, "This resurgence of contemplative prayerfulness in Christianity is a most welcome and even 'providential' turn of events. The rediscovery of mystical Christian spiritual practice will allow many Christians of a meditative, yogic and/or intuitive temperament to nourish themselves at the banquet table of their own tradition. They will not feel compelled to leave Christianity altogether behind in search of contemplative experience within mystical Buddhism, Vedanta, Taoism, Jainism or Sufism. Therefore, I heartily agree with the contemplative Catholic teacher, Father Thomas Keating: 'We will be in a better position both to examine the religious experience of the East and to represent our own tradition if we can first rediscover the forgotten richness of contemplative Christianity.'"[278] Some conservative evangelical contemplatives deny such allegations, but people like Keating, Merton, and Meister Eckhart destroy that myth.

It is noteworthy that a growing number of Catholic websites warn of the similarities between "centering prayer" of Christian mysticism and the occult, New Age practices. I highly recommend an article about

---

[276] Noted Harvard professor and clinical psychologist Richard Noll writes about the Jungian theory and movement, noting how Jung favored producing a master race, using people of Aryan heritage. See: Richard Noll, *The Jung Cult: Origins of a Charismatic Movement* (Glencoe, IL: Free Press Paperbacks, 1994).

[277] For a more in-depth, thoroughly researched study of Carl Jung, see this significant article by Ed Hird, Anglican minister of North Vancouver: www3.telus.net/st_simons/CarlJungPaper.pdf

[278] www.enlightened-spirituality.org/Christian_contemplative_meditation.html This article by Timothy Conway is titled "Contemplative Meditation in Christianity" and begins with a painting of Jesus meditating, done by a monk of the Vedanta Society. Conway is involved in Hinduism and open to about every form of "spirituality."

Trappist Abbot Thomas Keating, written by former Catholic priest John D. Dreher. [279]

Occult leader Alice Bailey (1880–1949) prophesied that New Age illumination would someday arrive via Christianity, so she told her followers to leave the outer shell of Christianity intact for the moment so as to change things from the inside.[280] Are we there yet?

Laurie Cabot, a practicing witch for over forty years, says, "The science of witchcraft is based upon our ability to enter altered states of consciousness we call *alpha*. . . . In alpha the mind opens up to non-ordinary forms of communication . . . it is the heart of witchcraft." She explains how "to put yourself into alpha" by finding a quiet place, seated, comfortable, with eyes closed and with controlled breathing. "When you feel *centered* then begin to visualize certain things. She says wise people of all ancient cultures possess this ability to communicate with spirits. Cabot is hopeful as she says, "As people become fed up with *revealed truths* handed down from ministers and clergy, they will ask us to show them the ways of alpha. . . . As other religions build walls around themselves and divide people into categories of insiders and outsiders, of *saved* and *damned*, of *saints* and *sinners* people will gravitate to us where all are welcome."[281] (Note: *beta* is the normal awake state of consciousness.)

Former New Age medium, Brian Flynn, says mind-altering mysticism cannot bring us closer to God. He writes about the striking similarities between what he experienced in New Age and what is now practiced in Christian contemplative spirituality.[282]

Committed Christ-followers with a background in New Age need to be heard. They know whereof they speak. One such powerful testimony is that of Marsha Montenegro. She begins her story by saying, "Spirit guides, meditation, astrology, the 'higher Self,' raising the kundalini, developing psychic abilities, praying to gurus, astral travel, numerology, Tarot cards, contacting the dead, hanging out with

---

[279] www.catholiceducation.org/en/religion-and-philosophy/apologetics/the-danger-of-centering-prayer.html

[280] See: Alice Bailey, *The Externalisation of the Hierarchy* (New York: Lucis Publishing Company, 1957), 510.

[281] Laurie Cabot with Tim Cowan, *Power of the Witch* (New York: Delta, 1989), 297.

[282] Brian Flynn, *Running Against the Wind* (Silverton, OR: Lighthouse Trails Publishing, 2007).

witches, Sufis, followers of Muktananda, Rajneesh, Sai Baba, Maharaji—all these and more were part of my journey."[283]

Islamic Sufism

Thomas Merton and some other Christian mystics study and like the ancient mystical Islamic branch called *Sufism*. Like mysticism in general, the Sufi Way includes self-discipline, privations, introspection, and a strict study and practice of the Qur'an along with Sharia laws, the Psalms of David, Gospels of Jesus, the Torah, and other holy scriptures from Sufi Saints. (Note the syncretism.) Sufis eventually arrive at the mystical stage where they begin to experience the spirit of Allah within them. They trust in their intuition rather than talking or using words to arrive at truth. Tenets include the belief that Allah is in your heart. These are interesting parallels.

At the beginning of 2012 I read that Hasan-al-Banna, founder of the Muslim Brotherhood, was Egyptian Sufi, as is Al Qaeda. Until his death Osama bin Laden was the Brotherhood's spiritual leader.[284]

The Sufi seek a worldwide Islamic Caliphate. One article about Sufism says, "The extent to which Sufism was influenced by Buddhist and Hindu mysticism, and by the example of Christian hermits and monks, is disputed, but self-discipline and concentration on God quickly led to the belief that by quelling the self and through loving ardor for God it is possible to maintain a union with the divine in which the human self melts away."[285]

Atheistic Philosophy and Psychology

Carl Jung, whom we've looked at, also figures here, along with Emanuel Swedenborg. The majority of contemplative authors, even some evangelicals, follow Jung's ideas about our false self and true self. He in turn was influenced by Swedenborg. Jung himself stated his

---

[283] www.wri.leaderu.com/pages/montenegro.html
[284] www.globalsecurity.org/military/intro/islam-sufi.htm
See especially the last paragraphs of this article.
See many articles by doing a Google search of "Sufi al Qaeda."
See also: www.jihadwatch.org/2014/02/raymond-ibrahim-exposed-the-muslim-brotherhoodal-qaeda-connection Note also that on December 8, 2015, the Egyptian newspaper, *Daily News,* stated, "Al Qaeda chief declares solidarity with Muslim Brotherhood." (This chief is Al-Zawahiri.)
wikiislam.net/wiki/Sufism_Spawned_The_Muslim_Brotherhood
[285] mwcnews.net/focus/analysis/20404-sufism-updated.html

psychology was rooted in ancient Gnosticism.[286] We can add William James to this category, American philosopher and psychologist, who wrote *The Varieties of Religious Experience*. His father, Henry James, was a Swedenborgian theologian.

Mystics within Protestant Liberalism

For some mystic authors, the first eleven chapters of Genesis are "prehistory" instead of being real history, thus relegating the Creation, fall, Noah, Tower of Babel, and so forth to mythology, although the rest of the Bible treats these people and events as historical reality. They also deny justification by faith alone. Mystic Tilden Edwards laments that rational thought "helped pave the way for the Reformation's justification by faith alone."

William Blake (1757–1827), steeped in the occult and Hinduism, said Jesus "is the only God . . . and so am I, and so are you." Theologian Millard Erickson says, "The gap between God and man has also been reduced by liberalism" which "pictures human nature as itself containing God. There is a spark of the divine with man."[287] Erickson notes liberalism's idea that human nature is basically good, and needs no conversion. Like many theological liberals, Blake also rejected the God of the Old Testament who was so full of restrictions, and did not hold to divine inspiration of the Scriptures.

Jakob Boehme (1575–1624), German mystic who influenced William Blake, the Quakers, as well as many mystical movements, thought Christ's incarnation was not a sacrifice to cancel out sins, but as an offering of love for humanity. He was a major forerunner of theological liberalism.

Friedrich Schleiermacher (1768–1834), German liberal theologian and philosopher and "father of modern liberal theology," is another key player who emphasized that the essence of piety is not knowing but *feeling* the infinite. He once wrote his father, "I cannot believe that he who called himself the Son of Man was the true, eternal God; I cannot believe that his death was a vicarious atonement." Richard Foster and Gayle Beebe highlight this liberal theologian and refer to "the vitality of his experience with Christ."[288]

---

[286] This and similar articles discuss the Jung-Gnosticism relationship:
www.gnosis.org/gnostic-jung/Jung-and-Gnosis.html

[287] Millard Erickson, *Christian Theology* (Grand Rapids: Baker, 1994), 305.

[288] *Longing for God* (Downers Grove, IL: InterVarsity, 2009), 196–202. This statement is hard to believe! What "Christ" are they referring to? What sort of

Ernst Troeltsch (1865–1923), theologically liberal theologian, was both anti-Semitic[289] and interested in Christian mysticism. He asserted that mysticism is "the real universal heart of all religion." But he saw in mystical spirituality a de-institutionalization of religion. He said "mysticism means that the world of ideas which had hardened into formal worship and doctrine is transformed into a purely personal and inward experience" at the expense of community.[290]

---

experience can we have with Christ if we don't believe he died for our sins? Richard Foster is a major factor in the renaissance of "ancient wisdom" of Catholic mysticism/contemplation. I heard him say at Wheaton College that he recognizes such heresy in many of the Christian mystics he continues to quote so freely. He prays for protection from evil spirits before entering the thought-suppressing contemplative *silence* by mantra-like repetition of a sacred word. He even says this mystic path is not for everyone, yet says it is the *only* way to know God intimately. How very wrong! Something does not add up quite right about this *mystic path,* a practice that Thomas Merton, Richard Keating, and some other key mystic writers admit is not found in the Bible. If its roots are not biblical, but just what we've discovered here in this section, I am increasingly assured it is based upon some very shaky grounds and should be avoided. May our Lord God give us his wisdom and enlightenment! And help us to examine all things and retain what agrees with the reality of God's Word. Let's be like those Bereans of old (Acts 17:11). Let's eat the fish but keep spitting out the bones. This entails speaking the truth in love, love for God and his Word and love for all people, both those fellow pilgrims and those who still need to become pilgrims and disciples of our Lord.

[289] My niece, Constance L. Benson, uncovered this fact about this well-loved icon of liberal Protestantism. See her book *God & Caesar: Troeltsch's Social Teaching as Legitimation* (New Brunswick: Transaction Publishers, 1999).

[290] Joel Rasmussen, "Mysticism as a category of inquiry into the philosophies of Ernst Troeltsch and William James," in *Exploring Lost Dimensions in Christian Mysticism,* ed. Louise Nelstrop and Simon D. Podmore (New York: Ashgate Publishing, 2013).

Chapter 5:
Christian Mysticism's Main Attraction

Why are so many evangelical Christians reading the Christian mystics/contemplatives and practicing mystic contemplation? I suggest the following possible factors:

- Many people truly seek spiritual reality, genuine renewal, and an intimate walk with God.
- If these people do understand the gospel, maybe they do not realize that most Christian mystics misunderstand the gospel and biblical sanctification. Many mystics use much of the same terminology as nonmystic Christians but with different meanings.
- It is possible they do not understand the gospel or comprehend the biblical teaching about initial justification followed by lifelong sanctification. If this is so, they are not bothered by the teachings and practices of Roman Catholic, Quaker, and liberal Protestant mystics who teach "a different gospel" (see Galatians 1:6).
- They may realize their need for help, so they are attracted to spiritual disciplines or the help of a spiritual guide or mentor.
- They may be influenced by someone they trust. Or, they may be influenced by an author or publishing house they trust. Many books by Christian mystics are now published by InterVarsity Press, Focus on the Family, Navigators, and so forth.
- For some it may include the yearning for connectedness with something old and authoritative, like Catholicism.
- Most of us live in the fast lane and are overbooked, tired, and stressed to the limit. Time spent in quietness and solitude is appealing. Contemplation is relaxing and helps with stress reduction.
- Christian mysticism/contemplative spirituality, like its New Age cousin, fits well into our postmodern and post-Christian nonjudgmental mentality and subjective mindset, where all truth is relative. In an altered state or trance there is a complete lack of "checkability." Nobody can deny or confirm what the mystic/contemplative feels or experiences in "the silence."
- Some people are rightly turned off by a Christian fundamentalist mentality that too often goes beyond what is written in Scripture.

Or they are bothered by preachers trying to explain what God has clearly left unexplained, for example all the minutiae in the book of Revelation.

- Many are rightly offended by certain fundamentalists with all the answers and who are unloving, ungracious, proud, overly judgmental, harsh, unwilling to listen or care, and seemingly unconnected with God and unrepentant about their favorite sins. Too many church leaders and authors seem more in love with themselves and their ideas than with Jesus. During our Lord's public ministry, he had some pretty strong words for such religious hypocrites.

- Mystical, nonverbal prayer can be quite appealing to people turned off by rationalistic spirituality with too little real emotion or real contact with God.[291] Even Jesus told a Samaritan woman that God seeks those who will worship him "in spirit" instead of mere legalistic worship (John 4:24). Of course it's easy to forget that Jesus also added "and truth," i.e., centered in Christ who is the Truth, and is in accordance with all that God has revealed in the Scriptures.

- Christian mystics/contemplatives do adhere to some principles that are biblical and helpful, including the desire to better our world, really walk with God, and be more disciplined so as to follow Jesus' example. People love this good teaching.

- Many of them undoubtedly love the mystics' educated way of expressing themselves, in spite of what one commentator calls their "copious eloquence."[292]

- We cannot rule out satanic deception, delusions, and blinding of our minds, especially after experimenting with the mystic path that leads to the spirit world.

- Some people are seeking something that could unite all religions.

- Nor can we ignore the appeal of novelty.[293]

---

[291] Jewish Christian, Randy Newman, expresses this in his article "Mystical Prayer vs. Biblical Prayer," found at
www.randydavidnewman.com/2012/07/16/mystical-prayer-vs-biblical-prayer/

[292] Quoted by John F. Nash, citing Rudolf Otto, "Prayer and Meditation in Christian Mysticism," *The Esoteric Quarterly*, Fall 2011.

[293] bradlittlejohn.com/2016/07/18/on-theological-novelty-and-atonement-theory-delivered-from-the-elements-review-pt-ii/ Bradford Littlejohn's thoughts have much to do with the present attraction to Christian mysticism including what he terms to "caricature traditional doctrines, making them sound transparently ridiculous. . . ."

Chapter 6:
Warnings about Christian Mysticism

An increasing number of Christian leaders, including Catholics, are beginning to push back at some of the dangerous practices and beliefs of Christian mysticism. They are waking up to see that these are not found in Scripture, and some are definitely prohibited by God.

Some of these writers do their homework and are helpful, but all of them need checking out. Citations from other writers can be taken out of context and be mistaken. We need to allow for others to grow and get their eyes opened and actually change their views as they rethink their positions and practices in light of the Scripture. Any links I have included in this book can contain both helpful and harmful ideas. We can all be mistaken, just as were the original twelve disciples, and even Jesus' own family members. We all have our blind spots, and can learn so much more about basic biblical truth, and get to know better our Lord and how to walk with him.

Here are a few books and articles that, among many others, have been of help to me to sort out truth from fiction. Each of these sources can help us better understand Christian mysticism and its subtle dangers.

Warnings from Within the Christian Mystic Movement

Christian mystics unsuspectingly enter the spirit world in their attempt to draw closer to God. Both Richard Foster and Thomas Merton include warnings when writing about that mystic path.

In his book *Prayer,* Richard Foster gives us a rather lengthy word of "warning and precaution" about contemplative prayer, i.e., prayer without words leading to spiritual ecstasy. Foster says, "In the silent contemplation of God we are entering deeply into the spiritual realm, and there is such a thing as supernatural guidance that is not divine guidance. . . . There are various orders of spiritual beings, and some of them are definitely not in cooperation with God and his way!" He then offers us a suggested prayer of protection and suggests we pray, "All dark and evil spirits must now leave," when practicing contemplative prayer.[294]

When I read this passage to a group of mature Christians, their immediate reaction was, "Then we shouldn't go there at all." They said such a practice is not biblical but more occult and New Age than anything else. Entering the spirit world via the mystic path is both dangerous and unbiblical. So why go there? A lady converted to Christ from New Age says about Foster's warning: "I could not help but think of my New Age days when I was taught to invoke a white light of protection before psychic activity or contact with the dead. Jesus, in teaching the disciples to pray, said, "Keep us from the evil one," but this was a petition to guard us from Satan's schemes, not a formula for warding off evil spirits while we pray."[295]

Foster continues to worry about this topic as seen in his recent book *Sanctuary of the Soul*, in which he devotes a whole chapter to spiritual warfare, titled "Like a Roaring Lion" and ends the chapter with a number of prayers of protection.

In his book *Celebration of Discipline*, Foster discusses the use of imagination as "a route into God's presence," while warning us that "the imagination can be distorted by Satan" as well as human manipulation and self-deception.[296]

As already noted, Catholic mystic Thomas Merton warned that contemplative methods could be dangerous and frightening.

Catholic physician John B. Shea writes this significant article, "The Church and the New Age Movement," which warns us about centering prayer and Christian mysticism in general.[297]

Catholic musician and contemplative John Michael Talbot says of monastic, centering prayer: "It can be most destructive if used unwisely. . . . I would not recommend too much integration of these things without proper guidance for those newer to the Catholic or Christian faith."[298]

---

[294] Richard Foster, *Prayer: Finding the Heart's True Home* (HarperSanFrancisco, 1992), 164–66.

[295] www.christiananswersforthenewage.org/articles_contemplativeprayer1.html

[296] Richard J. Foster, *Celebration of Discipline: The Path to Spiritual Growth* (HarperSanFrancisco, 1988), 25ff.

[297] www.catholicculture.org/culture/library/view.cfm?recnum=7091

[298] johnmichaeltalbot.com/many-religions-one-god See also: www.wayoflife.org/reports/john_michael_talbo.html

Some Mennonite Brethren express their warnings and fears about the contemplative spirituality movement, referring to it as apostasy via mysticism.[299]

One writer, Eric Ackroyd, says Carl Jung saw the dangers of becoming possessed by supernatural powers that he called *mana personalities* ("*possession* meaning letting these powers subdue the conscious mind and ignoring all reason.") Ackroyd says, "In individual psychology, Jung used it to describe the inflationary effect of assimilating autonomous unconscious contents, particularly those associated with anima and animus."[300] Jung was an expert about the occult and parapsychology from his personal involvement in it.

Some friends of mine involved somewhat in contemplative spirituality insist they do not follow everything the mystics write about, but pick and choose. I admire them for their discernment. Many people who read the mystics lack such ability.

Warnings from Nonmystic Catholics

Dreher, John D. "The Danger of Centering Prayer."

This lengthy warning was penned while he was still a Catholic priest.[301] He affirms that "the techniques of centering prayer are neither Christian nor prayer." He says, "The intent of the technique is to bring the practitioner to the center of his own being . . . to experience the presence of the God who indwells him." Dreher uses the term "centering prayer" as a synonym for Christian mysticism or Christian contemplation. It is a term coined by Trappist monks Thomas Keating, William Meninger, and Basil Pennington in the 1960s and 1970s. Like Eastern religions, "It makes use of a 'mantra,' a word repeated over and over. . . ." Dreher says, "In short, true prayer goes to God *from* the center of one's being, not *in* the center of one's being. . . . Such techniques can bring people in touch with the spiritual realm. But the spiritual realm includes not only God but human and angelic spirits," and even demonic influence. He sees such mysticism as "a part of a conflict of the Kingdom of God and the kingdom of darkness," and refers to 2 Thessalonians 2:6-10 "about the lawless one and the force that restrains him."

---

[299] mbcontemplativearchive.blogspot.com/
[300] www.mythsdreamssymbols.com/mana.html
[301] www.catholiceducation.org/en/religion-and-philosophy/apologetics/the-danger-of-centering-prayer.html (Dreher has left Catholicism and is now Episcopalian, but this article still appears on several Catholic websites).

England, Randy. *The Unicorn in the Sanctuary: The Impact of the New Age Movement on the Catholic Church.*

England, a Catholic attorney and expert on the New Age, writes this well-researched book as a warning about Christian mysticism whose followers he sees as "Catholic New Agers." He quotes G. K. Chesterton who decried the religion of worshiping the "inner light," the god supposedly within us all. England sees visualization as "probably the single most important New Age technique and basis for witchcraft." This book, full of concrete examples, is a strong warning about mystic contemplation including mind-altering use of a word or phrase in order to feel God's presence.

See this footnote for listing of some nonmystic Catholic apologetics websites.[302] The first blog says centering prayer (mysticism) is not really prayer and is not Christian but simply pagan: "Fr. Keating, founder of the Centering Prayer Movement, states in his books that the goal of centering prayer is to find the *True Self.* Fr. Keating further claims that the True Self is the human soul and that the True Self is also God. We know that the soul is created by God and tainted with sin. . . . Claiming that our soul is God is blasphemy! . . . Centering prayer teaches something that is Hindu and not Christian. . . . Another flaw in centering prayer is the promotion of universalism."

Warnings from Nonmystic Protestants and Other Christians

Alnor, Jackie. See her article about Thomas Merton![303]

Bennett, Richard (ex-Catholic priest), especially his article "Can Mysticism Lead to God?"[304]

---

[302] See these Catholic websites and articles:
www.ourladyswarriors.org/dissent/centerprayer.htm,
www.michaeljournal.org/newage.htm, www.spiritbattleforsouls.org/id47.html,
and www.catholicculture.org/culture/library/view.cfm?recnum=6819 (critical of
Richard Rohr)

[303] www.apostasyalert.org/Merton.htm

[304] www.christiananswers.net/q-eden/mysticism-bennett.html

CANA (Christian Answers for the New Age)

Former New Ager Marcia Montenegro gives us a few excellent articles including "Contemplating Contemplative Prayer: Is It Really Prayer?"[305]

Challies, Jim

Challies is a pastor in Toronto, Ontario. See his article, "The Boundaries of Evangelicalism."[306] Challies discusses Don Whitney's fears and warnings concerning nonevangelical contemplative spirituality that is leading many evangelicals into Christian mysticism. He agrees with Whitney in saying it is a dangerous practice to send our disciples "to learn their sanctification and spirituality from those we would consider heretical on justification." Challis says, "There are few mystics who hold to a robust doctrine of justification by grace through faith alone."

Cloud, David. *Contemplative Mysticism, A Powerful Ecumenical Bond.*

Christian Research Network[307]

See for example their article, "Contemplative Prayer."[308]

Evangelical Resources on Mysticism[309] is an excellent resource. It is one of the best starting points for learning about and evaluating Christian mysticism.

Flynn, Brian. *Running Against the Wind.*

Flynn, a former medium, warns about New Age beliefs and practices infiltrating Christianity.

Gangle, Kenneth O. and James C. Wilhoit, *The Christian Educator's Handbook on Spiritual Formation.*

This is one of the few books on spiritual formation that has a whole chapter dedicated to the need of initial salvation as the point of regeneration and justification. The author of this chapter, Robert P.

---

[305] christiananswersforthenewage.org/Articles_ContemplativePrayer1.html
[306] www.challies.com/articles/the-boundaries-of-evangelicalism
[307] christianresearchnetwork.com/
[308] christianresearchnetwork.org/topic/contemplative-prayer/#identifier_2_42750
[309] www.evangelicalresources.org/mysticism.shtml

Lightner, states, "Salvation is birth; spiritual formation is growth" (p. 42).

Gilley, Gary.
Gilley is pastor of Southern View Chapel, Springfield, Illinois. He writes extensively about Christian mysticism as well as many other helpful topics.[310]

Horton, Michael.[311]
Presbyterian professor of theology, Westminster Seminary of California. See especially his book *The Gospel-Driven Life*. Horton insists all our knowledge of God must come from Scriptures.

Inquisitive Christianity
This website is evangelical, nondenominational, and has an assortment of helpful articles about Christian mysticism, including contemplative prayer, labyrinths, *Lectio Divina*, spiritual formation, the paranormal, homosexuality, and some other contemporary issues.[312]

Johnson, Arthur L. *Faith Misguided: Exposing the Dangers of Mysticism.*
This Moody Press book is out of print, but the paperback edition can sometimes be found on Amazon.com. It is an outstanding critique of Christian mysticism. He says of Richard Foster's *Celebration of Discipline*: "Foster promotes a very mystical view of Christianity. . . . Much of what the Protestant Reformers opposed is promoted by Foster" (p. 153).

Lawson, Chris.
A former Calvary Chapel pastor, Lawson now heads up the Christian Research Network. In this video[313] he warns us about

---

[310] www.tottministries.org/articles
[311] rr–bb.com/showthread.php?114137–Michael–Horton–versus–Richard–Foster–on–Contemplative–Spirituality
See also:
www.modernreformation.org/default.php?page=articledisplay&var1=ArtRead&var2=1215&var3=main
[312] www.inquisitivechristianity.com
[313] vimeo.com/76998440

contemplation, which he says is serious deviation from historic Christianity.

Malan, Johan. "Eastern Meditation Sneaks into the Church."[314]
This online article from a retired Christian professor of anthropology at the University of Limpopo, South Africa, is a short, very helpful overview of Christian mysticism.

Newman, Randy (Jewish Christian). "Mystical Prayer vs. Biblical Prayer"[315]

Patton, C. Michael. "Why I Don't Think Much of the Spiritual Formation Movement."[316]
Pastor and professor, and founder of Credo House Ministries.

Piper, John.
Piper does not endorse contemplative spirituality. Note a retraction of his, as well as other people's involvement in contemplation.[317]

Whitney, Donald.[318]
Southern Baptist scholar and pastor Donald Whitney presented the paper, "Defining the Boundaries of Evangelical Spirituality," to the annual meeting of the Evangelical Theological Society, November 15, 2001. This deals with the growing inroads of a type of Christian mysticism that is nonevangelical. He says, "Just try to find a recent volume on spirituality written by an evangelical that isn't brimming with quotations from Catholics, mystics, and Quakers, and directly or indirectly promoting them as models and teachers of spirituality despite their theologies of revelation and salvation." He calls us back to the

---

[314] www.bibleguidance.co.za/Engarticles/Contemplation.htm
[315] www.randydavidnewman.com/2012/07/16/mystical-prayer-vs-biblical-prayer/
[316] www.reclaimingthemind.org/blog/2012/01/why-i-dont-think-much-about-the-spiritual-formation-movement/#comments
[317] www.desiringgod.org/articles/a-system-for-praying-in-2012 Piper says: "Update: Formerly I listed *Lectio Divina* as a third system for prayer. I've since removed it for the confusion it has caused. *We do not endorse contemplative spirituality.* The main point I'd like to recommend is using the text of Scripture as an organizer for our prayers—prayers that are exegetically faithful and gospel rich. I am sorry for introducing the category." (emphasis added)
[318] biblicalspirituality.org/wp-content/uploads/2012/02/boundriesspirituality.pdf

true gospel, and to the Reformation emphases of *faith only* and *Scripture only*. Whitney is professor of biblical spirituality at the Southern Baptist Seminary of Louisville. Note article in *The Tennessean*, Sept. 4, 2008, that quotes him about Christian mysticism.[319] He says the idea of emptying the mind is not biblically based. His website[320] seems quite balanced and is delightfully and amazingly nonjudgmental. The website contains many helpful resources including his recently revised and updated masterpiece, *Spiritual Disciplines for the Christian Life*. Unlike past versions, he no longer cites Christian mystic authors, neither favorably nor otherwise.

Witte, Mark.
See his significant list of quotations about Christian mysticism.[321]

Yungen, Ray. *A Time of Departing*.
A very thorough treatment of Christian mysticism, constantly quoting Christian mystics to back up all he says.

Other
Some Seventh Day Adventists are alarmed at intrusions of mysticism within their denomination.[322] See also the comments about the book *Hunger: Satisfying the Longing of Your Soul* by Jon Dybdahl, reviewed by Adventist pastor John Witcombe.[323] Also see his articles on the Seventh Day Adventist website, *Amazing Discoveries*.[324]
Some Nazarenes are also concerned.[325]

---

[319] www.appliedmeditation.org/About_IAM/articles/Tennessean.html
[320] www.biblicalspirituality.org
[321] witte2020.wordpress.com/quotes-2/christian-mysticism/
[322] adventistvalues.tripod.com/seventhday_adventism.htm
[323] www.communityadventist.com/wp–content/uploads/hunger–critique.pdf
[324] amazingdiscoveries.org/S–deception_New–Age_meditation_centering
[325] reformednazarene.wordpress.com/category/contemplative-spiritualitymysticismnew-age/

Section 2

Biblical Spirituality

Chapter 7:
Biblical Sanctification

In the first section of this book, we focused on one particular approach to knowing and walking with God: traditional Christian *mystic* spirituality. We did some evaluating, trying to retain what is biblical while rejecting what is heretical and harmful. We have noted that the essence of that mystic path is the attempt to know God intimately by means of mantra-like repetition of a sacred word and thereby entering "the silence."

This second section is the *biblical approach*—the better path to intimacy with God. It focuses on the dynamics of Christian growth from a nonmystical, biblical viewpoint. This chapter is based upon an assignment that I gave my seminary students in Argentina. It is about *biblical sanctification*, which may best be understood as the biblical path for holiness and increased intimacy with God.

Peter sums up this biblical path, with both a warning and an encouragement: "Be on your guard so that you may not be carried away by the error of lawless men and fall from your secure position. But grow in the grace and knowledge of our Lord and Savior Jesus Christ" (2 Peter 3:17-18).[326]

When I think of biblical examples of bold God-followers who truly walked with God in the middle of much opposition, a few men and women stand out in my mind: Joseph, Enoch, Noah, Anna, her son Samuel, David, Mary and Joseph, eleven of the twelve apostles, those men and women listed in Hebrews 11, and so many more. Now think for a moment of someone you know, or know about, who is a bold, Holy-Spirit-filled follower of Jesus Christ. What qualities stand out? Are there any clues to how they got that way?

When talking about what helps us mature spiritually, theologians have often used the terms "means of grace," "means of blessings," or

---

[326] Matt Slick has a helpful meditation on this text: carm.org/christianity/sermons/2-peter-317-18-growing-grace Matt is founder of CARM (Christian Apologetics and Research Ministry). Also check out his article, "Centering Prayer," about another path to spirituality: carm.org/centering-prayer

"holy habits." Wayne Grudem, in his book *Systematic Theology,*[327] discusses such means of grace which help people to know Christ personally and grow in their spiritual formation. Many Christians now prefer the term "spiritual disciplines." David Mathis used the term "habits of grace."[328]

Roman Catholicism has historically stressed the corporate means of grace via the seven sacraments, by means of duly ordained bishops and priests. The Catholic Church sees these as part of the process of justification (salvation) which Catholicism terms "infused justification." In some respects, monasticism with its mystic contemplation was an acceptable means *within* the church to resist the overpowering sacerdotal and clerical stranglehold. It was an effort to return to a more biblical and personal relationship with God.

We cannot stress enough the glorious fact that salvation is not something we work *for*. Yet it is something we work *out* (Philippians 2:12; see also Ephesians 2:8-10; Titus 3:5, 8). This process of sanctification, of becoming like Christ, involves many factors, corporate and personal, foremost of which is our daily walk with God. Some would call it *hiking* with God. Such a relationship results in Holy Spirit control and the fruit he produces—"love, joy, peace, patience, kindness, goodness, faithfulness, gentleness and self-control." Enoch and Noah "walked with God." I'd like to know which "spiritual disciplines" they used. Or what gave Joseph and Daniel such power with God. Jesus told people, "Follow me." Paul says, "Follow me as I follow Christ." Then he tells Timothy, "*Train yourself* to be godly" (1 Timothy 4:7, emphasis added). Any training involves discipline, self-control, a right goal, and correct methods. Encouragement and good role models also help.

Once I was born into God's family by personal faith in Christ's atoning sacrifice, I entered God's "rest" that the book of Hebrews talks about—rest from trying to merit salvation. Now I can begin to grow in Christlikeness. The Bible mentions basic *practices* which help me in this process.

---

[327] Wayne Grudem, *Systematic Theology* (Downers Grove, IL: InterVarsity, 1994), 950ff.).

[328] David Mattis, *Habits of Grace: Enjoying Jesus through the Spiritual Disciplines* (Wheaton, IL: Crossway, 2016). Mattis is part of John Piper's team in Minneapolis, MN.

There are also some essential *attitudes* and *values* in the Scriptures that are essential for Christian growth and service, and for knowing Christ more intimately. These include humility, honesty, integrity, love, sorrow for sin coupled with repentance, faith in God, desire to obey God in everything, and a strong desire to serve others and God. We will unpack these seven attitudes in Chapter 9.

But first we'll mention the biblical *practices*, those actions and disciplines that the Scriptures mention that are so basic for knowing, loving, and serving our Lord and Savior. This following list of biblical disciplines began as an assignment I gave my Argentine seminary students. I had asked them to analyze their lives and come to class with a list of what helps them mature in Christ and serve him better. I then added a few topics from my own reflections.

Don Whitney says, "The Spiritual Disciplines are those practices found in Scripture that promote spiritual growth among believers in the gospel of Jesus Christ. They are habits of devotions and experiential Christianity that have been practiced by the people of God since biblical times." [329] He also says we need to practice these both personally and with other Christians. Whitney stresses these are practices both taught and modeled for us in the Bible. The disciplines are not an end in themselves but meant to help us become more like Jesus. I do not list these disciplines in any special order, although the Scriptures should probably be near the top of anyone's list of priorities. We all need to analyze what helps us walk with God and become more like Jesus.

Paul practiced self-control and strict training, "so that after I have preached to others, I myself will not be disqualified for the prize" (1 Corinthians 9:24-27). He urged Timothy, "Have nothing to do with godless myths; . . . rather, train yourselves to be godly. . . . Be diligent in these matters; give yourself wholly to them, so that everyone may see your progress. Watch your life and doctrine closely" (1 Timothy 4:7; 15-16). What I seek most of all is a constant relationship with God, one that is real, authentic, robust, healthy, open, and transparent. I need a bold, open walk with God! I may need a decisive spiritual "coming out" from behind the mask of just pretending, of just acting a part.

---

[329] Donald Whitney has written much about spiritual disciplines. He is Professor of Biblical Spirituality and Associate Dean at The Southern Baptist Theological Seminary in Louisville, KY.

Most of these are *disciplines*, and most of them are divine commands. Some of these might fit more into the category of attitudes, like for instance trust in God, fear of the Lord, integrity, and so forth.

Saturate My Mind with the Inspired Scriptures

"Let the word of Christ dwell in you richly" (Colossians 3:16, ESV). I once read about a lady who creates new Lego projects. She said, "It enters every crevice of my life." She eats and sleeps Lego projects. In a similar way, the Scriptures need to permeate every crevice of my life. I must make Christ and his Word my only Teacher (Matthew 23).

Following Jesus' example in his use of Scripture is a good place to begin. He quoted the Old Testament Scriptures from memory. He boldly told religious leaders they woefully lacked both knowing the Scriptures and experiencing the power of God in their lives.

I need courage to take God at his word, whether or not I fully grasp its meaning or like what I read. The Scriptures must remain my final spiritual authority for doctrine and conduct. Church councils and ancient traditions and creeds can get it wrong. Neither are my feelings normative; they can be deceiving.

Meditation on God's Word is biblical, and when coupled with prayer, is so life transforming. Jesus told the devil: "People do not live on bread alone, but on every word that comes from the mouth of God" (Matthew 4:4). I live in a hurried, noisy culture, way too dependent upon electronic devices. I need regular times of silence and solitude to help me concentrate and meditate on God and his Word.

I appreciate Wheaton College professor Scott Moreau saying: "Meditation for the Christian is not a meaningless emptying of the mind. It is focused on filling the mind with God's truths, allowing them to percolate within us so that they become part of our 'mental programming.'"[330]

Ronald Whitney compares biblical meditation on Scripture to dipping a tea bag into a cup of hot water. Each dunk of the bag gives more flavor but nothing like "immersing the bag completely and letting

---

[330] A. Scott Moreau, *Essentials of Spiritual Warfare* (Wheaton, IL: Harold Shaw Publishers, 1997), 112.

it steep until all the rich tea flavor has been extracted and the hot water is thoroughly tinctured reddish brown."[331]

Some things that hinder me from proper meditation on Scripture are laziness, lack of a plan or place, busyness, unconfessed sin, conflict with people, getting bogged down with unessential topics in Scripture, anxiety, finding it hard to concentrate, forgetting Who is speaking to me through the Scriptures, and forgetting to converse with God about what I read.

Avoid Adding To or Subtracting From Scripture

I must use good hermeneutical principles, seeing each part in its biblical and historical context. Inspiration of Scripture means that even statements by Satan or by mistaken people are accurately quoted. The Bible is true in all that it affirms. At the same time, all of the Bible is profitable, for learning truth and avoiding bad examples and teaching. "Do not go beyond what is written" (1 Corinthians 4:6). I need to avoid being either broader or narrower than the Bible. I should avoid both adding my ideas or taking scissors to what God has said. Years ago the comic strip character Jeff found Mutt in a dark closet with the door shut and an open book in his hands. Jeff asked, "How can you read in here with no light?" Mutt explained he was just reading between the lines. I guess we don't need much light for that.

Inspiration ended with the apostles and prophets. Now is the time for perspiration in Bible study, with the illumination of the Holy Spirit. Divine leading may include my thoughts, other people's counsel, events, even dreams, but I must pass everything by the inspired Scriptures. Although God supernaturally guides me, I must go to the Scriptures for doctrinal truth.

It is wonderful to muse and ponder what God has said in Scripture, then to experience that spine-tingling "Aha!" moment. That sudden insight. When the text has come alive. I may still need to run it by the rest of Scripture, to see all the nuances and implications of this idea. I attempt to arrive at what the text actually meant to the original hearers. I also try to squelch the urge to come up with something unique, to

---

[331] Donald S. Whitney, *Spiritual Disciplines for the Christian Life* (Colorado Springs: NavPress, 1991), 44.

make myself appear smarter than the average reader or theologian. It is wonderful discussing the text with the divine Author.

Keep in Mind Three Levels of Spiritual Authority

The three levels of spiritual authority are as follows: [332]

God's commandments, for all cultures and all times: Some examples include the following: regular observance of the Lord's Supper, evangelism, baptizing new believers, praying much, loving God, loving people, total submission to God, and so forth.

Apostolic practices, but not commanded: These are descriptive but not prescriptive. Again, the Lord's Supper is an example. If you follow exactly what Christ did when first instituting it, you will have men only, in an upper room, at night, reclining around a table, using one cup, breaking one loaf of unleavened bread, and ending the service by singing a hymn.

Traditions and human customs: These are not mentioned in the Bible. For instance, my church observes the Lord's Supper once a month. Other present day customs may include using a pulpit, confessing sin to a priest, having a church membership list, church steeples and bells, etc. Such practices are not required for all Christians everywhere, and should be prohibited if they impede obedience to God. It is possible to break God's commandments by our traditions. Each church decides what customs help them to obey God.

Pray All the Time with Every Kind of Prayer

Prayer is conversing with God. Biblical prayer is always with words and thoughts. When I pray as I should, God shows up in some special way, whether or not I feel anything special. The Bible commands us to "Pray in the Spirit on all occasions with all kinds of prayers and requests" (Ephesians 5:16). That's pretty all-inclusive. Cognitive, biblical prayer, *is* the very essence of intimacy with God. This kind of prayer is a relationship with the Creator of the universe! Australian

---

[332] Adapted from *La Educación y la Obediencia*, and used by permission from its author, George Patterson. This was written in Spanish for his distance seminary ministry in Honduras, serving with Missions Door (formerly CBHMS).

missionary John Edmiston discusses how to pray at all times, as we practice sensing God's presence.[333]

There is nothing I know of that compares with living consciously in God's presence, in awe and worship, with words or in serene silence, knowing and feeling that all is now well in this divine-human companionship. In 1 Peter 4:7 we are told to be clear minded and self-controlled, "so that you can pray." I sin by not interceding for others (1 Samuel 12:23). Satan hates to see me in contact with God through honest and open prayer! So, I'll do it—a lot!

The godly Scottish minister Horatius Bonar stressed *intimacy with God* via prayer when he wrote the following:

> Be much alone with God. Do not put Him off with a quarter of an hour morning and evening. Take time to get thoroughly acquainted. Talk everything over with Him. Pour out every thought, feeling, wish, plan, and doubt to Him. He wants to converse with His creatures. Shall His creatures not want to converse with Him? He wants, not merely to be on "good terms" with you, if one may use man's phrase, but to be intimate. Shall you decline the intimacy and be satisfied with mere acquaintance? What! Intimate with the world, with friends, with neighbors, but not with God? That would look ill indeed.[334]

Tim Challies says three key factors in powerful praying are having a quiet place, a quiet hour, and a quiet heart. At the end of his article his example from Jesus shows that "quiet" does not eliminate use of words and concepts, even experiences like Jesus had in the Garden of Gethsemane which at times were not "merely peaceful meditations, or rapturous acts of communion. They were strenuous and warlike, from that hour in the wilderness when angels came to minister to the prostrate Man of Sorrows, on to that awful 'agony' in which His sweat was, as it were, great drops of blood." [335]

---

[333] www.aibi.ph/eternity/eternity51.htm
[334] See p. 29 in www.chapellibrary.org/files/1014/0294/0678/tobo.pdf
[335] www.challies.com/articles/3-keys-to-a-powerful-prayer-life

Pray Through the Scriptures

Learning to pray through the Scriptures takes time, but it is time well spent! I listen to God speak as I read the Bible, then stop and reply to him as I go along, like conversing with another person. I sometimes ask God, *Lord, what does this really mean? How should this change my life?* Or *Thanks, Lord, for this much-needed reminder.* John Piper encourages us to read and meditate on the Scripture *with prayer*: "Prayer does one of its most deep and satisfying works when it intersects with the Word of God in our lives. Without prayer the Word lies before us as a blank page."[336]

An excellent example of Scripture linked with prayer is seen in the life of George Müller (1805–1898). Instead of beginning the day in prayer alone, he found that starting with God's Word quickly led him to be in tune with God, with his heart warmed. When he prayed over the Scriptures, he says his heart was "comforted, encouraged, warned, reproved, instructed; and that thus, whilst meditating, my heart might be brought into experimental *communion with the Lord.*" (Emphasis mine) He did so, not to get preaching material but "to get blessing out of it . . . for the sake of obtaining food for my own soul . . . after a very few minutes my soul has been led to confession, or to thanksgiving, or to intercession, or to supplication; so that though I did not, as it were, give myself to *prayer,* but to *meditation*, yet it turned almost immediately more or less into prayer."[337]

Müller feared "spiritual deadness, which is so frequently the result of much study" when not accompanied by appropriate falling on one's knees in prayer (page 31 of his autobiography). Any true follower of Christ, born again by repentance and faith, can experience full fellowship with God Almighty by means of prayer, whether or not they feel anything special. Such a blessed relationship results in a changed life, a life of obedience to God.

---

[336] www.desiringgod.org/messages/parenting-for-the-glory-of-god-part-2

[337] *The Autobiography of George Müller*, compiled by G. Fred Bergin, (London: J. Nisbet and Co., 1914), 152–54.

Obey God

"You are my friends if you do what I command" (John 15:14).
1 John 2:3 echoes this: "We know that we have come to know him if
we obey his commands." King Saul learned the hard way that God
wants obedience instead of mere sacrifice and ritual worship (1 Samuel
15). This is sometimes hard to learn.[338] In the book of James we learn
that faith unaccompanied by a changed life is worthless, dead, fake. It
is so easy to say "Lord, Lord" but not do what he commands. I need to
be careful to stop at all the "red lights" God has set in place, and go
ahead at the "green lights."

The more I know, the greater is my responsibility, and greater my
guilt and punishment if unrepentant. Obedience, even in an
insignificant way, makes it easier to obey God in other ways. Likewise,
the more I disobey God the easier it becomes to go my own sinful way.
As I obey God, I walk in the light and become the light of the world for
others. It also ushers me into full and intimate communion with God.

Worship God in Spirit and in Truth

Jesus said the place and form of worship is immaterial and
irrelevant. "God is spirit, and his worshipers must worship in spirit and
truth" (John 4:24).

In contrast to legalistic or hypocritical worship, God seeks
wholehearted devotion. Philip Wendell Crannell says it well: "The true
worship of God is essentially internal, a matter of the heart and spirit
rooted in the knowledge of and obedience to the revealed Word of
God."[339]

Like most Christians today, I am too worship-deprived. All of my
life as a Christ-follower should be filled with reverence, awe, worship,
and praise for God.

Nancy Missler quotes a letter addressed to her that describes the
kind of constant worship God desires: "We should adore Him. We
should always be mindful of Him. We should constantly want to
interact with Him. Ask Him things. Tell Him our thoughts. Cry our

---

[338] You might want to check out a nice sermon outline on this topic.
oakridgechurch.com/riggs/kingsaul.htm
[339] Baker's *Evangelical Dictionary of Biblical Theology*,
http://www.biblestudytools.com/dictionary/worship/

heart out to Him and set Him above everything else in our lives." This is cognitive and constant, and as Missler says, "is the most important thing a Christian can learn to do!"[340]

I need to flee from any other object of worship.

Humble Myself Daily

"Humble yourselves, therefore, under God's mighty hand" (1 Peter 5:6). This is not the same as putting myself down. It is recognizing the source of my gifts and capacities. When I readily admit that I do not know it all, others will more easily follow my example and keep on studying and seeking out the truth. I, too, will keep on learning and maturing. Humility does not glory in education, titles, position, or one's genealogy (Romans 12:3; Philippians 3). Pride grieves the Holy Spirit. Humility is a huge factor in my becoming like Christ.

Be a Woman or Man "after God's Own Heart"

I long to be like King David, "a man after God's own heart" (Acts 13:22). David had a lifestyle of conversing with God with much praise and worship. I know David was justified by faith alone (Romans 4:6-8, quoting Psalm 32:3-5). Yet he longed for something more, for that intimate walk with God.

Hunger and Thirst for God

I hunger and thirst for God, for constant communion with him, as the psalmist expresses in the middle of affliction, in Psalm 42: "As the deer pants for streams of water, so my soul pants for you, my God. My soul thirsts for God, for the living God. Where can I go and meet with God?" This needs to be daily thirsting and deep drinking. The Lord still "rewards those who earnestly seek him" (Hebrews 11:6). This is a vital facet of true, biblical spirituality! Donald Whitney has a good article about thirsting for God![341]

---

[340] www.khouse.org/articles/2005/557/

[341] bso.larryandpriscilla.com/wp–content/uploads/2011/01/Do–You–Thirst–for–God.pdf See also Donald Whitney's website: biblicalspirituality.org/

Long for a Deeper Walk with God

Enoch and Noah had a deep walk with God. So should I.

So much more is included in what Christ purchased for me on Calvary! Way too often I find myself trying to live a Christian life in my own strength, not really trusting in, or hiking with, my Lord Jesus who has provided life "to the full" (John 10:10). Psalm 23 says, "The Lord is my shepherd, I shall not be in want." Sheep aren't the smartest of animals, but are in good hands when they have a good shepherd. I have the greatest Shepherd anyone could ask for! Jesus is all I need. He says, "Come along; follow me. You will eat well, and you've nothing to fear. I'll even restore your soul by some quiet waters. And we'll walk in intimate fellowship, then spend eternity together."

Walk in the Spirit

The Bible emphasizes that I should walk in the Spirit, be constantly filled with the Spirit, be under his constant control, be led by the Spirit, keep in step with the Spirit, live by the Spirit, heed the Holy Spirit's promptings, and be in tune with the Spirit. All these are divine commands. God's controlling power in me by his Spirit, coupled with much prayer and meditation on the Scriptures, results in an intimate relationship with Jesus Christ.

I am filled with God's Spirit to the degree that I obey Christ in all things. Such obedience involves both Scripture and God's daily promptings in my life.

Our good friend Steve Green expresses a beautiful fact about Holy Spirit control when he sings "You Can Be as Full as You Want to Be." This reality is found in 2 Chronicles 15:1-2: "The Lord is with you *when you are with him.*"

See God, as Christ Promised in the Beatitudes

Christ says, "Blessed are the pure in heart, for they will see God" (Matthew 5:8). *The NIV Study Bible* points out that my "heart" is the center of my being, including mind and emotions. Heart purity is in stark contrast with the outward religiosity of the Jewish religious leaders. Our Lord desires purity of *heart*—i.e., my innermost being, my soul, the fountainhead, the core of my personality, my ego, my will, the seat of my emotions and thoughts, my true self, the essence of being *me*.

Purity of heart means walking with God in sweet communion. I "see" him, see him in all of creation. I see his sovereign hand in the affairs of mankind. I see his face shining upon me. I see his power, his blessing, yes and even a bit of his glory. I see his Spirit at work in me. Then one day, in his glorious presence, I will see him face to face! Hebrews 11:25-27 says Moses left Egypt, rejecting the pleasures of sin for a short time. It says, "He persevered because he *saw* him who is invisible." I can, too, in a spiritual sense, via prayer, worship, singing, meditating on his Word, obedience, etc.

Get to Know God More Intimately

I want to know Christ (Philippians 3:7-10). Eternal life is defined as knowing the Father and the Son (John 17:3; 1 John 1:1-4). Like marriage, this is a growing relationship, with increasing levels of intimacy. Behavioristic Skinnerian psychology says I can't change. My old nature says this is the way I am, and always will be. Satan comes along with that same lie. God says I can change. I can know him more intimately!

Draw Near to God

"Draw near to God, and he will draw near to you" (James 4:8 ESV). As I do so, in humility and repentance, I bask again in his presence. Once again all is well with my soul, even when my world is a disaster. "Those who seek the Lord lack no good thing" (Psalm 34:10). "If you seek [God] he will be found by you" (1 Chronicles 28:9). "O God, you are my God, earnestly I seek you" (Psalm 63:1). Seeking not merely God's gifts and blessings, but seeking the giver, God himself. I need to look upward, not inward. To seek is to pursue, crave, desire, search for something with my whole being.

God's prescription for spiritual revival and divine blessing is as true today as it was for Israel in Solomon's day: "If my people, who are called by my name, will humble themselves and pray and *seek my face* and turn from their wicked ways . . ." (2 Chronicles 7:14).

Jesus still says "Come to me, all you who are weary and burdened" (Matthew 11:28). The result is great joy (Psalm 16:11). Whenever I sense I am far from God, I can be assured which one of us has done the moving! Hebrews 10:19-21 tells me to take the initiative and draw near to God, via faith and the blood of Christ. In Hebrews 4:14-16, I am encouraged to approach God's throne of grace with confidence.[342] I enter God's presence via real prayer, praise, and worship, coupled with repentance and trust.

Trust in the Lord

"Trust in the Lord with all your heart, and lean not on your own understanding" (Proverbs 3:5). Trust is reliance, is leaning on, and believing God knows best. Trust is faith in God, banking our life and eternal future on him. It is taking God at his word and acting accordingly. I am convinced God knows what is best for me and is still Lord of history and in full control. He is working all things "for good," from his eternal perspective. He has all the right in the world to tell me what to believe and what to do. How very little I really understand, but I have an omniscient, omnipotent Savior and Lord. I trust him for daily grace, knowing I cannot be holy or please him by my own effort.

Keep My Eyes Fixed Upon Jesus

Hebrews 12:2 tells us: "Let us fix our eyes on Jesus." The next verse says "we are surrounded by such a great cloud of witnesses," those women and men of faith of church history! I do not grow weary and lose heart as I gaze upon Jesus in all his glory and worship him for all he endured for my eternal redemption. I also admire these heroes of faith and can learn much from their example, but never attempt to pray to them!

Walk in the Fear of the Lord

Walking in the fear of the Lord is the beginning of wisdom. "The eyes of the Lord are on those who fear him" (Psalm 33:18). We need to "worship God acceptably with reverence and awe, for our God is a consuming fire" (Hebrews 12:28-29). The fear of God is a constant theme throughout Scripture, found at least 300 times. I find it helpful

---

[342] Pastor George Toews of Winnipeg has a helpful message on this text, found at: gtmessages.blogspot.com/2008/01/let-us-approach-throne-of-grace.html

to begin each prayer thinking about whom I am talking to, remembering some of his attributes or what he has done. I often address the Lord as "maker and sustainer of heaven and earth." I fear the Lord instead of people or events. God told Isaiah, "The Lord Almighty is the one you are to regard as holy, he is the one you are to fear, he is the one you are to dread" (Isaiah 8:12-13). I cast all my anxieties upon him who cares for me (1 Peter 5:7). John Piper has a balanced devotional about serving the Lord with fear and rejoicing with trembling.[343]

Acknowledge God in All My Ways

"In all your ways acknowledge him, and he will make straight your paths" (Proverbs 3:6, ESV). I must bring God into every part of my daily life. Pass everything by him. Some versions of this text say "submit to him" which is probably the essence of such acknowledgement. It is saying, "Yes, Sir!" to our spiritual commander in chief.

What I See and Hear Should Prompt Worship and Closeness with God

All my senses can serve to nudge me closer to God, especially as I redeem those senses, remembering the One who created and still sustains everything. All of created matter, the macro and the micro of things, animate and inanimate, should serve to lift me to God in tingling awe and praise (see Psalm 19:1-6). Redeemed senses involves taking care of what we see, hear, feel, taste, and touch.

Be Still and Listen to God

Being still and listening to God is what Psalm 46:10 is all about—not stilling my mind but my big mouth, to acknowledge that God is the sovereign Lord, God Almighty, the God of Jacob, my fortress. I recommend an excellent study on this text by Sarah Geis and Doug Groothuis of Denver Seminary.[344] Basically, God is telling us in this

---

[343] mail.google.com/mail/u/0/?shva=1#inbox/153e020e34a88338
This devotional appeared the week of April 4, 2016.
[344] www.equip.org/PDF/JAP363.pdf

text to be quiet and listen to him for a change. God told Peter on the Mount of Transfiguration to be quiet *and listen* to his Son!

Plan Some Extended Times for the Kind of Silence and Solitude Found in the Scriptures

It could be either a private or a group retreat, to pray and meditate on God's Word, to pray the Scriptures into my life and to center myself on God and his Word. Jesus' disciples knew where to find their Master when they awoke and he was gone—out communing with the Father in some quiet spot. A church we worked with in Argentina made a path up a low hill near town where believers would often go for prayer. Any place can become a place where I draw near to God the Father, through the Son, and with the aid of the Holy Spirit.

Be Holy, Like God

The Apostle Peter quoted Leviticus[345] when he wrote, "Be holy, because I am holy" (1 Peter 1:16). Jim Challies says, "Holiness ... characterizes all of God's attributes."[346] God wants nothing less than for us to be like him, yet never becoming divine.

Holiness is sanctification. It is the goal of biblical spirituality. The basic idea is separation: to be set apart, dedicated to God alone, removed from all that opposes God. In computer terminology, we talk about a "dedicated computer," meaning for a specific use, like personal banking, printing, or strictly company business. And whatever you do with it, avoid iffy and suspicious websites! Likewise, Peter says, "In your hearts *set apart* Christ as Lord" (1 Peter 3:15). That's where it all begins—in my heart,[347] my true self, the essential *me*. Holy living begins with my heart in sync with God, harmonious and in tune, on the same wavelength, living with the mind of Christ, bringing every thought into obedience to him, governed by his Spirit. If I get too adrift and far from the Lord, I may need a spiritual reboot. Like King David

---

[345] Leviticus 11:44-45 and 19:2

[346] www.challies.com/articles/the-essential-holiness Don't miss Challies' other articles on this topic: www.challies.com/topics/holiness

[347] Baker's *Evangelical Dictionary of Biblical Theology* gives us this definition of *heart*: "It denotes a person's center for both physical and emotional-intellectual-moral activities; sometimes it is used figuratively for any inaccessible thing." www.biblestudytools.com/dictionary/heart/

hitting the "reset button" in Psalms 51 and 32. Not reconverted but just a renewed relationship where we can again look God straight in the eye, so to speak. Holiness involves dying again to selfishness, godlessness, and all those old deeds of darkness (see Ephesians 5:11).

Hate What is Evil

Romans 12:9 says, "Hate what is evil; cling to what is good." Sara Sumner's doctoral dissertation ended up as a book, *Angry Like Jesus: Using His Example to Spark Your Moral Courage.* In a recent interview, she cited Psalm 7:11 which says, "God is a righteous judge, a God who expresses his wrath every day." She reminds us of Romans 12:9, "Hate what is evil," and says, "Many Christians brag of being loving or nonjudgmental. But if we don't abhor evil, we end up participating in it . . . we hate evil enough to tell the truth. . . . There needs to be a greater moral courage to do the right thing, even if it costs you. And then we will find that God has our backs."[348] Loving God and people means hating whatever comes between people and God's love. Real love means showing mercy to the unlovely and rebellious people all around us while hating what they do. Jude writes about this balance: "Rescue others by snatching them from the flames of judgment. Show mercy to still others, but do so with great caution, hating the sins that contaminate their lives" (Jude 23, NLT).

Flee All Temptation

My college Spanish teacher was always so concerned for our spiritual well-being and urged us to flee sin rather than go check it out. He used an unforgettable illustration of a stinky garbage can: "You can smell the rottenness from far away. You don't need to go take off the lid and stick your head in it."

I need to flee anything that keeps me from pleasing God. Head in the other direction. Do whatever it takes. I'm too much like one of Pavlov's dogs, responding to a stimulus. It might be what I see, hear, or even smell.

---

[348] "Righteous Anger: Not Just for Jesus," *Christianity Today,* December 2015, 72.

Joseph fled sexual temptation, trusted God through years of unjust imprisonment, and was used by God in a mighty way (Genesis 39; 45:4-8; 50:19-21). King David did not flee lust and suffered the consequences, yet he returned to the Lord in genuine repentance and was forgiven. Psalm 1:1 talks about the danger of godlessness pulling me down. Jude verses 22-23 are a good balance in this regard. So is the example of Jesus himself, always a friend of sinners yet without sin.

I need to flee the many land mines that surround us all, including minimizing sin as not so bad, or thinking it is impossible to overcome it. By his grace, God helps me daily to flee my "former way of life" and "my old self" (Ephesians 4:22), the old way of darkness (Ephesians 5:8).

The Christ-follower is called to flee many things, but not called to flee the devil. As I humble myself and submit to God, I am empowered to resist the devil—and he will flee from me! (James 4:7-10).

Walk Before God with Honesty and Integrity

I want to be trusted, counted on, faithful. "The Lord detests lying lips, but he delights in people who are truthful" (Proverbs 12:22). George Müller, known for his orphanage ministry in nineteenth century England, determined to stop including letters inside parcels so as to save money, since it was illegal to do so. God is honored and pleased when we resist the "father of lies," the devil, with the belt of truth (Ephesians 6:14).

Practice Fasting

Fasting can help me draw closer to the Lord, especially when coupled with physical solitude for prayer and praise, along with Bible meditation. Fasting also helps me seek God's solution when facing some daunting challenge or decision.

Do Some Journaling

Journaling or keeping a diary of my thoughts and reactions to Bible reading and to life in general has helped me in so many ways, from college days onward. My journal includes important world news items and my reactions to them. This helps me better understand the times and serves as a prayer guide.

Ask God to Search My Heart

Psalm 139 ends with this prayer: "Search me, O God, and know my heart; test me and know my anxious thoughts. See if there is any offensive way in me, and lead me in the way everlasting." My true self, my heart, needs constant cleansing and pardoning.

Live a Life of Daily Repentance and Confession, or Suffer the Consequences

Living with unconfessed sin distances me from warm communion with God and with others. King David is a classic biblical example (see Psalm 32:1-5). I can be assured all is well with my soul and with my God every time I sincerely repent and confess my sins. What relief and joy it brings. Those around me will probably know, at least by seeing the results. I need to remember that repentance is more than mere sorrow and contrition. It is a change of direction and purpose. I know I cannot lose my salvation by sinning, but willful disobedience brings on a cluster of bad consequences, both in this life and in the life to come. As the saying goes, "Your sin will find you out" (Numbers 32:23), or as some have put it, "Your sin will find you *ouch*." The devil only shows me Act One of the drama, not the horrific results of my sin.

Let's unpack this a little by noting some of the disturbing consequences—things I may lose when living with unconfessed sin:

- First and foremost, I lose communion with God. Adam and Eve found this out the moment they first sinned. Even Jesus on the cross lacked communion with the Father, but not because of his sins! Ezra 8:22 says, "[God's] great anger is against all who forsake him." Now that's something to worry about. Proverbs 6:16-20 lists seven things God hates. How can a loving God also hate and get angry? An Internet article explains it well: "God hates sin because it is the very antithesis of his nature."[349]
- I lose communion with other people. Sin destroys relationships, even with those I love the most. This, too, is so very sad.
- I lose the "fruit of the Spirit." When David sinned, he lost the *joy* of his salvation (Psalm 51:12). This was replaced by guilt, fear, shame, and much more (see Psalm 32). Sin keeps me from

---

[349] www.gotquestions.org/God-hate-sin.html

experiencing Spirit-given love, joy, peace, patience, kindness, goodness, faithfulness, gentleness, and self-control (Galatians 5:22-23).

- Though I don't lose the gifts of the Spirit when I coddle my favorite sins, I do end up using these gifts with wrong motives and without God's power and full blessing. 1 Corinthians 13:1-3 describes how this happens, and how it can result in more harm than good.
- I lose God's blessings, his *shalom*. Nehemiah wrote, "The gracious hand of my God was upon me" (Nehemiah 2:28 and several times in Ezra). How rotten I feel when God's gracious hand is absent from my life.
- My ministry for the Lord may be curtailed if I live in open, unrepentant sin.
- My power and effectiveness in prayer is affected. God feels distant. "If I had cherished sin in my heart, the Lord would not have listened" (Psalm 66:18. See also 1 Peter 3:7).
- I may lose my health, or even my life (Psalm 32; 1 Corinthians 11:30; Acts 5:1ff.).
- God's guidance is momentarily lacking.
- Rewards in heaven (Luke 14:13-14; 1 Corinthians 3:10-15; Galatians 6:9; Revelation 22:12).

Employ the God-Promised "Way Out" of Every Temptation

"But when you are tempted, he will also provide a way out so that you can endure it" (1 Corinthians 10:13). Ever watch the movie *Sabrina*? Remember what Linus says to her at the very end? "Save me, Sabrina fair. You're the only one who can." I need to pray: "Lord Jesus, save me! Rescue me! You're the only One who can!" Then not reject that "way out" when God provides it!

Love God with My Whole Being, Heart, Soul, and Mind, All the Time

When asked what the greatest commandment is, Jesus answered, "'Love the Lord your God with all your heart and with all your soul and with all your mind.' This is the first and greatest commandment" (Matthew 22:37-38).

Picture Jesus cooking breakfast by the Sea of Galilee after his resurrection. He looks at Peter who had denied him but had vowed he never would do so. So Jesus asks him: "Do you *love* me? Really? Then feed my lambs. Shepherd my sheep." The Greatest commandment in all the Law is to love God.

Former president of Denver Seminary Vernon Grounds once said: "The Lordship of Christ means that you must love Him with the top of your mind as well as the bottom of your heart."[350]

Love People

In his later years, Abraham Herschel, a Jewish rabbi and theologian, said: "When I was young, I admired clever people. Now that I am old, I admire kind people."

God calls each of his followers to be kind instead of nasty, accepting instead of damning, caring in place of narcissistic. Psychologist Albert Ellis wrote about how to live with neurotics. He said they can give another person just so much and no more, since they are utterly self-absorbed.

God calls each of us to love and care, as he himself does. First Corinthians 13 describes clearly such godly love. I show my love and devotion to God when I truly care for the disenfranchised, the poor, the lonely and lost, the stunted and broken by abuse. Even the broken rich of this world. So many people all about us are living in their own "hell on earth" of addictions, trouble, guilt, and rejection. Many are sick, unemployed, abandoned, or abused in some way. Some are refugees, widows, orphans, unloved, misunderstood, even hated. For these neighbors of ours, life is out of control.

Tragically, too many have no hope, thinking that nobody cares, that there is no way out. E. V. Hill said, "The one thing worse than being poor is believing that no one cares." James wrote, "Religion that God our Father accepts as pure and faultless is this: to look after orphans and widows in their distress and to keep oneself from being polluted by the world" (James 1:27).[351]

---

[350] *Eternity*, March 1972, 72.

[351] One church we worked alongside in Argentina took this biblical teaching quite literally. Their program of caring for needy widows reminded us of the New Testament teaching and practice (see Acts 6:1ff.; 1 Timothy 5:3-16).

Some have just stepped out of prison with no support and little knowledge of how society works. Recent immigrants come to our land needing to acculturate and learn English. They often tell us how their children are shunned and have no friends.

How do I receive such people? Do I value them as persons and truly accept them with all their wounds? Do I listen without condemning? Can they see Jesus in me? Or just more rejection? Will they give up, or lash out in frustration and anger? Or turn to prostitution and other sexual perversions, alcohol, drugs, gangs, or even a mind-altering cult of total control? Some will become suicidal or mentally damaged. Maybe kidnapped and enslaved. They desperately need acceptance, love, care, and practical help. On top of all that, everyone needs to find Jesus.

All lives matter! The worldwide needs are overwhelming. I may not be able to help very many people, but I can help one. The story is told of someone who picked up a stranded starfish and tossed it out to sea. Their friend said, "What difference will that make, seeing there are so many more?" They replied: "it will make all the difference in the world to that starfish."

Jesus says, "As I have loved you, so you must love one another. By this everyone will know that you are my disciples, if you love one another" (John 13:34-35). What does a spiritually mature Christ-follower look like? They love—just like God.

"Be kind and compassionate to one another, forgiving each other, just as in Christ God forgave you. Be imitators of God. . . . Live a life of love, just as Christ loved us" (Ephesians 4:32ff.).

Have God's Vision and Compassion for the Whole World

All people need to know *about* Christ in order to know him personally. Faith still comes by hearing the Word of Christ (Romans 10:17). "Jesus . . . went throughout Galilee, teaching in their synagogues, preaching the good news of the kingdom, and healing every disease and sickness among the people" (Matthew 4:23). This is holistic ministry, caring for body and soul.

Nothing opens hearts like true love, listening, caring, making time for people, showing compassion, encouraging, and being gracious and kind. What the Apostle Paul said regarding Timothy is sadly too often the case today: "I have no one else like him, who takes a genuine interest in your welfare. For everyone looks out for his own interests, not those of Jesus Christ" (Philippians 2:19-22).

Do Everything in Jesus' Name, as His Representative

"And whatever you do, whether in word or deed, do it all in the name of the Lord Jesus, giving thanks to God the Father through him" (Colossians 3:17). It helps to ask myself, "What would Jesus do in this situation?"

I well recall a story told by Vernon Grounds, of a young shoe shine boy many years ago, working in a busy train station. One day a busy businessman bumped him and kept going. The unfortunate boy was not able to retrieve his polish, brushes, and other equipment. A well-dressed man found him crying on the floor, then helped him find his box and each polish, brush, and rag, but the little guy kept on crying. When asked why he was still crying, he said, "I'm missing a nickel." At that, the businessman put a whole dollar in the boy's hand. The boy, looking up at that kind man, asked, "Sir, are you Jesus?" How often do people see Jesus in me?

As a Christian, I bear God's name. Former Wheaton College professor of Greek, Gerald Hawthorne, said Christians can "blaspheme the name of God by living in a way contrary to the nature of God."[352]

Rejoice in God and Be Thankful

This should happen in both the good times and when the bottom falls out. (Ephesians 5:4, 20; 1 Thessalonians 5:16-18) Quit being a grouch. Be optimistic with much faith. Stay positive. "Do everything without complaining or arguing" (Philippians 2:14). That's a tough assignment! Don't you just want to delete that word "everything"? Do "rainy days and Mondays" always get you down? Well, so does being around a chronic complainer and whiner who can only see the dark side of everything. Instead of lamenting what this world is coming to, maybe we should highlight *who* is coming to this world. That we are on his side, the winning side! We've read the last page of the Book and know how it is all going to end! Now that's something to rejoice about.

---

[352] G. F. Hawthorne, "Name," in *The International Standard Bible Encyclopedia*, *Vol. 3* (Grand Rapids: Eerdmans, 1986), 482.

Do Everything for God's Glory

"So whether you eat or drink or whatever you do, do it all for the glory of God" (1 Corinthians 10:31). "If anyone speaks, they should do so as one who speaks the very words of God. If anyone serves, they should do so with the strength God provides, so that in all things God may be praised through Jesus Christ. To him be the glory and the power for ever and ever. Amen" (1 Peter 4:11). A chorus says it well: "In my life, Lord, be glorified today."

Do Everything as if I Were Doing It for Jesus

"Whatever you do, work at it with all your heart, as working for the Lord, not for human masters, since you know that you will receive an inheritance from the Lord as a reward. It is the Lord Christ you are serving" (Colossians 3:23-24). Even when I give someone a cup of cool water, I should do so as if I were giving it to Jesus (Matthew 25:31-46).

Live in Constant Awareness of God's Presence

The mystics have no corner on sensing God's presence. What sometimes hinders this? Sin? World in turmoil? Losses and hardships? Accidents and sickness? Psalm 16:8 says, "I have set the Lord always before me. Because he is at my right hand, I will not be shaken." Though I know Christ is always with me, I too often act as if this were not true.

Keep in Mind the "Blessed Hope" of Jesus' Return

The blessed hope should lead me to blessed holiness. "We know that when he appears, we shall be like him. . . . Everyone who has this hope in him (Christ) purifies himself, just as he is pure" (1 John 3:2-3). Virtually every major New Testament passage dealing with the end of the end times also tells us in that very context how we ought to live now! As for the minutia of eschatology, I am increasingly a "wait and see" guy. When a prophecy someday is fulfilled I will have an "Aha!" moment, able finally to say, "So this is what God was predicting. Now I get it." I need to get out of Acts 1:6-7, wondering when Christ will return, and get into Acts 1:8 and be involved in God's agenda for worldwide evangelism. C. T. Studd, cricketer turned missionary, once said, "Some wish to live within the sound of Church or Chapel bell; I want to run a Rescue Shop within a yard of hell." Jesus is in full control of history, bringing it to his foreordained conclusion.

Die Daily to the World, the Flesh, and the Devil

Paul talks about putting off the old self and putting on the new self in order to be like God. Ephesians 4:17ff. says I should "no longer live as the Gentiles do . . . darkened in their understanding and separated from the life of God." Verse 22 says, "You were taught, with regard to your former way of life, to put off your old self . . . and to put on the new self, created to be like God in true righteousness and holiness."

Constantly Yield My Will to God

I need to follow Jesus' example of submission, yielded to the Father: "Nevertheless, not my will, but yours, be done" (Luke 22:42, ESV). In bold contrast, the essence of magic is seeking power by means of certain rituals and incantations, wanting those mystical powers to do *my* bidding. Biblical spirituality is *submission*. Genuine submission to God pleases him, and that is all that really matters. It is trust in God Almighty, so worthy of such love and trust. Instead of "selling my soul" to God's enemy, I yield my soul to God.

Seek the Renewing of My Mind

"Do not conform to the pattern of this world, but be transformed by the renewing of your mind. Then you will be able to test and approve what God's will is—his good, pleasing and perfect will" (Romans 12:2). Instead of turning it off in order to enter God's presence, I need to seek the renewing of my mind. Such renewal of my mind helps me make holy responses and decisions and to be able to discern the will of God in every situation. John Piper says this entails "the path of wisdom and spontaneous godliness—wisdom where we consciously apply the word of God with our renewed minds to complex moral circumstances, and spontaneous godliness where we live most of our lives without conscious reflection on the hundreds of things we say and do all day."[353]

---

[353] www.desiringgod.org/messages/the-renewed-mind-and-how-to-have-it

Seek First and Foremost the Kingdom of God

How well do I understand the term *Kingdom*? Matthew 19:16-30 helps me get a handle on this concept. Note the synonyms in this passage. This *Kingdom* is redemption, salvation, and eternal life! We are to seek God's Kingdom and his righteousness as top priority (Matthew 6:33). Jesus taught his disciples to pray, "Your kingdom come, your will be done" (Matthew 6:10). To sum it up, it is redemption, both personal and universal. Wheaton College's motto says it all: "For Christ and his Kingdom." It's all about Christ and the gospel he came to provide and proclaim. It's all about redemption that includes justification, sanctification, and ultimate glorification. Becoming Godlike, but never divine! I will finally be totally righteous, both in position and practice. That last part is so unfathomable right now. What a blessed hope, finally seeing Christ and being like him. No wonder Christ urges us to seek first his Kingdom. Note in the book of Acts how preaching the "kingdom of God" is synonymous with teaching "about the Lord Jesus Christ" (Acts 28:31). This is typical Hebrew parallelism. (See also Acts 1:3; 8:12; 19:8; 20:25.)

Grow in the Grace and Knowledge of Jesus Christ

"But grow in the grace and knowledge of our Lord and Savior Jesus Christ" (2 Peter 3:18). We grow in both knowing about Jesus and knowing him intimately as we remain firmly tethered to him. That's what this whole topic of "spirituality" is all about! As we walk with Jesus we become increasingly like him. When at last we see him, we'll then know as we are known, in blessed perfection, but never divine.

Follow Jesus' Example

Christ told his disciples, "I have set you an example that you should do as I have done for you" (John 13:15). Again, in verse 34, he says, "As I have loved you, so you must love one another." See Appendix 1.

Consciously Serve as an Example for Others

The Scriptures are overflowing with such examples, some more intentional than others. Paul says to follow his example of following

155

Christ. He also tells Timothy to "set an example for the believers in speech, in life, in love, in faith and in purity" (1 Timothy 4:12). A good example is powerful motivation! Someone asked a young person which Bible translation he favored. He replied, "My Grandma's. She translated it into life." In Hebrews 11 we have a long list of great examples of people who showed their faith by godly living, in spite of some incredible obstacles.

Avoid Idolatry and Every Form of Syncretism

After the ten northern tribes of Israel were taken into Assyrian captivity (722/721 BC), the remaining mix of people in Samaria "worshiped the Lord, but they also served their own gods in accordance with the customs of the nations from which they had been brought. . . . Even while these people were worshiping the Lord, they were serving their idols" (2 Kings 17:33, 41). About a hundred years later, Jeremiah quotes the Lord saying, "Do not learn the ways of the nations" (Jeremiah 10:2). See also Deuteronomy 12:29-31; 18:9. Isaiah 2:6 says, "You have abandoned your people, the house of Jacob. They are full of superstitions from the East; they practice divination like the Philistines, and clasp hands with pagans." Psalm 106 rehashes Israel's sordid history, as the Hebrews soon forgot what God had done for them. Verse 35 laments, "They mingled with the nations and adopted their customs."

Occult leader Alice Bailey (1880–1949) prophesied that New Age "illumination" would someday arrive via Christianity, so she told her followers to leave the outer shell of Christianity intact for the moment so as to change things from the inside.[354] Religious syncretism is the fusion of differing belief systems, blending and incorporating ideas and practices from various religions.[355] *Merriam-Webster* defines it as "the combination of two or more forms of belief or practice." Western

---

[354] Alice Bailey, *The Externalisation of the Hierarchy* (New York: Lucis Publishing Company, 1957), 510.

[355] This helpful article includes examples of such syncretism of Catholic Christianity in the Americas among animistic peoples: www.gotquestions.org/syncretism-religious.html We saw this firsthand in northwest Argentina, where many Catholics still worship and appease the Incan earth god, *pacha mama*. Sometimes a converted *curandero*, the tribal traditional healer, will be tempted to continue healing in the old magical ways but now "in Jesus' name."

interest in Eastern mysticism continues to grow at an alarming pace, following the pattern set for us by syncretistic Desert Fathers.

Catholic author Randy England has written extensively about the dangers and heresy of Eastern New Age ideas and practices pervading the West. He says the Christian church is sanctifying pagan practices with mantric prayer, visualization, and promising divinity for humans.[356] He contrasts the pagan repetitive prayer of the Baal worshipers on Mt. Carmel with the simple prayer of Elijah (1 Kings 18).

We all know the best way to detect counterfeit money is to study the genuine thing. Likewise, we need to know the Scriptures to detect counterfeit teaching and practices.

Seek Counsel from Mature Believers

The Bible is full of examples of mentoring.[357]

I need to heed warnings from Christians who have roots in New Age, the occult, and shamanism. They know the signs—that same evil darkness, now found in Christian mysticism.[358] The Guaraní in Argentina who became followers of Christ could easily recognize practices that they once knew all too well, those old ways associated with Shamanism.

I must avoid association with, or seeking the counsel of any "guru" (Hindu term for *a personal spiritual teacher*) or spiritual guide who denies the gospel and other essential biblical doctrines. I need to heed

---

[356] www.ewtn.com/library/newage/nwmystic.htm See also his book *Randy England, The Unicorn in the Sanctuary: The Impact of the New Age Movement on the Catholic Church* (Rockford, IL: Tan Books, 1991), with stern warnings about the impact of the New Age movement on the Catholic Church, including "Christian" mysticism.

[357] This helpful article on biblical mentoring includes some key examples: http://www.lifeway.com/Article/Biblical-model-of-mentoring

[358] Matt Slick writes: "Before I became a Christian I was involved in the occult. One of the practices I would undergo when trying to contact the spiritual realm and/or trying to receive some mystical experience would be to empty my mind, remain motionless, and completely open myself up to receive whatever would come. Essentially, I was seeking an altered state of consciousness and contact with the spiritual world. This is one of the hallmarks of occult practices and it opens the person to demonic contact." See whole article: https://carm.org/centering-prayer

God's warning found in Psalm 1 about not hanging around with ungodly mockers of Christianity, or adopting their thinking and lifestyle.

Good counsel is so needed, but I must always remember that Christ, not friends or tradition, must remain my supreme authority.

Be an Active Member of a Local Church

I need to live connected with other Christians instead of being a spiritual nomad. In Ephesians 4:11-16, Paul underscores the importance of corporate spirituality where Christ has given the church the gifts of apostles, prophets, evangelists, pastors, and teachers. These God-given roles could be seen as the biblical equivalent of what some people now call "spiritual directors." Their task is "to prepare God's people for works of service, so that the body of Christ may be built up, till we all reach unity in the faith" (i.e. the body of truth as seen in Jude 1:3, 20). Like the Old Testament illustration of "iron sharpening iron," I need to stimulate a *reciprocal* ministry where I give and take, teach and learn; where we minister together with common goals and mutual respect. I am of value to you, and you also can enrich me. Each believer has both needs and resources. I need to love and be loved, to accept and to be accepted. It is not me doing something for you, but allowing and expecting God to do great things in both of us. This demands a lot of humility; it results in mutual growth, and God gets the glory. Even Paul expressed such a reciprocal ministry, writing the believers in Rome, "I long to see you . . . that you and I may be mutually encouraged by each other's faith" (Romans 1:11-12). Hebrews 10:24-25 talks about urging "one another on toward love and good deeds," then underscores the need for meeting together in larger groups.

The local church is prominent in the New Testament, as was the synagogue and temple worship prior to Jesus' ascension and the Day of Pentecost experience of Acts 2.

Set Apart One Day a Week for Rest and Renewal

This is easier said than done for most of us, especially those in Christian ministry. I need to set apart one day a week for rest and renewal, a change of pace, chilling out and drawing closer to God, and ministering to others. This includes both corporate as well as private worship. "Remember the Sabbath day by keeping it holy" (Exodus 20:6-11). My body and spirit need a change of pace, a time for renewal. I need to turn off the electronics, slow down, smell the roses, and enjoy life and all God has made. A sacred moment of quiet is so vitally essential for time to think, to ponder, to plan. A time for heart searching, and to find out God's priorities for my life. To be still before God. Sometimes I need a total disconnect from the ordinary, a time to crash, get some needed sleep and nourishing food. Like tired Elijah after fleeing from Jezebel and her threats.

Restore Christians Who Fall

"Whoever turns a sinner from the error of his way will save him from death and cover over a multitude of sins" (James 5:19-20). "Correct, rebuke and encourage—with great patience and careful instruction" (2 Timothy 4:2). Not condescendingly, but lovingly and graciously, not gossiping about them but confronting them directly. Galatians 6:1 says I need to restore gently a fallen believer, encouraging them to repent, confess the sin to God and to others whom they have offended, and embrace God's forgiveness. Jesus taught that I need to "go and show him his fault, just between the two of you" (Matthew 18:15-17). I need to forgive the repentant and help restore them to ministry and spiritual fruitfulness. After David's repentance and public confession, he writes, "Then I will teach transgressors your ways, and sinners will turn back to you (Psalm 51:13). God forgives and gives me another chance, which of course greatly displeases the devil whose very name means *slanderer* or *accuser*. As I help another to walk closer to the Lord, I will probably need the same kind of help someday. We all fall, more often than we care to admit, like Paul mentions in Romans 7.

Finally, Make Your Own List

As you glance over my list, I encourage you to make your own. Try distilling from the Scriptures and your personal experience what helps you walk with God, to love and serve him with your whole being. Some people refer to these spiritual disciplines as *holy habits,* as we daily make holy decisions.

I must make sure each of the above practices is solidly backed by biblical theology, that is, making sure the "spiritual theology" conforms wholly to biblical theology. I also need to make sure all my thoughts conform to the Scriptures. I want to finish well someday, able to say, "I have kept the faith."

All the items in the above list require a fully-engaged mind as I seek to walk in full communion with the Lord.

I might want to underline or highlight the topics I need to work on. Memorizing a key verse of Scripture about that topic could be of great help. I also need to talk to God about it, and maybe discuss this with a trusted friend and pray together.

Enoch walked with God. So did Noah. And so can we, my dear friend and fellow pilgrim. We can and should hike daily with him in joyous intimacy.

Chapter 8:
Right Motives for Loving, Obeying, and Serving

Peter once said to Jesus, "We have left everything to follow you! What then will there be for us?" (Matthew 19:27). In other words, "What's in it for me?"

At that point Peter still had much to learn about loving and serving God. So do I. So do we all. *Why* should I be holy? Quite often my motive is as important as what I actually do. I'm sure many more motives could be found, but here is a start. It's interesting to look at these in terms of what I get out of it versus what God gets out of it.

God demands holiness. "Be holy, because I am holy" (1 Peter 1:15-16, quoting Leviticus 11:44-45). God wants me to be holy, like him! 1 Thessalonians 4:3 says, "It is God's will that you should be sanctified." That alone should be enough. God knows what's best for each of us. Now we will look at some other possible motives.

I want to experience full, intimate communion with God. Ah, now there's a great motive! Still slightly selfish, but not at all bad. The psalmist wrote: "For the Lord is righteous; he loves righteous deeds; the upright *shall behold his face*" (Psalm 11:7, ESV, emphasis added). The phrase "behold his face" speaks of free access to God, basking in his presence, sensing him near. It means having his approval, protection, power, love, cleansing, and much more.

I want God to "be with me" in a special way. We sing, "God be with you till we meet again." What does this mean? Philippians 4:9 says, "Whatever you have learned or received or heard from me, or seen in me—put it into practice. And the God of peace *will be with you*" (emphasis added). James 4:8 says, "Come near to God and he will come near to you." In 1 Chronicles 22:11, King David tells Solomon, "Now, my son, the Lord be with you, and may you have success and build the house of the Lord your God." In Nehemiah 2:8 and 18 we read, "The gracious hand of my God was on me." (See also Ezra 7:6, 9-10, 28; 8:18, 22, 31.) Our word "goodbye" originally came from "God be with you." Living in communion with God means being with God, with his gracious hand upon me.

Holiness increases God's glory. "So whether you eat or drink or whatever you do, do it all for the glory of God" (1 Corinthians 10:31). According to the Westminster Shorter Catechism, "Man's chief end is to glorify God, and to enjoy him forever."[359] Now here's a pure motive! All about Jesus! Like a well-known hymn says, "To God be the glory, great things He hath done."

I want to make God look good and the Christian life attractive. In contrast, my sin drives people from God and his redemptive love.

I want to be a good example for other Christians. Paul urges Timothy to "set an example for the believers in speech, in life, in love, in faith and in purity" (1 Timothy 4:12).

I love and serve God simply because he is God, fully worthy of all my love, worship, and obedience.

I wish to please the Lord. Colossians 1:10 says, "And we pray this in order that you may live a life worthy of the Lord and may *please him* in every way" (emphasis added).

I do not want to grieve the Holy Spirit (Ephesians 4:30).

Nor do I want to quench the Holy Spirit's promptings in my life (1 Thessalonians 5:19).

I love him because he first loved me. It's all about gratitude and appreciation. 1 Corinthians 6:20 says, "You were bought at a price. Therefore, honor God with your body." An old chorus says, "After all he's done for me . . . how can I do less than give him my best, and live for him completely, after all he's done for me." This is a powerful motive.

I wish to have all the "fruit of the Spirit" always functioning. These are the first to go when I'm disobedient, unrepentant, living with unconfessed sin.

---

[359] www.reformed.org/documents/wsc/index.html?_top=www.reformed.org/documents/WSC.html

I await heaven and spending eternity with God, in that glorious place prepared for me in a new heaven and earth (2 Peter 2:11-13; Hebrews 11:10 ff.). A story is told of a missionary couple arriving in New York on a steamer from Africa, along with US President Teddy Roosevelt where a band was playing and many people waving. This missionary was a little sad, with nobody there to welcome them back from years of service. So his wife turned to him and said: "Honey, you're forgetting something. We're not home yet." 1 Corinthians 15:58 says our labor in the Lord is not in vain. A chorus says it well: "It will be worth it all, when we see Jesus."

I wish to avoid bad consequences for disobedience, both now and in heaven where we will enjoy degrees of reward and ministry according to our earthly faithfulness (Matthew 6:19-21, 25:14-30; Luke 19:11-27; 1 Corinthians 3:12-15, 4:5; 2 Corinthians 5:10). Walking with God in holiness is good for *me* (Romans 8:28; 1 John 5:3). "The Lord disciplines those he loves" (Hebrews 12:6). "It is a dreadful thing to fall into the hands of the living God" (Hebrews 10:31). I await the "judgement seat of Christ" where I will be rewarded according to my motives as well as faithfulness.

I remember God *sees* me, all the time. People attempt to go incognito with masks, camouflage, stealth technology, but they can never hide from God. "For your ways are in full view of the Lord, and he examines all your paths" (Proverbs 5:21). At Peter's denial Jesus looked out and *saw* him (Luke 22:60-62). God knows all about us, even our every thought, and our whole future. Even the hairs of our head are all numbered. Christ told each of the churches in Revelation chapters 2 and 3 he knows all about them, as "the one who searches hearts and minds" (Revelation 2:23).

I want God's blessing and approval, God's favor, and the *shalom* he gives to those who truly walk with him.

I desire to have divine power and grace (Colossians 1:11; Acts 1:8; Titus 2:11-14). Then I can say with Paul, "I can do everything through him who gives me strength" (Philippians 4:13).

I wish to be Christ's ambassador, his representative, his envoy (2 Corinthians 5:20; Colossians 3:17).

Holy living gives me assurance of salvation. Christ's sheep follow him (John 10:27). 1 John 2:3 says, "We know that we have come to know him if we obey his commands."

The assurance of Christ's Second Coming is also a great motive for holy living and service. It's noteworthy that most major passages in the New Testament that treat the Second Coming and related events also discuss how we ought to live.

Holy living will draw others to faith in Christ by their seeing Christ in me (1 Peter 3:1-2; Matthew 5:16; Philippians 2:15). I wish to be "salt" and "light." At Christmas, some of our outside lights came unplugged. I don't want to become like those lights, or like others that became covered with leaves and snow and barely glowed. As is written in Matthew 5:14-16, "You are the light of the world. A town built on a hill cannot be hidden. Neither do people light a lamp and put it under a bowl. Instead they put it on its stand, and it gives light to everyone in the house. In the same way, let your light shine before others, that they may see your good deeds and glorify your Father in heaven."

I wish to be "an instrument for noble purposes . . . prepared to do any good work" (2 Timothy 2:21).

I wish to have a clear conscience before God. In 2 Timothy 1:3 Paul talks about serving God "with a clear conscience." Then I don't have to be glued to the rearview mirror!

Holiness gives me perspective and hope. Suffering produces hope (Romans 5:4-5). "May the God of hope fill you with all joy and peace as you trust in him, so that you may overflow with hope by the power of the Holy Spirit" (Romans 15:13). God is the source of my hope. That great hymn says it well: "My hope is built on nothing less, than Jesus' blood and righteousness." We know where we're going and what we'll be. 1 John 3:2-3 says, "We know that when he appears, we shall be like him, for we shall see him as he is. Everyone who has this hope in him purifies himself, just as he is pure." What a glorious thing to know! We know we have passed from death unto life. We know we have eternal life, are forgiven, that we have peace with God. For us, there is "no condemnation" and no separation from the love of God and from the God of love. We know that when Christ appears, we shall be like him. Ours is not a hope-so religion but a know-so faith in God.

I desire to have divine guidance. Isaiah 30:21 says, "Whether you turn to the right or to the left, your ears will hear a voice behind you, saying, 'This is the way; walk in it.'" Note all the expressions of guidance in Psalm 23. The hymn "He Leadeth Me" well expresses this desire.

I want to see my country experience God's blessing. In Proverbs we read, "Righteousness exalts a nation, but sin is a disgrace to any people" (Proverbs 14:34).

I want to love, worship, and serve God with my whole being, and with all the right motives. This is the only life worth living! Peter had much to learn about motivation. By the time his martyr's death occurred, I'm sure he had learned much about loving, worshiping, and serving the Lord Jesus for all the right motives. In his first epistle we read, "But just as he who called you is holy, so be holy in all you do. . . . But you are a chosen people, a royal priesthood, a holy nation. A people belonging to God, that you may declare the praises of him who called you out of darkness into his wonderful light" (1 Peter 1:15; 2:9). Try rereading those two epistles he wrote, thinking about all these motives we've listed! Note how far Peter had progressed spiritually. Surely, there's hope for us, too!

Chapter 9:
Core Values and Attitudes
Essential for Growth and Service

Here are some basics for all true followers of Christ, members of God's family by faith in Christ's atoning sacrifice for them. Once we are born again, we can begin to grow in Christlikeness, greatly helped by these core values. The first three are also found in Micah 6:8—what the Lord requires of us (do what is right, show mercy, and walk humbly with God.) The brief descriptions of each of these basic attitudes (shown in italics) were written by my good friend David Korb, a former pastor and then a regional director for WorldVenture.

Humility

I will recognize Jesus Christ as the Source of my gifts and abilities and maintain a right understanding of my own limitations so that he receives all the glory.

I still have much to learn and to modify. I am far from perfect or mature. In *Mere Christianity*, C. S. Lewis said, "When a man is getting better he understands more and more clearly the evil that is still left in him. When a man is getting worse he understands his own badness less and less." God still opposes the proud and gives grace to the humble (1 Peter 5:5). Humility does not glory in education, titles, position, or genealogy (see Philippians 3). Jesus must receive absolutely all the glory (see 1 Peter 4:11). It is amazing how much can be accomplished when nobody cares who receives the credit.

True humility is strength. With humility, I recognize the source of my gifts and capacities. If I readily admit that I do not know it all, others will more easily follow my example of trusting in God and making Christ their Lord. They will keep learning to know Christ and walk in communion with Him.

Am I the proverbial "ugly American" who has to be in control, thinks he knows it all, and is constantly seeking praise and status?

Honesty and Integrity

In my interactions with self, God, and others I will strive for sincerity and authenticity, undergirded by love. I will seek God's wisdom to make right choices and ethical decisions.

I need to be truthful, upright, sincere, transparent, open, genuine, authentic, real, ethical, honorable, and reliable. I need to be honest with myself (Romans 12:3), with God and his Word (2 Corinthians 2:17, 4:2; Revelation 22:18-19), and with others (Colossians 3:9; Acts 5:3). I thus pattern my life after God who does not lie (Titus 1:2; Hebrews 6:18) and am controlled by his Spirit of truth (John 14:17, 15:26). I resist the devil with the belt of truth (Ephesians 6:14).

In 2 Corinthians 6:11-13, Paul pleads with the Corinthians to open wide their hearts, just as he has done with them. Being honest does not mean "spilling your guts" or saying everything you think. Charles Spurgeon once said, "Tell-all is thought a fool." Love often covers a multitude of sins (1 Peter 4:8) but at the same time recognizes sin for what it is. Before speaking, we need to ask: 1) Is it true? 2) Do I really need to say this? and 3) Am I saying it with love and all the right motives?

It is said that character is what we are when no one is looking. We need the courage to believe and do what is right and truthful, no matter what the cost; otherwise we end up as hypocrites, living an illusion, and we fail to mature. If we're not maturing, we too often end up doing things *to* others instead of *with* them.

Love

I will demonstrate love in a way that seeks the welfare of others, allowing them to grow and mature with dignity.

Egotists are overly concerned with their own Bible study and growth. The person who truly loves seeks the welfare and maturity of others, as we read about Pastor Timothy (see Philippians 2:19-21). True, divine love does not dominate or drown the other person, but allows them to grow and mature with dignity. A false, egotistical love says, "You are my only friend in the world. I need you to care for me." It creates dependence, and neither person will mature normally. Sometimes a false love will be easily offended and run away when there are problems. In Romans 13:10, Paul says, "Love does no harm to its neighbor." Love is the fulfillment of God's law, the essence of all God desires of us (see Romans 13:8-9; Galatians 5:14). I show real love when I take time to actually listen to others.

Constant Repentance

I will consistently entreat God to show me what needs to be changed or abandoned in my life, seeking his pardon (and that of others, if they are involved) and committing to change by faith.

God needs to show me what needs to be changed or abandoned in my life. Constant repentance and seeking pardon leads to a fruitful, Spirit-filled life and the extension of God's Kingdom. It results in the lordship of Jesus Christ and intimate communion with him. It involves a constant renewal of our minds (Romans 12:1-2).

Constant Faith in the Lord

I will trust in God and depend on his strength.

I put my whole trust in God almighty. Faith in God is my response to everything he has said and has provided for all those who truly love him. Christ once condemned the Pharisees for knowing neither the Scriptures nor the power of God (Matthew 22:29). Some err in seeking only God's power. Others err with just a dry, legalistic study of the Bible that does not affect their lives. True biblical Christianity unites these two essentials. Faith is another piece of our armament for resisting the enemy (Ephesians 6:16).

An atheist in China once said, "If I believed just a tenth of what you Christians say you believe, I'd be ten times more enthusiastic." Even with the smell of decay all about us, we are encouraged, for we know we are on the winning side. We await that trumpet blast (1 Thessalonians 4:16-18; 1 Corinthians 15:51ff; Matthew 24:29-31), and know we will either return with Christ, or receive a transformed body, and will forever serve him in his never-ending Kingdom. He is in full control of history, bringing it all to his foreordained conclusion. What a tremendous worldwide fellowship we belong to. This is God's world, every square centimeter of it! Biblical faith includes the awareness of God's constant holy and loving presence.

Obedience

I will believe God's Word and do what it says, regardless of how I feel, knowing that God promises a good result.

Christ said, "You are my friends if you do what I command" (John 15:14). Biblical faith and walking with God results in a changed life. In Romans 14:9 we read that Christ died and rose again, to be our Lord. Once we obey one thing God commands, then he can teach us one more thing. We are filled with the Spirit to the degree that we obey Christ. It does no good to beg or sing for that filling if we are not willing to obey even the most insignificant thing God says or guides us to do. "My food, said Jesus, is to do the will of him who sent me" (John 4:34). This *putting into practice* is what Brazilian Paulo Freire calls "praxis." James' epistle denounces faith without feet, or mere empty words. Jesus had no harsher words than those for the proud, hypocritical religious leaders (see Matthew 23). Paul told Titus, "They claim to know God, but by their actions they deny him" (1:16).

Courageous Service

Following the example of Jesus, I will lay down my rights and choose to serve rather than be served.

My perception is that many people wish to lead, but few want to serve. Jesus came not to be served but to serve, and to give himself as a sacrifice. As the Father sent him, so he sends us. We may have that servant heart, be competent, and have all the other core values, yet still do nothing, out of fear or laziness. Veteran missionary Jim Cook once challenged me by saying, "Bruce, have the courage to take God at his Word!" God told Joshua, "Be strong and courageous. Do not be terrified; do not be discouraged" (Joshua 1:9). It is truly amazing how often the Bible tells us to be courageous, and not afraid or discouraged. God calls us to serve him courageously, fearlessly, bravely, and confidently, as we walk in the fear of the Lord and in full communion with him.

Chapter 10:
Concluding Thoughts

There's a story about the elderly Dr. Albert Einstein leaving Princeton by train. When the conductor came by, old man Einstein couldn't find his ticket. The conductor recognized Dr. Einstein and assured him, "That's all right, Dr. Einstein, I'm sure you paid." As the conductor was entering the next car he looked back to find Dr. Einstein on his hands and knees looking under his seat. Rushing back, he said, "Oh please, Dr. Einstein, we all know who you are. You don't need to find your ticket." Dr. Einstein looked up at him and said: "Young man I too know who I am. What I don't know is where I am going."[360]

Many of the followers of historic mystic Christianity, with faith rooted in the Desert Fathers, are not sure of who God/Ultimate Reality is, are confused about the nature of humans, about salvation, about how to pray, about how to enter into intimacy with God while avoiding bad spirits who are also there in *the silence*. They are confused about how to evaluate non-Christian religions. They reject the Judeo-Christian Scriptures as their final authority for Christian belief and living. They do not know for sure where they will spend eternity, or even if they will enjoy personal existence.

We need to return . . . go back . . . way back, even further than the mysticism of the "Desert Fathers." How about going all the way back— to Christ and the Apostles, back to "Moses and the prophets," and to all the other inspired writers of the Bible? We can easily fall into either the deadly error of not knowing the Scriptures or not having the power of God (Matthew 22:29). Both are constantly needed.

We need to read the short epistle of Jude once again, and become more discerning and aware of the false prophets now invading biblical Christianity, as the Bible foretold. At the same time, we need to be positive, like our Lord and the Apostles. We need to be holy, fill our minds and hearts with the Scriptures, pray at all times, and really love both God and people (see Jude 1:20-21). Only then can we be bold witnesses as we rescue the perishing with mercy and compassion.

---

[360] themennonite.org/opinion/god-taking-us/

171

Neither scholasticism nor mysticism are the answer. Shaun Bryant, pastor of an Orthodox Presbyterian church in Modesto, California, points out that historically the scholasticism of the Middle Ages, with its emphasis on knowledge, was usually too weak on the personal relationship with God, divorcing Bible study from the heart and ending up with formalism and driving some to mysticism. Mysticism, on the other hand, is the opposite extreme, downplaying or ignoring the Scriptures in its quest for direct contact with God via mindless contemplation and forgetting the objective authority of the Bible. In biblical Christianity truth should never be divorced from the heart nor should the mind ever be turned off.[361]

Martin Luther came to see that neither scholasticism nor mysticism by themselves led to God but were just other forms of justification by works. Spiritual techniques were of no value until he discovered the gospel and trusted in Christ and Christ alone for his eternal redemption. Christ is still the perfect balance of true wisdom and power.[362] Much of modern-day contemplative spirituality would have us undo the Reformation and return us to Catholicism and to a false gospel of infused righteousness in an attempt to climb up to heaven by God's "grace" *and* our own merits. Martin Luther found that sinful mankind was far from God. Maybe we should paraphrase the Apostle Paul to the Galatians: "You foolish contemplatives! Who has bewitched you?"

The old gospel of God's grace through Christ is the only Path, the only Way, the Truth, and the Life. His full pardon and real fellowship with him is ours, free for the taking, via repentance and the new birth. Justification is by faith alone, resulting in real union with God and the start of a life of getting to know Christ even better day by day. It is not so much about being rule-oriented but relational, of loving Jesus and being tethered to him. Then if we truly love him we'll want to obey him (and will have the power to do so). The Reformers returned to biblical Christianity, finding that God satisfies both our intellectual and heart desires, both wisdom and power. This is the balance God desires for us. The enemy of God always has attempted to knock people off this balance. My theology professor at Denver Seminary, Gordon Lewis, often told us, "Do not ever separate the head from the heart . . . not even with something as thin as a razor blade." Now that could be downright deadly!

[361] gcmodesto.sermons.io/sermons/mysticism-and-scholasticism
[362] See 1 Corinthians 1:18-31.

The antidote to false teaching is the real thing. We need to be experts in knowing and loving God and experts in loving and really caring for all people. We need to be more relational with God than merely rules-oriented. We need to become "more like our Master" as that old hymn put it, living daily in his power, a life of repentance and faith. We should seek a warm, intimate, personal, and authentic walk with the Lord. It is a constant challenge to avoid nonbiblical extremes and maintain equilibrium. This is the history of biblical faith in God from Genesis to Revelation and all down through the ages. It is true Christianity. We have many enemies (world, flesh, and the devil), and we have an almighty and loving God who indwells every true follower of Christ. He alone is worthy of our trust and worship.

One expert at knowing and loving God was George Müller. In the 1800s, this godly man of prayer and faith showed great compassion for orphans all across England. He learned to combine Bible meditation with prayer at the start of each day. Müller feared "spiritual deadness, which is so frequently the result of much study" when not accompanied by appropriate falling on one's knees in prayer.[363] In my estimation, this is biblical piety and true spirituality.

Several friends of mine love the writings of contemplative spirituality but assure me they do not go along with everything that many of the mystics say or do. I personally heard Richard Foster say the same when questioned about Meister Eckhart and other mystics who go beyond historic orthodox Christianity. I pray for discernment for writers like Richard Foster. This may be fine for them, but how many others will follow them in reading the mystics and, unlike my friends, will be less discerning and will be taken in by these writers' heresy? This grieves me deeply. I, too, read the contemplative authors as well as narrower-than-the-Bible right wing conservatives as I attempt to examine all things and hold to that which agrees with God's written Word.

Why immerse ourselves in heresy in our quest for a speck of truth? Why remove the lid of the religious garbage can in search of something edible?

I have concluded that contemplative spirituality is in varying degrees a syncretism of general mysticism and Christianity. No wonder some New Age websites appreciate almost all of the Catholic mystics being quoted by Christian mystics like Richard Foster, Henry Nouwen,

---

[363] *Autobiography of George Müller* (London: J. Nisbet and Co., 1914), 31.

Adele Ahlberg Calhoun, and so forth.[364] Many Christian mystics learn from Buddhism and Hinduism and see very little difference between them.[365]

Pastor Gary Gilley, in his series on mysticism, says that through the present revival of Christian mysticism, via Foster and others,

> Classical, Medieval Roman Catholic mysticism has been dusted off and offered as the newest and best thing in spirituality. But there is one little problem. If this is how God wanted His followers to connect with Him why did he not bother to say so in His Word? If contemplative prayer . . . is the key that will unlock this greater dimension of spirituality, as we will see is being claimed, why did God not give us instructions on how to pray in this manner? Why did He leave it up to monks and nuns hundreds of years later to unveil this key to true godliness? Of course, the answer is that He did not. God's Word is sufficient; all that we need for life and godliness is found there (See 1 Peter 1:4; 2 Timothy 3:16, 17).[366]

We may be approaching the end of the end times. Satan well knows this. He knows his days are numbered, and his cancerous lies are today invading Christ's body the church and are metastasizing at an alarming rate. Nonbiblical mysticism is becoming pandemic. What profound blindness and lack of discernment on the part of evangelical Christians! Could this form of mysticism be a sign of the nearness of Christ's return and the end of the end times? Is contemplative spirituality preparing the world for an anti-Christian and antibiblical ecumenism and

---

[364] www.enlightened-spirituality.org/Christian_contemplative_meditation.html This article by Timothy Conway is entitled: "Contemplative Meditation in Christianity" and begins with a painting of Jesus meditating, done by a monk of the Vedanta Society. Conway is involved in Hinduism and open to about every form of "spirituality." (A significant article)

[365] www.stolaf.edu/people/huff/classes/religion/Essay.html This website by contemplative Teresa Tillson of St. Olaf College introduces typical methods of contemplative prayer, *Lectio Divina*, etc., then proceeds to discuss in a positive light the practices of Zen Buddhism, then Ignatius of Loyola's prayer of active imagination, then more guidelines for contemplative prayer.

[366] www.tottministries.org/mysticism-part-1

eventually the global religion the Scriptures mention? Is the restrainer ceasing to restrain? (See 2 Thessalonians 2:5-7)

The New Testament often warns us of being deceived. Why? Because it is so easy to be misled and fooled.

Not all mystics are the same. Within so-called Christian mysticism there exists a gradation, or shading from conservative evangelical Protestantism to theologically liberal Protestantism, to Catholicism, and to varying degrees of Eastern non-Christian spirituality. As I see it, the biggest danger is getting started down that road, since the most conservative books also recommend the more liberal or Catholic authors with varying degrees of non-Christian mystic influence. It is little wonder then that New Age writers talk positively about the revival of contemplative meditation in Christianity!

The antidote to "deceiving spirits and things taught by demons" (see 2 Timothy 4:1) involves regeneration, then holy living and biblical teaching on the basics, including how to walk with God in love, awe, and full fellowship.

How should we show contemplatives a better way? How should we treat them with true respect as we disagree? Are we merely experts at reproving, rebuking, and exhorting? Do we know how to cut people some slack instead of just cutting them to pieces? Do we speak the truth but always in love and with mercy? Do we follow Jesus' and the apostles' example of forgiving and rescuing as well as exposing and warning of false teachers and prophets and doctrines of demons? Are we concerned for removing the beam from our own eye before attempting to remove the speck from someone else's? Or are we hypocrites and frauds with moral and ethical failures? Are we selfish, narcissistic, self-righteous, and impeding the spiritual growth of a younger generation?

I want to be more like Jesus who said, "Do not judge" but in almost the same breath said "Watch out for false prophets" (Matthew 7:1, 15).

Christian mysticism jolts me with the truth I have known for many years, that merely knowing the Scriptures does not automatically result in changed living. Obedience to the little we know of God and his Word is vastly more important than much knowledge with little obedience. Hypocritical knowing without really walking with God only leads to greater condemnation and drives people from God. The old hymn sums up this needed balance: "When we walk with the Lord, in the light of his Word, what a glory he sheds on our way. While we do his good will, he abides with us still and with all who will trust and obey . . . there's no other way to be happy in Jesus . . ."

Fortunately, Jesus knows all about me and seeks my renewal. In Revelation 2 and 3 Jesus repeatedly says, "These are the words of him who . . ." then follows a glimpse of Jesus. Jesus says he knows all about me and is the one "who searches *hearts* and *minds*" (Revelation 2:18-29). Jesus knows all about my actions and motives. He knows my heart, knows what trips me up, knows that I, too, live in an idolatrous and immoral society where people are still learning "Satan's so-called deep secrets"[367] (Revelation 2:24). He knows my hard work, that I have kept the faith, have daily devotions, attend church, even participate in a small group. He also knows of my indiscriminate love and that I too easily put up with people as evil as old Jezebel. And that I am enticed by immorality like that which was introduced to the ancient Hebrews by Balaam and Balak.

If Jesus should send me such a letter, what might he say? I can imagine Jesus saying: Wake up! Repent! Learn to love me as you did at the first. Prepare for severe worldwide persecution. Be faithful no matter what happens. Remember that I will protect you through the trials and tribulations (Revelation 3:10). Be an obedient overcomer. Move through the doors I am opening for you. Be a bold witness, with life and lips. Really think about me as you sing praises and pray. Learn what true worship is all about. Talk to me about what you read in the Scriptures.

Finally, Jesus would tell me, as he did those churches, "Whoever has ears, let them hear what the Spirit says to the churches" (Revelation 2:7). I need listening ears that take God's admonitions to heart, as Revelation 1:3 says, even though I fail to understand much of what Revelation describes. I should read it all, then when it comes to pass I will be able to say, "Ah, now I see. Now I get what the Holy Spirit was talking about." Like what happened at Jesus' first coming. I am encouraged. Jesus is going to win! Hallelujah! And I belong to him. I will be like him, but never divine. No, I'll never share God's infinite essence! Not as the serpent, and many of the Christian mystics would have us believe.

---

[367] Already the Christian church was facing syncretism of pagan Greek mystery religions and philosophy, including Gnosticism, all of which later impacted Christianity in a big way via the "Desert Fathers" of Egypt, Palestine, and Syria. The New Testament book of Colossians is also combating this insipient Gnosticism, extreme Judaism, and mysticism.

Today sin is again crouching at our doors, as in Genesis 4:7. God pleads with us: Don't go there. Don't even think of it. Stop! Danger! Beware the mystic cancer so subtly invading and seeking to destroy the Kingdom of God and to deviate even faithful followers of Christ.

Paul wrote to the Corinthian followers of Christ in Greece: "The message of the cross is foolishness to those who are perishing, but to us who are being saved it is the power of God" (1 Corinthians 1:18). No universal salvation is envisioned here! Then he says, Christ is both the power and wisdom of God. Jews were seeking signs and wonders. The Greek philosophers chased after human wisdom, looking in all the wrong places because of their erroneous Greek mystery religion's concept of divinity, coupled with their rejection of divine revelation. Paul says, Jesus and the true gospel are all we need! He is the alpha and omega, A-Z, and everything in-between. (See Revelation 1:8; 21:6; 22:13.) He, along with the Father and Holy Spirit, is eternal, divine, creator, and sustainer of all that exists, the sovereign ruler of history.

As a Christ-follower, I need to learn to walk in the Spirit, be continually filled with the Spirit, learn not to grieve the Spirit, or repress and quench the Spirit's promptings in our life. The Spirit of Jesus who gave us the Scriptures wants to control me, all of me, all the time. He wants to do a mighty work in and through me. Am I too content merely to know about God? Am I ignorant of, or afraid of his power and control in my life? Am I too sophisticated to believe in a God of miracles? Angels and Jesus are still appearing to people today, including Muslim religious leaders. How much do I hunger after God, after real communion with him? Do I enjoy basking in God's presence and sensing his nearness? Do I know how to express genuine awe and worship of God at any moment? Don't I know that listening to Scripture is God speaking to me, personally? And that responding in prayer and genuine praise and worship is real communion with Him? All this without shutting down the mind. This occurs as I center on *Jesus*, instead of centering on something inside of me! I need to look upward rather than inward. The "good life" is Jesus! The song "Knowing You," by Graham Kendrick, describes well this truly biblical form of *centering*.

Appendix 1: Following the Example of Jesus

To begin with, this activity is only for true followers of Christ. Professor Ed Hayes of Denver Seminary wrote a short article, "Who is Jesus?" He refers to *The Imitation of Christ*, written in the thirteenth century by Thomas a Kempis. This little book has had a long and widespread influence.

Hayes encourages us to meditate on the life of Jesus Christ and to follow his example. He says, "This means to live as he lived, to think as he thought and to conform ourselves to His image." But he adds a much-needed corrective to what many Catholics and liberal Protestants mean by simply following Jesus: Hayes says, "Single-hearted focus reaps great reward, but it does not guarantee our salvation. We do not become saints by imitation, but by transformation. Martin Luther, who was profoundly influenced by Thomas a Kempis, gave a gentle warning, 'It is not imitation that makes sons, but sonship makes imitators.'"

We need to look at Jesus' life as the perfect example and live in constant communion with him. This results in Christ being our source of power for holy living. On numerous occasions Jesus said, "Follow me." Check out these texts about following Jesus' example.

Ephesians 5:1-2 says we are to "Be imitators of God, therefore, as dearly loved children and live a life of love, just as Christ loved us and gave himself up for us." In other words, live like God! Be like Jesus. Pattern your life after him. See Ephesians 5:25: "Husbands, love your wives." How? "Just as Christ loved the church and gave himself up for her."

Other verses to consider:

- Colossians 3:13 says, "Forgive as the Lord forgave you."
- 1 Thessalonians 1:6 says, "You became imitators of us and of the Lord."
- 1 John 2:6 tells us we should "walk as Jesus did."
- Paul tells the Corinthians (1 Corinthians 11:1), "Follow my example, as I follow the example of Christ."
- Romans 15:7 says, "Accept one another, then, just as Christ accepted you."

- John 13:14-15, After washing his disciples' feet Jesus said: "Now that I, your Lord and Teacher, have washed your feet, you also should wash one another's feet. I have set you an example that you should do as I have done for you."
- In Matthew 11:28-29 Jesus says, "Come to me, all you who are weary and burdened, and I will give you rest. Take my yoke upon you and learn from me, for I am gentle and humble in heart, and you will find rest for your souls."
- 1 Peter 1:15-16 quotes the Old Testament, where God tells us, "Be holy, because I am holy." Then 1 Peter 2:21 says, "To this end you were called, because Christ suffered for you, leaving you an example, that you should follow in his steps."

I love studying Jesus' example, observing his competence, character, courage, and his style of leadership. He called his disciples, lived with them, taught them, oriented them, sent them out, and then helped them evaluate their ministry upon their return. He, the perfect teacher, taught his disciples little by little, helping them reflect and process ideas, and to think for themselves. Much of his teaching began with a parable or by asking questions. (I have often happily watched the Guaraní church leaders in Argentina lead in this same way.) Jesus was in constant communion with the Father and was guided by the Spirit. He often spent a night in prayer, or rose early to seek solitary communion with the Father. He came to seek and to save the lost, with a servant attitude. He proclaimed the good news and went about doing good and showing compassion. He adapted culturally, speaking the language of the common people of northern Galilee. He never discriminated, but was the object of discrimination for being poor, speaking Aramaic, and being from Nazareth. He was always eating with a variety of people, walked a lot, admired the beauty of the flowers, enjoyed children, touched people, attended weddings and funerals, patiently and persistently preached, was never rushed, spent much time with a small group of personal friends, knew and trusted the Scriptures, accepted and worked with all true believers, prayed for the spiritual unity of the universal church (his body), resisted the devil, cast out demons, and warned his followers about false prophets and religious hypocrites.

We should never forget that Jesus wants to be more than a mere example. The saying "like father, like son" is especially true when the two of them spend both qualitative and quantitative time together. So, we need to walk with God, mindful of him all the time, both in times of silence and solitude as well as in the heat of the daily battle with its pitfalls and challenges.[368] Jesus Christ, our perfect leader and example, also wants to be our daily friend, our companion, and our power. Could this constant communion with God be what 1 Thessalonians 5:17 means when it tells us to "pray continually"? God does not "hang up" when we say "Amen." Nor should we.

---

[368] The old hymn, "Blessed Quietness," by Manie P. Ferguson, expressed this reality.

Appendix 2: Questions for Reflection

Could, or should, an evangelical Christian sometimes practice a form of mystical contemplation without the common nonbiblical premises of Catholic and Quaker contemplatives? Might we have a time where we no longer consciously think about anything but merely bask in God's glorious presence and sense his being with us in a special way? And listen to God? Just feeling forgiven and accepted by his grace? Maybe such an occasion could shift back and forth from thinking with words to some form of nonthinking, but avoiding intentionally turning off our minds.[369]

Are mindless contemplative techniques appropriate for children and youth? Richard Foster's book *Sanctuary of the Soul* (pages 125ff.) suggests that such techniques are not suitable for busy new parents. So, if contemplation with its accompanying ecstatic state is the only means of really knowing God and being in communion with him (as some affirm), how can busy people and children know and enjoy God?

How does one distinguish between grace and illusion?[370] If you seek greater intimacy with God by means of the mystic path, do you ask God to protect you from the unclean spirits that also lurk there in "the silence" and "darkness"? How can you be sure you hear *God's* voice instead of messages from our own desires or even from the evil one? Thomas Merton asks, "How does one know that he is guided by God and not by the devil?" Dallas Willard attempted to answer this by noting "the quality of God's voice."[371]

The Apostle Paul urged the Thessalonians to "test everything. Hold on to the good" (1 Thessalonians 5:19-20). The Bereans were more careful, or less gullible, than the Thessalonians. Acts 17:11 says they checked out the Apostle Paul by listening to him, then "examined the Scriptures every day to see if what Paul said was true" (Acts 17:11).

---

[369] Randy Newman's comments on this topic are well worth the reading! See: www.randydavidnewman.com/2012/07/16/mystical-prayer-vs-biblical-prayer/

[370] Thomas Merton, *The Inner Experience: Notes on Contemplation* (HarperSanFrancisco, 2003), 76.

[371] Richard Foster, *Sanctuary of the Soul* (Downers Grove, IL: InterVarsity, 2011), 83–84.

Is it possible to practice contemplative prayer in groups? Or is it strictly a private, individual practice?

What do you find in Christian mysticism/contemplation that is both unique to mysticism and genuinely helpful for you (something you never experienced in traditional Christianity)?

If you have become a Christian mystic, what was it that kept you from a close walk with God before practicing the mystic path of silent contemplation?

Which Christian mystic authors have helped you the most?

Which Christian mystic authors should be avoided?

Which Christian mystic *practices* should probably be avoided?

In your estimation, is entering the mystic silence and ecstatic state by means of repeating a sacred word:
- The only way to know God intimately and sense communion with him?[372]
- One of several ways?
- Not the way at all? What helps you to *know* God instead of just know about him?

Can we practice and teach "spiritual formation" apart from Christian mysticism?

---

[372] If repetition of a sacred word or phrase is the *only* way to enter God's presence and hear his voice, as most Christian mystics assert, how are we to explain the absence of this mystic path in the Bible? (As some prominent Christian mystic authors admit).

Can we know God intimately with our minds fully engaged? Are we really in God's presence when we pray with words and ideas? Or when we worship and praise God with our minds engaged?

Does mystical, contemplative prayer really work for you, or for anyone you know? In what ways? What are the results? Have you found it to be all that the mystics promise? Do you enjoy victory over temptation as well as power for holy living and evangelism?

Are you fully convinced that people need personal conversion, without which they will spend eternity separated from God?

Appendix 3: List of Christian Mystic Leaders

The Old and New Testament Scriptures abound with warnings about heretical, gospel-denying false prophets, teachers, and religious movements.

An increasing number of our much-respected evangelical leaders and organizations are using and promoting Christian mystic authors. These evangelicals firmly believe and preach the true gospel of salvation by faith alone in the vicarious death of Christ. They are looking for ways to have a deeper walk with God and grow in Christlikeness and are fed up with dead orthodoxy. I am leaving their names off this list unless they are definitely *practicing and promoting* the "mystic path" of an altered state of consciousness brought about by a mantra-like repetition of a sacred word or phrase.

We all need to ask ourselves which emphases of contemplative spirituality are biblical or at least compatible with the Bible, and which ones are not.

Ávila, Teresa of: (1515–1582), worked closely with John of the Cross and Anthony of Jesus in Spain. She wrote *The Interior Castle* which Richard Foster and many other mystics love. (See also pages 196–201 of Foster's *Devotional Classics*). In *The Interior Castle* she described the seven stages one goes through to arrive at union with God: 1) Humility, 2) Practice of Prayer, 3) Meditation, 4) Quiet, 5) Illumination, 6) Dark Night, and 7) King of Glory (or Union with the Divine). These stages correspond to the Seven Chakras found in Yoga and Hinduism.

She often saw visions, heard audible voices, and tortured herself with ceremonial flagellation in order to be more holy. Frequently her experiences were frightening. Mysterious noises would come from her throat. People sometimes accused her of being under satanic power. In fact, she herself often feared she was possessed by demons. At least she claimed to have seen many demons. One of these, in her own words, "made me thrash about with my body, head, and arms, and I was powerless to prevent him."[373]

She would use holy water to protect herself from these spirits. As all Carmelites, Teresa was extremely devoted to Mary and was quite devoted to Joseph. She said she had seen and talked with many dead people and to have seen Jesus, the Holy Spirit, and even the Father. She would arrive at a state of ecstasy, a state of complete passiveness where all senses quit, including memory. She described this as sweet, happy pain, alternating between a fearful fiery glow and a spell of strangulation. She was sometimes seen levitating during mass.[374] Teresa hated Protestants, thinking they were damning themselves by rejecting the Mass and the authority of the papacy. She was a writer of the Counter Reformation.

Richard Foster says on page 201 of *Devotional Classics*: "For some reason, Teresa of Ávila has always been difficult for me to read." He still attempts to glean lessons from her and is seemingly unbothered by her aberrations, heretical doctrines, and occultist practices. Foster favorably quotes Teresa in about every book he writes including his latest, *Sanctuary of the Soul.* And Bruce Demarest, on page 269 of his book *Satisfy your Soul,* says Teresa "enjoyed deep communion with Christ."

Barton, Ruth Haley: (1960–) Ruth Haley Barton is the founder of the Transforming Center based in Wheaton, Illinois. She was a staff member of Willow Creek Church. Her training includes the Shalem Institute for Spiritual Formation, which was begun by Tilden Edwards.[375] Edwards calls this institute "The Western Bridge to Far Eastern spirituality." She talks a lot about "the false self" and "the true self." The jacket of her book *Invitation to Solitude and Silence,* says "Much of our faith is about words—preaching, teaching, talking with others. Yet all of these words are not enough to take us into the real presence of God where we can hear his voice. . . ." Dallas Willard wrote the foreword. She freely quotes many contemplatives such as Thomas

---

[373] *The Life of Saint Teresa of Ávila by Herself,* trans. J. M. Cohen (London: Penguin Books, 1957), 222.

[374] www.themystica.com/mystica/articles/l/levitation.html This article treats both Teresa and many other mystics who would levitate. Mystic expert Evelyn Underhill also writes on this topic: www.sacred-texts.com/myst/myst/myst19.htm

[375] Tilden Edwards laments that rational thought "helped pave the way for the reformation's 'justification by faith alone.'"

Merton, M. Basil Pennington, Richard Foster, and Richard Rohr (see below).

Blake, William: (1757–1827) Highly influenced Thomas Merton, and was influenced by Hinduism. He communed with angels and was steeped in the occult. He claimed he talked daily with his dead brother. He was influenced by Emanuel Swedenborg and Jacob Böhme. A recent study shows how Blake used erotic Kabbalistic and tantric sex techniques, using sexual arousal to produce his spiritual visions.[376] Knowing all this, it surprises me that Blake is quoted so favorably by Richard Foster in *Celebration of Discipline*; and also in Renovaré's *A Spiritual Formation Journal*, 1996. On "tantra" or "tantric" see Wikipedia article[377] which shows us how incompatible it is with Christianity.

Böhme (or Boehme), Jakob: (1575–1624) German mystic who influenced William Blake, the Quakers, and many mystical movements. Quaker founder, George Fox, had some of Böhme's books in his library. Böhme thought Christ's Incarnation was not to cancel out sins, i.e., not a sacrifice, but as an offering of love for humanity. His mentor, Balthasar Walther, introduced Kabbalistic ideas into Böhme's thought. Behmenists (Böhme's disciples), who merged with the Quakers, were strongly influenced by him. Böhme taught that through the contemplative mystical state "hereby you may arrive at length to see all manner of divine sensations and heavenly communications."[378]

Bourgeault, Cynthia: (1947–) Episcopal priest, writer, president of "The Contemplative Society" and the "Aspen Wisdom School." One Internet site says of her: "She passionately promotes the practice of Centering Prayer, and has worked closely with Thomas Keating, Bruno Barnhart, Richard Rohr, as well as many other contemplative teachers and masters within Christianity and other spiritual traditions."[379]

---

[376] Martha Keith Schuchard, *William Blake's Sexual Path to Spiritual Vision* (Rochester, VT: Inner Traditions, 2008). This shows how morally sick Blake was! I do not plan to order this book nor do I recommend it.

[377] en.wikipedia.org/wiki/Tantra

[378] Hugh Ross, ed., *George Fox: A Christian Mystic* (Ireland: Evertype, 2008), 50.

[379] www.contemplative.org/cynthia-bourgeault

Calhoun, Adele Ahlberg: (1949–) She is pastor of spiritual formation at Christ Church, Oak Brook, Illinois, and teaches some courses at Wheaton College and Northern Baptist Theological Seminary. She is author of *Spiritual Disciplines Handbook,* which includes instruction about "centering prayer" and "contemplative prayer" along with many mystic practices as well as Bible-based spiritual disciplines like Bible study, memorization, worship, service, etc. Counted as her spiritual tutors she knows through books are M. Basil Pennington, Thomas Keating, Phyllis Tickle, Gerald May, Richard Foster, Henri Nouwen, Richard Rohr, Julian of Norwich, Thomas Merton, Teresa of Ávila, and many more.

Campolo, Tony: (1935–) American Baptist, professor emeritus of sociology, Eastern University. He questions that Christ is the only way to God, and believes that Christ is in every human being whether Christian or not.[380] He says mysticism is the common ground between Christianity and Islam and other religions. He says people can experience Jesus without even being aware of it, under a different god's name. He says: "I've got to believe that Jesus is the only Savior but being a Christian is not the only way to be saved."[381] Campolo says in *Partly Right,* "We affirm our divinity by doing what is worthy of gods."

Catherine of Sienna: (1347–1380) Italian Catholic mystic who had revelations and visions of Jesus and many dreams and trances. She claimed to have drunk the blood of Christ as well as the milk of Mary, Christ's mother. She claimed to have had a mystical marriage with Jesus which included some pretty erotic sentiments. She flagellated herself three times a day with an iron chain and would levitate off the floor several times a day. She was quite an activist, writing fearlessly to both cardinals and popes. She is lauded on pages 287–92 in Richard Foster's book *Devotional Classics*, although Foster admits her writings are hard to grasp. Demarest says, "Catherine opened her heart to God and enjoyed deep, lifelong devotion to the Lord."[382] See this footnote for more information about levitating mystics.[383]

---

[380] Tony Campolo, *A Reasonable Faith* (Nashville: Nelson, 1983), 192.
[381] www.crosscurrents.org/CompoloSpring2005.htm
[382] Bruce Demarest, *Satisfy your Soul: Restoring the Heart of Christian Spirituality* (Colorado Springs: NavPress, 1999), 286.
[383] www.themystica.com/mystica/articles/l/levitation.html

Chardin, Pierre Teilhard de: (1881–1955) French philosopher and Jesuit priest who greatly influenced the rise of the New Age movement. He rejected the idea of original sin, rejected the Genesis account of creation, and said man is evolving mentally and socially toward a final spiritual unity. He said, "I believe that the Messiah whom we await . . . is the universal Christ." (This universal, cosmic Christ he speaks of is not the Jesus of the Bible. See Matthew Fox for a fuller treatment of this). Although Chardin rejected almost every major doctrine found in the Scriptures, Richard Foster includes a favorable review of him in at least one of his books.[384]

Demarest, Bruce: (1935–) Retired Denver Seminary professor. He is an evangelical contemplative who relies heavily upon traditional Catholic and other mystics down through the ages, referring to "ancient wisdom of the church . . . treasures from ancient Christian spirituality . . . the spiritual masters of history," including Teresa of Ávila, Francis of Assisi, Brother Lawrence, John of the Cross, and many others. Denver Seminary students would often accompany Demarest to a Catholic monastery in Pecos, New Mexico, for lectures, Lauds, and the celebration of the Eucharist. The back cover of his book *Satisfy your Soul*, says, "Demarest clears away misunderstandings, offers safeguards against a nonbiblical Christian mysticism . . ." which for Demarest includes the practices of TM and Yoga.[385] He is saddened that many Christian mystics, these "spiritual masters," ignore or deny the need for personal conversion.

Eckhart, Meister: (1260–1327) German theologian, Dominican monk, philosopher, and mystic. He had pantheist ideas; was into the occult, Buddhism, and Hinduism; and he believed the human soul is one with God and not merely united to God. He expressed the idea of the divinity of the soul in saying, "As fire turns all that it touches into itself, so the birth of the Son of God in the soul turns us into God."[386] He said, "The core of the soul and the core of God are one" and, much

---

[384] See: Richard J. Foster and Emilie Griffin, ed., *Spiritual Classics* (New York: HarperOne, 2000), 320. This book is a Renovaré Resource for Spiritual Renewal.

[385] Bruce Demarest, *Satisfy your Soul: Restoring the Heart of Christian Spirituality* (Colorado Springs: NavPress, 1999), 149–151.

[386] William Ralph Inge, *Christian Mysticism: The Bampton Lectures, 1899: Considered in Eight Lectures Delivered before the University of Oxford* (London: Methuen & Co., 1899).

like the Quakers 300 years later, he referred to the divine Light within every human. He fits what is called "nondualistic" or, monistic mysticism (no essential difference between our soul and God).[387] Eckhart said, "I pray to God to make me free of God for my essential being is above God. . . . According to my unborn mode I have eternally been, am now, and shall eternally remain . . . I and God are one."[388] He referred to people penetrating into the "divine darkness." Eckhart influenced many mystics and philosophers over the centuries, including George Fox (founder of the Quakers), Carl Jung, Thomas Merton, and Aldous Huxley. Eckhart believed in reincarnation and denied Christ's substitutionary atonement. Richard Foster and many other mystic authors favorably quote him without any disclaimers.

Edwards, Tilden: (1939–) Episcopal priest, founder of the Shalem Institute for Spiritual Formation in Washington, DC. He refers to his institute and to contemplative prayer as "the Western bridge to Far Eastern spirituality." This institute is very ecumenical and syncretistic. An increasing number of evangelicals are now on such a bridge. Edwards called interfaith dialogue "the wider ecumenism." Edwards laments that rational thought "helped pave the way for the Reformation's 'justification by faith alone.'" Ruth Haley Barton studied at his institute. Richard Foster includes Edward's book *Spiritual Friend*, on his list of "excellent books on spirituality."[389] Even a Buddhist website includes an enlightening article written by Tilden Edwards which reveals much about his interspirituality.[390] This is a significant article you shouldn't miss!

Findley, James: (1943–) Former Trappist monk at the Abbey of Gethsemani, Kentucky, where Thomas Merton was his spiritual director. He earned his PhD from Fuller Seminary's Graduate School of Psychology. His writings include a lot about Merton, Christian meditation, and contemplation. Besides working as a clinical psychologist he hosts silent retreats and workshops.

---

[387] A review of C. F. Kelley's book *Meister Eckhart on Divine Knowledge* says: "It is also the greatest exegesis of Christian nondualism ever published." www.amazon.fr/Meister-Eckhart-Divine-Knowledge-Kelley/dp/0300020988

[388] "Meister Eckhart Sermon 52" in *The Essential Writings of Christian Mysticism,* ed. Bernard McGinn (New York: Random House, 2006), 442–443.

[389] See Brian Flynn, *Running Against the Wind* (Silverton, OR: Lighthouse Trails Publishing, 2007), 156–158.

[390] www.upanishad.org/dialogue/jesus_buddha.htm

Ford, Leighton: (1931–) President of Leighton Ford Ministries. Despite being Billy Graham's brother-in-law, he fervently promotes contemplative mysticism including all the historic mystics like Thomas Merton and Thomas Keating. He now believes that Catholics and Buddhists are in communion with the same God. He practices mantra-like praying several times a day.

Foster, Richard: (1942–) Quaker. Founded Renovaré. His book *Celebration of Discipline,* first appeared in 1978 and has a continuing widespread influence. He relies heavily upon the writings of a host of Catholic and Protestant mystics including Thomas Merton, Thomas Keating, Evelyn Underhill, Agnes Sanford, Francois Fenelon, Ignatius Loyola, Teresa of Ávila, Madame Guyon, Catherine of Sienna, Meister Eckhart (quite the heretic), Henri Nouwen, Tilden Edwards, M. Basil Pennington, Carl Jung, Julian of Norwich, Pierre Teilhard de Chardin, William Blake (steeped in the occult), just to mention a few. In fact, Loyola's *Spiritual Exercises* was a primary basis for *Celebration of Discipline.*

In *Celebration of Discipline,* Foster encourages us to read ancient Chinese mysticism of Lao-tse as well as Zarathustra of ancient Persia (Iran) who founded the Zoroastrian religion. Such reading serves to "guide us in the spiritual walk." Foster is promoting a vision of an all-inclusive community he thinks God is forming today, via the common ground of Christian mysticism. Foster is a big fan of the ecumenical Catholic monk, Thomas Merton, who held to universal salvation, believed that divinity inhabits every person on this globe, and ended up being more Buddhist than Christian. We heartily share with Richard Foster a desire for a greater in-depth walk with Jesus Christ and many of the "spiritual disciplines" he emphasizes are indeed helpful in our growth in grace. A friend of mine who has read most of Foster's books says Foster has cozied up too closely to Hindu philosophy in an attempt to make these disciplines "work." At Wheaton College I heard Foster tell students, "Meditative prayer ushers us into God's presence . . . mute language . . . opening ourselves to God's voice." He stressed that we learn from silent, meditative prayer. Foster is here describing the traditional mystical theory that God cannot really be known via the intellect and with words, but only by shutting down the mind with use of a mantra. Foster sounds much like what Pseudo–Dionysius taught so many hundreds of years ago.

Fox, George: (1624–1691), Founder of the Quakers. Fox was born the year Jacob Boehme died and was influenced by Boehme's writings. He claimed that all human souls have divine Inner Light, "that of God in everyone" as he phrased it. Tony Campolo, on page 199 of *The God of Intimacy and Action,* says, "George Fox, the founder of the Society of Friends, taught, in accord with what is written in John 1:9, that the Spirit of God is a sacred presence in every person who is born into the world."[391]

Fox, Matthew: (1940–) Defrocked Dominican scholar turned Episcopalian. Fox is now a priest of the San Francisco-based Episcopal Diocese of California. He was founder and president of the University of Creation Spirituality which, while it functioned, was "deep ecumenism" and rediscovery of Western mystical traditions along with Eastern and indigenous practices. He relies heavily on Meister Eckhart and likes Thomas Merton. He believes in "the cosmic Christ," instead of the historical Jesus. Wayne Boulton says, "Fox can draw freely from religions as archaic as Taoism and as primal as Lakota Indian spirituality, since their insights are assumed to be ultimately compatible with Christianity."[392] Boulton adds that Fox blurs the distinction between creature and creation, has no use for organized religion, and rejects the idea of original sin. Matthew Fox says "The Cosmic Christ is the Christian archetype for the divine image present in every being, indeed, every atom in the universe. It is the light in all things. It is also, with its incarnation in Jesus, the wounds in all things. Divinity is both the light and the wounds in all things. All beings, therefore, are other Christs. And every human is meant to be another Christ." Brennan Manning often quotes Matthew Fox. Fox once said: "The Black

---

[391] We note that John 1:9 does not say that Jesus indwells everyone. Scripture says that Jesus, the "light of men" (1:4) and "light of the world" (John 8:12; 9:5), gives light to everyone. There's the light of creation, natural conscience, and the Scriptures. Jesus is indeed "the true light" and not a counterfeit or just some human Eastern religious guru promising "enlightenment." Jesus' giving light to everyone (John 1:9) is connected in v. 12 with believing in him and receiving him. See also 3:16-21. In John 12:14 Jesus says, "I have come into the world as a light, so that no one who believes in me should stay in darkness." 2 Corinthians 6:16 states that only believers in Christ are temples of the living God, indwelt by God's Spirit. Other helpful texts on this topic include: Acts 2:38; 5:32; Romans 5:5; 8:9; John 7:39; 14:16-17; 1 John 3:24; 4:13. Only believers in Christ are anointed by God's Spirit: 2 Corinthians 1:21-22; 5:5; 1 John 2:20, 27.

[392] Wayne Boulton, *Christian Century*, April 1990, 428–32.

Madonna invites us into the dark . . . into our depths . . . where Divinity lies . . . where the true self lies."[393]

Fox advocates goddess worship and refers to the "divine feminine." In April of 2010 he led a seminar, "Earth Spirituality and Mystical Tradition," held at a Unitarian Universalist Church near Washington, DC, sponsored by the Shalem Institute for Spiritual Formation (See Tilden Edwards on this institute). A Catholic blog says this seminar was "a melding of Celtic spirituality, goddess worship, panentheism (which posits that God interpenetrates every part of nature, but also transcends nature), environmental activism, and a political rejection of American empire."[394] He also said: "We've been told by bad preachers that Jesus died on the cross for your sins." Check out this short interview[395] with Fox before his expulsion from Catholicism in which he discusses the widespread influence of Thomas Merton.

Guyon, Madame Jeanne-Marie: (1648–1717) Wealthy French Catholic mystic aristocrat involved in "Quietism." She ended up with a type of pantheism closer to South Asian religions than to Christianity. Richard Foster praises her and often quotes her. She once said, "Make use of scripture to quiet your mind. First read a passage . . . once you sense the Lord's presence, the content of what you read is no longer important . . . you are reading to turn your mind from the outward things to the deep parts of your being . . . to experience the presence of your Lord." See Foster's latest book, *Sanctuary of the Soul,* for more details about Guyon.[396] She also held to ideas of perfectionism where

---

[393] Matthew Fox says: "The Black Madonna is Dark and calls us to the darkness. . . . Darkness is something we need to get used to again—the "Enlightenment" has deceived us into being afraid of the dark and distant from it. Light switches are illusory. They feed the notion that we can "master nature" (Descartes' false promise) and overcome all darkness with a flick of our finger. Meister Eckhart observes that "the ground of the soul is dark." Thus to avoid the darkness is to live superficially, cut off from one's ground, one's depth. The Black Madonna invites us into the dark and therefore into our depths. This is what the mystics call the "inside" of things, the essence of things. This is where Divinity lies. It is where the true self lies."
See: janicemasonsteevesartwork.blogspot.com/2010/02/black-madonna-my-journey.html

[394] wdtprs.com/blog/2010/05/matthew-fox-is-still-alive-and-is-still-an-idiot/

[395] www.youtube.com/watch?v=72-ByOYQtxU&feature=related

[396] On pages 71–72 of Foster's *Sanctuary of the Soul* he quotes Guyon as saying, "We are not reading the Scripture to gain some understanding but to 'turn your mind from outward things to the deep parts of your being. You are not there to

sin is impossible. David Cloud quotes her as saying, "So was my soul lost in God, who communicated to it His qualities," then she spoke of being plunged "wholly into God's own divine essence."[397] She taught that we can know God by entering a mindless, meditative state in which we can eventually merge with Christ. She believed we could claim God's healing; she practiced kything (mind reading); and thought she was inspired in her writings, practiced automatic writing, and believed in sinless perfection. Mystic writer Evelyn Underhill refers to Guyon as a "medium." Gene Edwards, writing an introduction to one of her books, says, "The contents of a few of her writings can literally curl the hair of an evangelical. She was, first of all, a Roman Catholic. . . . Her eccentricities I ignore. . . ." and says she was "a woman who saw Jesus Christ in virtually every circumstance of life." It's interesting that near the end of her life Guyon wrote about being justified before God by grace alone without works.[398]

Huxley, Aldous: (1894–1963) British agnostic mystic, part of the famous Huxley family of agnostic biologists. He lived the last part of his life in the United States. Thomas Merton read one of Huxley's books, *Ends and Means,* thus introducing Merton to mysticism.

John of the Cross: (1542–1591) Spanish priest and mystic involved in the Counter Reformation. He worked closely with Teresa of Ávila. He was very dedicated to the Virgin Mary. He was highly ascetic and often abused his body almost to the point of death, going through what he termed "the dark night of the soul." His famous book by this title mainly deals with purgation, the first step in the classical mystical way. This involves killing all desire, thought, imagination, affection, memory, intellect, and will; and is a thick and heavy cloud upon the

---

learn or to read, but . . . to experience the presence of your Lord! . . . The Lord is found *only* within your spirit, in the recesses of your being, in the holy of Holies." I wonder if Foster completely agrees with Guyon since in this same book, 73–77, he adds two other ways "of entering the experience of beholding the Lord," namely: 1) Reflecting the glory of the Lord in nature; 2) by means of worship music (so long as it is not too loud or exciting, he says).

[397] logosresourcepages.org/Believers/guyon.htm

[398] en.wikipedia.org/wiki/Jeanne_Guyon Guyon expressed this thought near the end of her life, as found in her autobiography. Moody Press printed this years ago (no date). See also: www.ccel.org/ccel/guyon/auto which mentions her ideas of *sola gracia* and *sola fide*. At times, we need to remember that only Christ knows who his sheep are.

soul keeping it in affliction and withdrawn from God. The next step in the mystical way is illumination where God floods your soul with his love. The final stage is union, where the soul is united with God in perfection, and means you can skip purgatory since you've already suffered enough on earth. Foster and many other mystics love his writings.[399] John once said, "The soul must lose entirely its human knowledge and human feelings, in order to receive Divine knowledge and Divine feelings."[400]

Johnston, William: (1925–2010) A Jesuit missionary who lived in Japan. Author of *Christian Zen*. He decried the "tyranny of dogma" in Western religion and advocated ecumenical mysticism as the alternative for bridging East and West and all religions. He was an expert at mixing Catholicism and the religions of Asia. He said contemplative meditation "goes beyond ordinary reasoning" and it enters into "the silence, without words, without reasoning, without thinking . . . into the nothingness, into the emptiness, into the darkness."

Julian of Norwich: (1342–1423) Catholic mystic in England. Thomas Merton called her "the greatest of the English mystics." She thought God is all love, that there is no wrath in him, and that sin is necessary and not shameful and not to be confessed. For her, sins were but disguised virtue. She held to the controversial belief in God as mother as much as father. She believed that God not only lives in *all* people, but that our inmost being (i.e., our soul) is divine. She wrote, "And I saw no difference between God and our Substance: but as it were all God."[401] She lived during the time of the influential, anonymous book, *The Cloud of Unknowing*. Richard Foster and Thomas Merton love to quote her, as do many other Christian mystics.

Jung, Carl: (1875–1961) Swiss psychiatrist with a huge and growing influence on Christians, especially those with leanings toward Christian mysticism. Jung was especially interested in the mysticism of Ignatius

---

[399] See Richard J. Foster, *Celebration of Discipline: The Path to Spiritual Growth* (HarperSanFrancisco, 1988), 102–05. See also: Richard Foster, *Devotional Classics*, 33–39.

[400] William Ralph Inge, *Christian Mysticism: The Bampton Lectures, 1899: Considered in Eight Lectures Delivered before the University of Oxford.* (London: Methuen & Co., 1899), 209.

[401] cac.org/julian-of-norwich-part-iii-2015-07-22/

Loyola. He is quoted by Foster.[402] Jung was obsessed with the occult and eroticism and studied Hinduism and other eastern religions. He studied pagan cults of Mithras and concluded their idea of self-deification could repair the damage done by Christianity. He saw himself as a spiritist. He was anti-Christian, a wolf among lambs if there ever was one, as seen in his letter to Freud. He was bent on changing or eliminating Christianity, which he saw as a myth.

Religion was for him a useful and necessary myth.[403] Jung thought it regrettable that God lacked a shadow side, thinking that good must be integrated with evil, "the spirit of darkness" as he termed it, to reach wholeness.[404] He thought all religions were imaginary but useful. He was influenced by Swedenborg and Jakob Böhme. Jung wrote at times under the guidance of a demon spirit guide. He wrote his doctoral thesis on parapsychology, and was involved in séances with his mother and two female cousins. He was also involved in alchemy, fortune telling, and channeling spirits. Jung taught we all have a "collective soul" as the Divine Child and our "true self" as opposed to our "false self." Jung saw the true self, or Divine Child, as the Aryan god within, perhaps the sun god or even Mithras. The "true self" is connected to all other humans in a "collective unconscious." Noted Harvard professor and clinical psychologist, Richard Noll, writes about the Jungian theory and movement, noting how Jung favored producing a master race, using people of Aryan heritage. [405] On page 215 of Noll's book, he also notes that Jung believed that "by contacting and merging with the god within, true personality transformation would then follow." In 1997 Noll wrote again about Carl Jung, *The Aryan Christ: The Secret Life of Carl Jung*. Anglican priest, Richard Kew, wrote a helpful review of this book that I highly recommend.[406] Jung's theories continue to exert an enormous influence on psychological, religious and spiritual thinking today. Kew's review says, "Jung is at least one of the midwives of the new age, while providing a veneer of respectability to occultism in sundry forms."

It is amazing that so many Christians are fond of Jung and his ideas, especially in light of his involvement in Spiritism; his self-deification;

---

[402] Richard Foster, *Celebration of Discipline*, 15.
[403] www.psychoheresy-aware.org/jungleg.html (A significant article).
[404] C. G. Jung, *Psychology and Religion: West and East, The Collected Works of C. G. Jung, Vol. 11* (Princeton University Press, 1958).
[405] Richard Noll, *The Jung Cult: Origins of a Charismatic Movement* (Glencoe, IL: Free Press Paperbacks, 1994).
[406] touchstonemag.com/archives/article.php?id=11–04–052–b

his racism and anti-Semitism; his seeing of all religion as an evil myth; and his bent on destroying Christianity. Jung himself stated his psychology was rooted in ancient Gnosticism.[407]

For a quick analysis and evaluation of Carl Jung read this article.[408] For a more in-depth, thoroughly researched study of Carl Jung, see this significant article by Ed Hird, Anglican minister of North Vancouver.[409]

Keating, Thomas: (1923–) Trappist monk, working closely with William Meninger and Basil Pennington at the abbot of St. Joseph in Massachusetts. They promoted the "centering prayer" method of contemplative prayer in 1975. In 1984 Keating cofounded Contemplative Outreach, Ltd., which is interreligious, ecumenical, and international, an ecumenical spiritual network that promotes mysticism including the dangerous Hindu Yogic Kundalini Energy. Kundalini deals with psychic energy at the base of the spine. It is called the serpent and often results in demonic manifestations. Keating has greatly influenced many people including mystics such as Henri Nouwen, Richard Foster, and Brennan Manning. He promoted Transcendental Meditation, Zen, and Yoga, which Bruce Demarest says "may involve traffic with dark, spiritual powers."[410] Keating and Pennington endorse the book *Meditations on the Tarot.* (Tarot is a deck of cards used in divination and fortune telling.) Like Carl Jung, Keating talks about finding one's True Self, saying that God and our True Self are not separate![411] Keating quotes Freud and follows the ideas of Carl Jung. Keating says: "God is not the fearful God of the Old Testament." He thinks contemplative prayer leads to divine union, i.e., sharing God's divinity. Contemplative prayer, he says, deepens our knowledge that we are already free and that we belong to God. Concerning his ecumenicity and syncretism, one former New Ager says of him: "When Keating was beginning this journey at St. Joseph's Abbey, Spencer, Massachusetts, he invited Buddhist monks and a former monk who had

---

[407] www.gnosis.org/gnostic-jung/Jung-and-Gnosis.html
[408] www.newswithviews.com/West/marsha5.htm
[409] www3.telus.net/st_simons/CarlJungPaper.pdf
[410] Bruce Demarest, *Satisfy your Soul: Restoring the Heart of Christian Spirituality* (Colorado Springs: NavPress, 1999), 149–51.
[411] In other words, Keating is nondualistic or monistic. See: www.newagedeception.com/new/free–resources/4–7–reasons–why–the–errors–in–the–centering–prayer–movement–should–not–be–in–your–parish.html

become a Transcendental Meditation teacher to give sessions to the monks at a retreat at his monastery."[412]

Kelley, Thomas: (1893–1941) He was born into a Quaker family and became a philosophy professor. While studying in Hawaii he did advanced research in Eastern philosophies. He liked Meister Eckhart's writings. As most Quakers, he believed each person has a divine center, a light within us all, a speaking voice.

Kelsey, Morton: (1917–2001) Episcopalian priest who, like most mystics, believed God dwells within everyone's soul. He saw little difference between New Age practices and mystic Christianity.[413] He was open to any methods that help us in our "inner journey." His extensive writings include *Christo-Psychology* (integrates Carl Jung's ideas with Christianity) and *Encounter with God*. Kelsey is favorably quoted by Richard Foster.

Kidd, Sue Monk: (1948–) A Sunday school coworker handed her a book by Thomas Merton, which started her on the mystic trail including Catholic retreat centers and monasteries. She is quoted favorably by Richard Foster. Kidd endorses Dallas Willard's book *The Spirit of the Disciplines*. She wrote the foreword of Henri Nouwen's *With Open Hands*. Sue Monk Kidd says, "We are one with all people. We are part of them and they are part of us. . . . When we encounter another person . . . we should walk as if we were upon holy ground."[414] In other places she says she worships the goddess Sophia. Obviously she believes God dwells in absolutely everyone. She states this clearly in her book *When the Heart Waits*: "The soul is something more than something to win or save. It is the seat and repository of the inner Divine, the God–image, the truest part of us."[415] In her book *The Dance of the Dissident Daughter* she says, "The ultimate authority of my life is not the Bible. . . . It is not something written by men and frozen in time. It is not from a source outside myself. My ultimate authority is

---

[412] christiananswersforthenewage.org/Articles_KeatingLecture.html

[413] Kelsey says: "You can find most of the New Age practices in the depth of Christianity. . . . I believe that the Holy One lives in every soul." ("In the Spirit of the Early Christians," *Common Boundary*, Jan./Feb. 1992, 19).

[414] Sue Monk Kidd, *When the Heart Waits* (New York: HarperCollins, 1990), 228.

[415] Ibid., 233.

the divine voice in my own soul. Period." [416] She goes on to say that when she traveled to Crete with a group of women they entered a cave and sang to "the Goddess Skoteini, Goddess of the Dark."[417] She also writes: "I came to know myself as an embodiment of Goddess."[418]

L'Engle, Madeleine: (1918–2007) Beloved writer. She was a part of Richard Foster's Renovaré organization. Her universalism is obvious in this quote of hers: "All will be redeemed in God's fullness of time, all, not just the small portion of the population who have been given the grace to know and accept Christ. All the strayed and stolen sheep. All the little lost ones."[419]

Manning, Brennan: (1934–2013) Former Franciscan priest. In 1982 he left the priesthood and married. He often cited Thomas Merton, William Shannon, Henri Nouwen, Basil Pennington, and many other mystics. He believed in the divinity of all people, universal salvation for all, and rejected the need for a bloody sacrifice.[420] He urged us to "listen to people in other denominations and religions." During "centering prayer" he urged people to stop thinking about God: "Enter into the great silence of God. . . . Choose a single, sacred word . . . repeat the sacred word inwardly, slowly, and often." Manning popularized Jungian Psychotherapy. In *Abba's Child* Manning said Dr. Beatrice Bruteau is a "trustworthy guide to contemplative consciousness." But Bruteau states: "We have realized ourselves as the Self that says only I Am." Manning often quoted extreme liberal mystic Matthew Fox.

Merton, Thomas: (1915–1968) Merton was a Catholic Trappist Monk. His mother was a Quaker. He highly esteemed and corresponded with skeptic Aldous Huxley and wrote his master's thesis on William Blake (see bio on Blake). In the 1960s Merton read Eckhart and Zen poetry

---

[416] Sue Monk Kidd, *The Dance of the Dissident Daughter* (New York: HarperCollins, 1996), 76–78.

[417] Ibid., 93.

[418] Ibid., 161.

[419] https://en.wikiquote.org/wiki/Madeleine_L'Engle

[420] On pages 58–59 of Brennan Manning's book *Above All* he says: "The god whose moods alternate between graciousness and fierce anger . . . the god who exacts the last drop of blood from his Son so that his just anger, evoked by sin, may be appeased, is not the God revealed by and in Jesus Christ. And if he is not the God of Jesus, he does not exist."

which radically changed him. He popularized Jungian Psychotherapy. Merton became a Catholic monk at age twenty-six. As a Catholic he believed we are justified by both faith and works and once referred to Protestantism's stress on *sola fide* (faith alone) as dangerous.[421] As a good Catholic, he stated: "God wills that all graces come to men through Mary."[422] He was highly influenced by Hinduism, Zen Buddhism, Muslim Sufism,[423] and Taoism and Vedanta (Hinduistic). He urged us to tell all people they are already united to God with divinity at their center.[424] He once said, "I intend to become as good a Buddhist as I can." Just before his death Merton told John Moffitt: "Zen and Christianity are the same."[425] Virtually all Christian mystics highly esteem Merton and quote him freely. But Bruce Demarest of Denver Seminary says of Merton, "Merton . . . suspected that Christian contemplation and Zen meditation pursue the same goal—the unmasking of the false or illusory self and the discovery of the true self. . . . Merton saw no contradiction between Buddhism and Christianity . . . when Merton delves into Eastern religions . . . he becomes unreliable. . . . The Dalai Lama even says, 'Buddhism is Buddhism, and not Christianity.'"[426]

Everyone should read this website article about Merton.[427] Merton thought highly of Yoga and Zen. Foster mentions about Merton that "his interest in contemplation led him to investigate prayer forms in Eastern religion. Zen masters from Asia regarded him as the preeminent authority on their kind of prayer in the United States."[428] For many

---

[421] *Cunningham, Lawrence, ed., Thomas Merton: Spiritual Master, The Essential Writings* (New York: Paulist Press: 1992), 155.

[422] Thomas Merton, *New Seeds of Contemplation* (KY: The Abbey of Gethsemani, 1961), 168.

[423] Check out this significant website about Islamic Sufi: www.wikiislam.net/wiki/Sufi See also: en.wikipedia.org/wiki/Sufism

[424] Merton's view of humanity led him to write, "It is a glorious destiny to be a member of the human race. . . . If only they (people) could all see themselves as they really are. I suppose the big problem would be that we would bow down and worship each other. . . . At the center of our being is a point of nothingness which is untouched by sin and by illusion, a point of pure truth. . . . This little point . . . is the pure glory of God in us. It is in everybody." (From Merton's book *Conjectures of a Guilty Bystander*, 157–58).

[425] www.thomasmertonsociety.org/altany2.htm

[426] Bruce Demarest, *Satisfy your Soul: Restoring the Heart of Christian Spirituality* (Colorado Springs: NavPress, 1999), 276–77.

[427] www.apostasyalert.org/Merton.htm

[428] Richard J. Foster and Emilie Griffin, ed., *Spiritual Classics* (New York: HarperOne, 2000), 17.

years Merton was in contact with a Muslim Sufi cleric, Abdul Aziz. Merton thought the monks of all religions share the same light as he did—and he was probably right! Foster cites Merton favorably and says Merton "has perhaps done more than any other twentieth-century figure to make the life of prayer widely known and understood."[429] In another book, Foster says, "I am constantly pleased at how applicable Merton's writings are to the nonmonastic world in which most of us live."[430]

Moreland, J. P.: (1948–) Professor of philosophy, Talbot School of Theology at Biola University. He promotes contemplative spirituality, including the use of a mantra. He loves using Catholic retreat centers and encourages gazing at pictures and statues of Jesus. He fears that evangelicals are overcommitted to the Bible in thinking that it is the sole authority for faith and practice. His book *Kingdom Triangle: Recover the Christian Mind, Renovate the Soul, Restore the Spirit is Power*, strongly promotes traditional contemplative spirituality and the writings of Richard Foster and Henri Nouwen.

Nouwen, Henri: (1932–1996) Originally from the Netherlands, Catholic priest, universalist (all will be saved), influenced by Eastern religions,[431] psychologist, theologian, and mystic who taught at Yale, Notre Dame, and Harvard. Toward the end of his life he was a pastor in Toronto to a group of people with developmental disabilities, a ministry he called his "true home." A 1994 survey of Protestant church leaders in the United States showed that Nouwen was second only to Billy Graham in influence. Nouwen was a friend to so many, and as one person writes, "He was so loving, so listening, and so generous with his time and his presence." Many of us thoroughly enjoy reading Nouwen, a man who enjoyed people, music, nature, and was knowledgeable about and cared for what was occurring in the world.[432] Ravi Zacharias once referred to Henri Nouwen as one of the greatest saints in recent

---

[429] Ibid.

[430] Richard Foster, *Devotional Classics* (HarperSanFrancisco, 1993), 66.

[431] Nouwen wrote the foreword to Thomas Ryan's book *Disciplines for Christian Living*, saying: "The author shows a wonderful openness to the gifts of Buddhism, Hinduism, and Moslem religion. He discovers their great wisdom for the spiritual life of the Christian and does not hesitate to bring that wisdom home."

[432] Henri Nouwen, *Sabbatical Journey* (New York: The Crossroad Publishing Company, 1998), vii.

memory. If this is so, we need to take a longer look at his life and beliefs.

While lauding and trying to follow his example of compassion and caring, some evangelicals have considerable concerns about his nonbiblical ideas of universal salvation and the common mystical heresy that God dwells in the depth of every human being.[433] In his book *Life of the Beloved* he wrote to a secular Jewish friend and said, "We are the beloved," "children of God," "God's chosen ones," "precious in God's eyes," and have eternal life. Nouwen said it was his call in life to help everyone claim his or her way to God. By the end of his life Nouwen had rejected the need for evangelism and missions.[434] This same book has some good advice, to be sure, including recognizing the blessings all around us—the blossoming trees and flowers, music, paintings, along with the words of encouragement and affection that come to us. But tragically, like most mystics, Nouwen ignored or repudiated the exclusive biblical message about sin and repentance, and the need to know Christ personally, and to receive by faith alone the full pardon and sonship that Christ provided for us on the cross. In his attempt to promote religious ecumenism he defined "diabolic" as meaning dividing, whereas "devil" actually means slanderer or accuser (see page 135 of *Life of the Beloved*). He said, "Wherever the Spirit works, divisions vanish and inner as well as outer unity manifests itself." It is true we need to attempt to live at peace with all people and to endeavor to keep the unity of the Spirit. But Jesus also said he came not to bring peace but a sword. (i.e., opposition from nonbelievers or carnal Christians).

Peck, M. Scott: (1936–2005) While studying at a Quaker seminary he read from the Upanishads and Zen Buddhism and realized he already was a mystic and called himself a Zen Buddhist at age 18. He was an

---

[433] Henry J. M. Nouwen, *Here and Now: Living in the Spirit* (New York: The Crossroad Publishing Company, 1994), 22: "The God who dwells in our inner sanctuary is the same as the one who dwells in the inner sanctuary of each human being." Nouwen called our souls "sacred centers" in *Bread for the Journey: A Daybook of Wisdom and Faith* (New York: HarperCollins, 1997), Jan. 15.

[434] Henri Nouwen said: "Today I personally believe that while Jesus came to open the door to God's house, all human beings can walk through that door, whether they know about Jesus or not. Today I see it as my call to help every person claim his or her own way to God." *Sabbatical Journey* (New York: The Crossroad Publishing Company, 1998), 50–51.

army psychiatrist for many years. He was profane, alcoholic, and took pride in use of pornography. He believed in open marriage, seeing no problem with sex outside of marriage. He denied Jesus was sinless and denied the biblical gospel of redemption. He was baptized in a liberal Christian church but never quit saying he was a "New Ager," thought Zen Buddhism prepared him for Christianity, that Zen should be taught in every fifth grade class. In his book *Further Along the Road Less Traveled*, he said, "Christianity's greatest sin is to think that other religions are not saved," and called the story of Adam and Eve a myth. On page 64 he said "Buddha and Christ were not different men." He thought that people of all religions would be found in heaven, that the "gates of hell" are wide open so that anyone can choose to walk out at any time. Peck taught that everything is relative, that we need to reject the religion of our parents and that we should not be dogmatic about any religious truth (*The Road Less Traveled*, 181–182). Peck said the New Age movement "is potentially very godly and its virtues are absolutely enormous." He said man can become God. On page 258 of *The Road Less Traveled*, he wrote: "God wants us to become Himself (or Herself or Itself). We are growing toward godhood. God is the goal of evolution. It is God who is the source of the evolutionary force and God who is the destination." Peck advocated a one world government.

Pennington, M. Basil: (1931–2005) In the 1960s he, along with Thomas Keating and William Meninger, helped popularize the ancient practice of "centering prayer" at Saint Joseph's Abby, a Trappist monastery at Spencer, Massachusetts. Pennington and Keating also endorsed participation in Transcendental Meditation, Zen, and Yoga.[435] One Catholic blog says that Thomas Keating endorsed the book *Meditations on the Tarot*. Both Keating and Pennington promoted the

---

[435] In their book *Finding Grace at the Center*, 5–6, Thomas Keating and Basil Pennington say: "We should not hesitate to take the fruit of the age-old wisdom of the East and 'capture' it for Christ. . . . Many Christians who take their prayer life seriously have been greatly helped by Yoga, Zen, TM and similar practices. . . ." No wonder a growing number of Catholics are saying the "centering prayer" of these Trappist monks is really New Age. Why then does Adele Calhoun attempt to deny this? (See her book *Spiritual Disciplines Handbook*, 208). Keating and other Catholic monks got involved with Zen Buddhist and Hindu meditative practices, fusing Eastern spirituality with Catholicism. Keating says they are following Thomas Merton's example who was also a Cistercian Monk who had pushed the boundaries writing about Zen.

use of tarot cards.[436] Pennington was a universalist who thought hell is but separation from God in this life. He thought the meditative practices of all religions lead to the same God.[437] He wrote *True Self, False Self.*

Rohr, Richard: (1943–) A very ecumenical Franciscan priest in New Mexico. He says Buddha and Christ are the same. He is a specialist on the Enneagram, an ancient tool for studying personality types. He says, "This is a very ancient Christian tool for the discernment of spirits, the struggle with our capital sin, our *false* self, and the encounter with our True Self in God." He wrote *Everything Belongs: The Gift of Contemplative Prayer.* One Catholic website, Catholicculture.org, strongly rejects Rohr and his heresies.[438] Apparently Rohr rejects the idea of hell, makes fun of pro-lifers, resists calling God "Father," and rejects the idea of the substitutionary atonement of Christ, saying his death was not necessary for salvation.

Scazzero, Peter: (1956–) Contemporary contemplative mystic. His book and seminar is called *Emotionally Healthy Spirituality.* He emphasizes the "Daily Office" with set times of prayer, and knowing your "true self." He favorably quotes Eckhart, Teresa of Ávila, Thomas Merton, Richard Foster, Dallas Willard, Brennan Manning, M. Scott Peck, Basil Pennington, Henri Nouwen, Tilden Edwards, and many other mystics. He says the following three books have helped him understand about this kind of wordless contemplation: Thomas Keating's *Open Mind, Open Heart,* Cynthia Bourgeault's *Centering Prayer and Inner Awakening,* and Basil Pennington's *Centered Living.*

Shannon, William Henry: (1917–) Thomas Merton's biographer. Rejects the God of the Old Testament.

Sweet, Leonard: (1961–) Sweet says the "old teachings" of Christianity must be replaced with the new teachings of "the new light," which draw from "ancient teachings" (i.e., the Desert Fathers and other mystics of the middle ages). He's a theologically liberal Methodist

---

[436] acatholiclife.blogspot.com/2007/05/errors–of–centering–prayer.html

[437] "It is my sense, from having meditated with persons from many different traditions (including Eastern religions), that in the silence we experience a deep unity. When we go beyond the portals of the rational mind into the experience, there is only one God to be experienced" (Pennington, *Centered Living,* 192).

[438] www.catholicculture.org/culture/library/view.cfm?recnum=6819

clergyman and professor. Sweet coauthored a book with the Emerging Church's Brian McLaren. On page 130 of his book *Quantum Spirituality*, Sweet writes, "One can be a faithful disciple of Jesus Christ without denying the flickers of the sacred in followers of Yahweh, or Kali, or Krishna." Note: Kali is the Hindu goddess of destruction and Krishna is the incarnation of the Hindu god Vishnu.

Taylor, Brian C.: (1951–) Rector of St. Michael and All Angels Episcopal church in Albuquerque, New Mexico. He is author of several books about contemplative spirituality including *Becoming Christ* and *Setting the Gospel Free*.[439] He is theologically liberal, denying the substitutionary atonement of Christ. He practices Benedictine Spirituality.

Thomas, Gary: (1961–) Professor, Western Seminary, Portland, OR. In his book *Sacred Pathways,* Gary Thomas tells people how to draw near to God: "Choose a word (Jesus or Father, for example) as a focus for contemplative prayer. Repeat the word silently in your mind for a set amount of time (say, twenty minutes) until your heart seems to be repeating the word by itself. . . ."[440] This book also introduced us to the mystic Mary Anne McPherson Oliver and her book *Conjugal Spirituality*.[441] In his book *Sacred Parenting,* Thomas devotes an entire chapter to mystic contemplative spirituality, where we "seize heaven and invite God's presence into our lives" (pp. 58–59). In this chapter he mentions two influential authors in his life: Teresa of Ávila and Frank Buchman, founder of Moral Rearmament. In the 1930s Buchman admired Hitler and he was involved in both mysticism and the occult.

---

[439] The book's synopsis says: "*Setting the Gospel Free* is an exploration of Christian faith and practice from an experiential and contemplative point of view. The book integrates elements of Buddhist techniques of mindful awareness and contemplative prayer as a means of fully experiencing Christian faith in our daily lives."

[440] Gary Thomas, *Sacred Pathways: Discover Your Soul's Path to God* (Grand Rapids: Zondervan, 2010), 185.

[441] Oliver suggests we include Hindu Upanishads and erotic Tantric writings in our religious practices. She suggests couples practice "Taoist visualizations and meditations, accompanied by breathing exercises" as well as the use of Yin and Yang movements. Lighthouse Trails says her book *Conjugal Spirituality* "is a primer on tantric sex (the union of mystical experiences and sexual activity) and other mystical practices." See: www.lighthousetrailsresearch.com/blog/?p=4803 On "tantra" or "tantric" see Wikipedia article: en.wikipedia.org/wiki/Tantra which shows us how incompatible it is with Christianity.

In this same book he favorably quotes Basil Pennington, a Catholic priest involved with the occult and who mixed Eastern religion with Christianity and promoted Yoga, Zen, TM, and similar practices. Although Gary Thomas has a lot of great insights in his writings, he seems to be increasingly influenced by the wrong kind of mysticism.

Underhill, Evelyn: (1875–1941) British Anglican, practiced and wrote a lot about mysticism. Her most influential book is *Mysticism*, written in 1911. She wrote about the "inward light" that all people find at their centers which she calls "the ineffable splendour of God." A Wikipedia article about her says, "More than any other person, she was responsible for introducing the forgotten authors of medieval and Catholic spirituality to a largely Protestant audience and the lives of eastern mystics to the English speaking world." She is quoted quite favorably by Richard Foster in both *Celebration of Discipline* and *Devotional Classics*.

Vanier, Jean: (1928–) Canadian Christian mystic. He founded L'Arche, a ministry to the disabled, where Henri Nouwen lived and ministered during his last ten years. Vanier is involved in interspirituality. He calls Hindu Mahatma Gandhi a great prophet and "a man sent by God." His idea of "opening doors to other religions" is to help people develop their own faith, irrespective of their religion.[442]

Vaswig, William: (1931–2011) Was codirector with Richard Foster of Renovaré. He was a former Lutheran pastor. He studied at Shalem Institute for Spiritual Formation in Washington, DC, (See "Tilden Edwards"), which is very ecumenical and syncretistic, an intentional blending of Christian mysticism with Eastern religions like Hinduism and Buddhism.

Willard, Dallas: (1935–2013) Was a professor of philosophy, University of Southern California and lectured at UCLA and other schools. He served on the board of Biola University. As mentioned before in a footnote, Dallas Willard was critical of "common and prescribed activities in Christian circles" and mentioned Bible study, prayer, and church attendance. He said these "generally have little

---

[442] Carolyn Whitney-Brown, ed., *Jean Vanier: Essential Writings* (New York: Orbis Books, 2008), 8.

effect for soul transformation, as is obvious to any observer."[443] He said nearly the same again in *The Great Omission*, 2006. Some evangelical Christians doubt Willard understood the biblical gospel. In chapter three of his book *The Spirit of the Disciplines* Willard asked, "Why is it that we look upon salvation as a moment that began our religious life instead of the daily life we receive from God?"[444] He apparently saw no need for the new birth experience and replaced initial conversion with discipleship. At any rate, he seemed to hold to pluralism, saying you can be in another religion and be a Christ-follower without being a Christian, whether or not you even know about Christ. Willard followed the typical pattern of Christian mystics in his love for the writings of universalists like mystics Meister Eckhart, Thomas Merton, and Henri Nouwen, all of whom were highly influenced by Eastern Religions.

Yancey, Philip: (1949–) Popular Christian author, editor at large for *Christianity Today*. He liked Brennan Manning and considered him to be his spiritual director. Yancey is a strong promoter of Christian mysticism. He quotes Meister Eckhart and recommends Thomas Merton. Yancey longs for unity between all religions, saying, "Perhaps our day calls for a new kind of ecumenical movement: not of doctrine, nor even of religious unity, but one that builds on what Jews, Christians, and Muslims hold in common. . . . Indeed, Jews, Christians, and Muslims have much in common."[445]

---

[443] Dallas Willard, "Spiritual Disciplines, Spiritual Formation and the Restoration of the Soul," *Journal of Psychology and Theology*, 26/1/1998.

[444] rcwollan.wordpress.com/tag/prodigal-son/

[445] From a 2004 interview with Yancey in *Whosoever*.

Selected Bibliography

These are books in my library that I have used for researching Christian mysticism. They range from theologically liberal to ultraconservative, from mystic to nonmystic; and they include authors who are Catholics, Quakers, and others.

Anonymous. *Cloud of Unknowing and Book of Privy Counseling.* New York: Image Books, 1973.

Baker, Howard. *Soul Keeping: Ancient Paths of Spiritual Direction.* Colorado Springs: NavPress, 1998.

Barton, Ruth Haley. *Invitation to Solitude and Silence: Experiencing God's Transforming Presence.* Downers Grove, IL: InterVarsity Press, 2004.

Calhoun, Adele Ahlberg. *Spiritual Disciplines Handbook: Practices That Transform Us.* Downers Grove, IL: InterVarsity Press, 2005.[446]

Campolo, Tony. *How to be Pentecostal Without Speaking in Tongues.* Dallas, TX: Word Publishing, 1991.

Campolo, Tony, and Mary Albert Darling. *The God of Intimacy and Action: Reconnecting Ancient Spiritual Practices, Evangelism, and Justice.* San Francisco, CA: Jossey-Bass, 2007.[447]

Cloud, David W. *Contemplative Mysticism: A Powerful Ecumenical Bond.* Port Huron, MI: Way of Life Literature, 2008.

———. *The New Age Tower of Babel.* Port Huron, MI: Way of Life Literature, Fourth Edition, June 2010.

---

[446] On page 144 of this book, along with many other pages about demonization, Calhoun shows the importance of discernment and how to "call upon God to move on someone who is caught up in dark things."

[447] On page 3, Campolo says that through contemplation one is born again and really gets to know Jesus. Mystical Christianity frees us from destructive legalism and scholastic Christianity "which can reduce faith to theological propositions . . . a loveless religion."

Corduan, Winfried. *Mysticism: An Evangelical Option?* Grand Rapids: Zondervan Publishing House, 1991.[448]

Cunningham, Lawrence, ed. *Thomas Merton: Spiritual Master, The Essential Writings.* Paulist Press: 1992.[449]

Demarest, Bruce. *Satisfy Your Soul.* Colorado Springs: NavPress, 1999.[450]

Eerdmans' Handbook to the History of Christianity. Grand Rapids, MI: Eerdmans, 1977.

England, Randy. *The Unicorn in the Sanctuary: The Impact of the New Age Movement on the Catholic Church.* Rockford, IL: Tan Books, 1991.[451]

Ferm, Vergilius. *Living Schools of Religion.* Ames, Iowa: Littlefield, Adams & Co., 1958.[452]

Flynn, Brian. *Running Against the Wind.* Silverton, OR: Lighthouse Trails Publishing, 2007.[453]

Ford, Leighton. *The Attentive Life: Discerning God's Presence in All Things.* Downers Grove, IL: InterVarsity Press, 2008.[454]

Foster, Richard J. *Celebration of Discipline: The Path to Spiritual Growth.* HarperSanFrancisco, 1998.

———. *Prayer: Finding the Heart's True Home.* Kent, Great Britain: Hodder & Stoughton, 1992.

---

[448] Corduan is professor of philosophy and religion at Taylor University in Upland, Indiana.

[449] The foreword is by Patrick Hart who served as Thomas Merton's secretary.

[450] Demarest recently retired from teaching at Denver Seminary.

[451] England, a Catholic attorney, writes this well-researched book as a warning about "Christian" mysticism whose followers he sees as "Catholic New Agers." He quotes G. K. Chesterton who decried the religion of worshiping the "Inner Light," the god supposedly within us all. He sees visualization as "probably the single most important New Age technique and basis for witchcraft."

[452] This contains helpful background about Hinduism and Quakerism as well as monasticism and mysticism.

[453] Flynn's book is excellent but nobody now knows what's happened to the author.

[454] Leighton Ford is Billy Graham's brother-in-law, and fervently promotes contemplative mysticism including all the historic mystics like Thomas Merton and Thomas Keating. He now believes that Catholics and Buddhists are in communion with the same God.

———. *Sanctuary of the Soul: Journey into Meditative Prayer.* Downers Grove, IL: InterVarsity Press, 2011.

———. *Streams of Living Water: Celebrating the Great Traditions of Christ.* HarperSanFrancisco, 2001.

Foster, Richard J., and Emilie Griffin, ed. *Spiritual Classics: Selected Readings on the Twelve Spiritual Disciplines.* New York: HarperOne, 2000. ("A Renovaré Resource for Spiritual Renewal")

Foster, Richard J., and Gayle D. Beebe. *Longing for God: Seven Paths of Christian Devotion.* Downers Grove, IL: InterVarsity Press, 2009.[455]

Foster, Richard J., and James Bryan Smith. *Devotional Classics.* HarperSanFrancisco, 1993.

Gangle, Kenneth O., and James C. Wilhoit, ed. *The Christian Educator's Handbook on Spiritual Formation.* Grand Rapids: Baker Books, 1994.[456]

Groeschel, Craig. *The Christian Atheist: Believing in God but Living as if He Doesn't Exist.* Grand Rapids: Zondervan, 2010.[457]

Guyon, Jeanne. *Intimacy with Christ* (Formerly titled *Guyon Speaks Again*). Jacksonville, FL: The SeedSowers, 2001.[458]

Inge, William Ralph. *Christian Mysticism: The Bampton Lectures, 1899: Considered in Eight Lectures Delivered before the University of Oxford.* London: Methuen & Co., 1899.

Keating, Thomas. *Open Mind, Open Heart: The Contemplative Dimension of the Gospel.* New York: Continuum, 1992.

---

[455] This is a book of readings of classic mystics but also includes the "Father of Liberalism," Friedrich Schleiermacher, of whom the author says: "I cannot escape the vitality of his experience of Christ." Schleiermacher denied the divinity of Jesus Christ and his substitutionary atonement.

[456] This is one of the few books on spiritual formation that has a whole chapter dedicated to the need of initial salvation as the point of regeneration and justification. The author of this chapter, Robert P. Lightner, states: "Salvation is birth; spiritual formation is growth." See page 42.

[457] This is a needed corrective to dead orthodoxy which just believes about God instead of really knowing him.

[458] This book consists of correspondence between Jeanne Guyon and Francois Fenelon in modern English.

Keller, Timothy. *Prayer*. New York: Penguin Books, 2014.[459]

Larson, Bob. *Larson's New Book of Cults*. Wheaton, IL: Tyndale House Publishers, 1989.[460]

Life with God Bible (formerly *The Renovaré Spiritual Formation Bible*). Harper Bibles, 2005.[461]

McColman, Carl. *The Big Book of Christian Mysticism: The Essential Guide to Contemplative Spirituality*. Charlottesville, VA: Hampton Roads Publishing Company, 2010.[462]

McGinn, Bernard, ed. *The Essential Writings of Christian Mysticism*. New York: The Modern Library, 2006.

Merton, Thomas. *The Inner Experience: Notes on Contemplation*. HarperSanFrancisco, 2004.

Noll, Richard. *The Jung Cult: Origins of a Charismatic Movement*. New York: Free Press Paperbacks, 1997.[463]

Nouwen, Henri J. M. *Life of the Beloved: Spiritual Living in a Secular World*. New York: The Crossroad Publishing Co., 1992.

——. *Sabbatical Journey: The Diary of his Final Year*. New York: The Crossroad Publishing Co., 1998.

——. *The Return of the Prodigal Son: A Story of Homecoming*. New York: Doubleday, 1994.

——. *With Open Hands*. Notre Dame, IN: Ave Maria Press, 2006.

---

[459] Keller is quite knowledgeable about Christian mysticism and rejects its major tenets, urging us to avoid what is termed "prayer without words" which serves to break down the boundary between us and God. He says words and thoughts are essential, both for hearing God's voice and our response to him in prayer. On page 59, Keller quotes J. I. Packer in saying Christian mysticism's mantra-like praying is but Eastern mysticism in Western dress.

[460] See especially pages 53–56 regarding meditation, which Larson says always involves shutting down the mind.

[461] Richard Foster is the chief editor and founder of Renovaré.

[462] McColman, a proponent of Christian Mysticism, is a lay associate of the Cistercian Monastery of the Holy Spirit, Conyers, GA. This well-researched book comes highly recommended by Richard Rohr, Phyllis Tickle, Brian D. McLaren, and many others.

[463] Noll also wrote again about Jung, *The Aryan Christ: The Secret Life of Carl Jung*. Noll is an expert about Carl Jung. He points out Jung wanted to produce a master race!

Ortlund, Raymond C. *Lord, Make my Life a Miracle!* Ventura, CA: Regal Books, 1974.

Packer, J. I. and Nystrom, Carolyn. *Praying.* Downers Grove, IL: IVP Books, 2006.

Petry, Ray C. *A History of Christianity: Readings in the History of the Early and Medieval Church.* Prentice–Hall, Inc., 1962.

Rea, Jana, with Richard J. Foster. *A Spiritual Formation Journal.* HarperSanFrancisco, 1996.

Ringma, Charles. *Dare to Journey with Henri Nouwen.* Colorado Springs: Piñon Press, 2000.

Ross, Hugh McGregor, ed., *George Fox, a Christian Mystic.* Ireland: Evertype, 2008.

Scazzero, Peter. *Emotionally Healthy Spirituality: It's Impossible to Be Spiritually Mature, While Remaining Emotionally Immature.* Nashville: Thomas Nelson, 2006.

Shannon, William H. *Silence on Fire: Prayer of Awareness.* New York: Crossroad Publishing, 1991.[464]

Schimmel, Annemarie. *Mystical Dimensions of Islam.* Chapel Hill: University of North Carolina Press, 1975.

Taylor, Brian C. *Becoming Christ: Transformation Through Contemplation.* Cambridge, MA: Cowley Publications, 2002.[465]

——. *Setting the Gospel Free,* London: SCM Press Ltd., 1996.[466]

Thomas, Gary. *Sacred Pathways: Discover Your Soul's Path to God.* Grand Rapids: Zondervan, 2010.

Underhill, Evelyn. *Mysticism.* New York: E.P. Dutton, 1911.

Waldron, Robert. *Walking with Henri Nouwen: A Reflective Journey.* New York: Paulist Press, 2003.

---

[464] Shannon is a well-known Merton scholar and Catholic priest.

[465] Taylor thinks that through the contemplative path "we become transfigured in Christ's light; we become him, he becomes us," see page 229.

[466] Taylor ends the book with instruction for practicing contemplative prayer, saying it is not for everybody. He has adapted his method from Zen meditation taught at the Zen Center of San Diego, California.

Walker, Williston. *A History of the Christian Church (Revised)*. New York: Charles Scribner's Sons, 1959.

Webber, Robert E. *Common Roots: The Original Call to an Ancient-Future Faith*. Grand Rapids: Zondervan, 1978.

Whitney, Donald S. *Spiritual Disciplines for the Christian Life*. Colorado Springs: NavPress, 2014.

Willard, Dallas. *The Spirit of the Disciplines: Understanding How God Changes Lives*. HarperSanFrancisco, 1988.

Yungen, Ray. *A Time of Departing: How Ancient Mystical Practices are Uniting Christians with the World's Religions*. Silverton, OR: Lighthouse Trails Publishing Company, 2006.

(Many other resources consulted can be found in the footnotes.)

Made in the USA
Lexington, KY
23 March 2017